THE ENTERPRISE ARCHITECTURE MATTERS BLOG

ADRIAN GRIGORIU

CONTENTS

INTRODUCTION TO THIS

This a collection of posts on Enterprise Architecture (EA) I posted during the last few years. I blogged, constantly, since the very beginning of 2007.

The blogs were hosted by eBizq, and ITToolBox, an online site that enables exchange of knowledge in IT.

The posts are inserted as is and as they were at the time of publication since they exhibit the freshness or crudeness of the time while they record the progress made in the maturity of profession and my own. They are informal. Some formatting and editing was applied to render the book more readable. Nevertheless, formatting is kept simple so that the book can be converted to most formats, on most devices or paper without problems or particular care. Links refer you to the original postings.

The posts were grouped in categories of interest to the reader and where necessary, were set in chronological order. Sometime you'll find duplication and overlapping because it was relevant, it is perhaps useful for immediate comprehension or it might simply happened at the time.

My inspiration was often drawn from the many issues raised in EA fora such as LinkedIn or from the blogs of reputed EA personalities and firms. At times, I need to sum up the state of art or objectively assess or even criticise current EA methods or the positions of various bodies with regard to EA. I also responded to my fellow bloggers' challenges or I commented on the opinions of the day.

The book makes references to the GODS-FFLV, my own EA framework.

You'll find that EA is still open to debate and that not even a definition, scope or framework was agreed upon. In the end, this is a collection of views. The book is not devised to be rigorous in an academic sense.

I hope you'll enjoy and even find useful the over 400 pages of thoughts on EA, its design, governance, role and benefits.

You'll find more information on my web site and book, "An Enterprise Architecture Development Framework".

THE ENTERPRISE PROBLEM AND THE EA PROMISE

The Enterprise problem and the Enterprise Architecture promise

March 5, 2010

http://www.ebizq.net/blogs/ea_matters/2010/03/the-enterprise-problem-and-the-enterprise-architecture-promise.php

"...Our natural inclination is to reduce matter first to molecules and then to atoms... But this approach...does not always work. In other words, the whole can often be more than the sum of the parts. Just consider the beautiful patterns created by large flocks of birds flying in the sky, which cannot be explained by understanding in ever greater detail the physiology of those birds. It is the *interactions* between the birds that are the key: the patterns form if each individual simply keeps a steady gap between it and its neighbours and flies in their average direction... This is the science of complex systems -- a rapidly growing field that tackles any system with lots of individual elements that interact in some way, be they birds flying in formation, car drivers moving along a highway or computers linking to form the Internet." Read more here about the network science.

An Enterprise is a complex system of people and technology. It is created by humans, typically and unfortunately, without a blueprint. We wish its parts fly in formation, like the ducks, to the same destination, but do they? We need to understand the alignment mechanism of the flight. But how do the birds do it, after all? For one, they follow a V formation, more often than not, that is a kind of flight architecture.

But how do we make the Enterprise fly? We should be able to do it better than the ducks, for sure.

Maybe the Enterprise Architecture approach would help us understand the flying formation of our organization and our CRM, ERP... systems that form the big picture of our firm and enable us comprehend what keeps these systems working together.

But what is an Enterprise?

It consists of a group of people, trained and organized to deliver a product, using technology.

What is Enterprise Architecture? It's the Enterprise structure and its operation blueprint. Simply architecture in our own words. EA documents stakeholders' use cases as business flows and the technology and organizational resources executing them.

An Enterprise has many problems today: the silo organization, the point solutions duplicating functionality, the unnecessary complexity and the poor understanding of the Enterprise operation causing poor implementations, a lengthening of the decision making, and a failure to deliver in time the business change. That renders the Enterprise unresponsive in a world of growing complexity and change.

The Solution is indeed Enterprise Architecture meant to streamline your Enterprise, enable faster product delivery at lower costs, handle the exploding amount of complexity and information and provide greater agility to cope with change.

What drives your business today?

Oct 31, 2008

http://it.toolbox.com/blogs/ea-matters/what-drives-your-business-today-19556

What are the main drivers for your business today? Of course the business has to return value to all its stakeholders: owners, employees, community...

But what are the main categories of issues a business always has to have in perspective? I would classify them in a few categories:

1. Streamline current Operations

Activities: automate as much as possible, reduce redundancies in function, process, platform and projects, reduce the tangled, spaghetti architecture, document current business functionality and implementation to get in control of your business

2. Built the Enterprise for the future (the Strategic view)

Analyze trends (industry, economical, social, political and regulatory, technological) and plan your strategy and business models accordingly (market segments, products, costs, new technology capabilities)

3. Enhance Corporate Social Responsibility to be a community and environment friendly and compliant enterprise

4. Improve customer satisfaction reflected in enhanced and new products, better customer response and relationship

5. And last but not least, increase profit and reduce costs for your stakeholders (the financial view)

But what is the impact on IT and Enterprise Architecture?

WHAT EA IS AND FREQUENTLY ASKED QUESTIONS (FAQ)

The definition of Enterprise Architecture, revisited (i)

Aug 17, 2007

http://it.toolbox.com/blogs/ea-matters/the-definition-of-enterprise-architecture-revisited-i-18045

Recently, I participated at the 5th Enterprise Architecture conference in Sydney Australia, which, by the way was informative. It is worth mentioning the fact that many speakers thought that the Enterprise Architects should be more business oriented and become a part of the business decision making process. What was also clear was that many delegates still did not have a clear definition of what Enterprise Architecture is. This is why I would like to return to the basics: what EA is!

But first the dilemma... Is it

- an Enterprise state
- a document
- a set of diagrams
- a process
- a program
- an organization design
- strategic planning and Enterprise portfolio management
- an Enterprise IT integration program
- Business Process Management (BPM) development
- an organization alignment to strategy and business objectives

Now a few definitions from reputed organizations...

CIO Definitions from SearchCIO.com, posted October, 2006:

"An enterprise architecture (EA) is a conceptual blueprint that defines the structure and operation of an organization. The intent of an enterprise architecture is to determine how an organization can most effectively achieve its current and future objectives. Purported advantages of having an enterprise architecture include improved decision making, improved adaptability to changing demands or market conditions, elimination of inefficient and redundant processes, optimization of the use of organizational assets, and minimization of employee turnover."

From General Accountability Office (GAO) of the US federal government, August 2006:

"An enterprise architecture is a blueprint for organizational change defined in models [using words, graphics, and other depictions] that describe (in both business and technology terms) how it operates today and how it intends to operate in the future; it also includes a plan for transitioning to this future state".

FEA definition:

"The FEA (Federal Enterprise Architecture) consists of a set of interrelated "reference models" designed to facilitate cross-agency analysis and the identification of duplicative investments, gaps and opportunities for collaboration within and across agencies. Collectively, the reference models comprise a framework for describing important elements of the FEA in a common and consistent way. Through the use of this common framework and vocabulary, IT portfolios can be better managed and leveraged across the federal government."

From TOGAF 8.1 FAQ:

"An EA defines the components or building blocks that make up the overall Enterprise "their interrelationships and guidelines governing their design and evolution"

They are all good definitions, but let me try to unify them in a single enduring one, in the next post.

The definition of Enterprise Architecture, revisited (ii)

Aug 24, 2007

http://it.toolbox.com/blogs/ea-matters/the-definition-of-enterprise-architecture-revisited-ii-18574

So what is Enterprise Architecture?

Let's ask this question again after we talked about and designed or even implemented one. In fact, what have we implemented? How do we define a definition though? What is the anatomy of a definition? Let us try Zachman's approach to this.

The EA is:

- What: The structure of an Enterprise and its blueprint describing.
- How: How the Enterprise operates and the processes executed by.

- Whom: People.
- Which: The technology implementing processes.
- Where: Showing the location of people and technology.
- Why: To streamline, align, blueprint, strategically plan, and confer agility.
- When: According to the Enterprise transformation plan to a target state.
-

  Described in artefacts such as:
- Business Architecture: Products, Value Chain, stakeholders' use cases, business model, strategy, business processes, rules, orchestration, B2B choreography... artefacts
- Technology & IT Architectures: Applications, Infrastructure, email, Content Management, network, SCADA... People & Organization architecture: organization chart with roles and responsibilities, culture, values... views
- Information architectures and many other Enterprise views: location, planning, security...
- The Enterprise transformation roadmap and its project portfolio artefacts

All mapped and linked through an EA framework.

In short though: the EA is the Enterprise structure and the operation blueprint describing the current and future states of the Enterprise, in terms of Business, Technology, People and Information views, and the transformation roadmap, process, program and portfolio, all linked together by an EA framework.

The EA ultimately will constitute the Enterprise Knowledge DB. But EA is more than the sum of its parts; it is about the governance (mind) and the culture (soul) of the Enterprise (body).

Enterprise Architecture definition, revisited

Aug 11, 2010

http://it.toolbox.com/blogs/ea-matters/enterprise-architecture-definition-revisited-40493

Here is Nick Malik's blog on the definition of EA.

The post is about Nick's own and quoted EA definitions from various sources:

Here is the EARF's definition:

"Enterprise Architecture is the continuous practice of describing the essential elements of a socio-technical organization, their relationships to each other and to the environment, in order to understand complexity and manage change."

The definition adds little to the standards one we all know from IEEE/ISO; in simple terms it translates to the practice (it implies repeatability, continuity anyway) of describing the elements of the Enterprise ("socio-technical organization"!) and their relationships between them and environment. Nothing specific to the Enterprise though. It serves to manage complexity and change, amongst others but it also serves the design or the strategic alignment purposes, as well.

The more than 1300 entries compressed definition of LinkedIn debate, mentioned by Nick and elaborated by Kevin Smith:

"The purpose of Enterprise Architecture is to enable an enterprise to realise its Vision through the execution of its Mission, whilst enabling it to respond to change and increasing its effectiveness, profitability, customer satisfaction, competitive edge, growth, stability, value, durability, efficiency and quality while reducing costs and risks by Strategic Planning, Architecture and Governance supported by a Decision Support framework in the context of aligning all parts of the enterprise using Models, Guidance, Processes and Tools."

It is more a definition of purpose rather than a definition of concept. It is also an essentialised version of more than a thousand opinions. It is long, probably incomplete in its enumeration, abundant in undefined terms (such as Vision, Mission, Decision Making framework, Guidance...), hard to memorise, and as such to use. Well the practice of attempting to pacify so many conflicting definitions may inevitably lead to this. Nice try though.

Nick had a few definitions of SMS length himself. They are all OK but partial and unique.

Definitions from other sources state that EA is the "organizing logic" of the Enterprise. This is not too relevant since what is "logic"? Does the current Enterprise and EA has much "logic"? "Logic" lives more in people minds while EA represents a structure, logical to us or not.

Many definitions refer to purpose but there are more ways to get to the same purpose. Other definitions refer to process, business function, profession or use cases such as EA for "strategic alignment".

Nevertheless, in describing the architecture of a house does one tell us what the architect's profession does or what the process is? The architecture is just the plan of the house. The constructor would plan and build it, not the architect.

We have to separate as such the EA profession or the process from what EA is.

All these efforts to define EA are worthy. The trouble is that people having discovered discord in the field, come out too easily with definitions of what they think the EA is or should be, without trying to consolidate existing definitions. True, there is no single accepted body of knowledge or definition.

I sanction though the EARF approach to define "definition" first.

In my view, definition should state an alternative term, synonym in the first place, reflecting the "what it is" in an analogy.

From this angle, EA is the architecture of the Enterprise that is the structure and its operation blueprint.

The blueprint shows the components and inter-relationships between elements and environment. So it is standards compliant. The blueprint can serve many stakeholders for multiple purposes. It will be associated with a process and an EA team and so on.

The definition of Enterprise Architecture, continued

Aug 15, 2010

http://it.toolbox.com/blogs/ea-matters/the-definition-of-enterprise-architecture-continued-40497

The issue seems to be that EA definitions are usually associated to a purpose and a single purpose at that. People associate EA with their own goal, work or understanding such as strategic planning or technology alignment etc and thus they come with partial definitions.

That is why we have such a proliferation of definitions.

Let's ask some questions from another angle: what is EA as seen by stakeholders?

- Is it an Enterprise wide IT architecture? Is it ITIL?
- Is it a tool to specify and execute strategy? Is it a strategy in itself? Is IT strategy?
- Is it a program? Is it a discipline? Is it a document, a web site, a tool, a process or organisational group?

All these are part of the same answer, the EA, and complement the EA definition, as implied in its "architecture" name: the structure and blueprint of the Enterprise describing its operation and technology and people resources.

Of course in your organization you would have to specify the EA scope, typically a part of IT, to avoid misleading expectations, match skills and assess costs. But you'll still have a process, a team, a project, a tool, or activity to execute the EA. You will come with a blueprint of sorts, a transformation roadmap, and you will support the strategy effort.

But EA is much more than the sum of its parts.

And EA is more than IT: it is about the real estate, fleet, business continuity, communications networks, production technology...

What would my Enterprise Architecture definition look like

Apr 11, 2012

http://it.toolbox.com/blogs/ea-matters/what-would-my-enterprise-architecture-definition-look-like-51031

Were I to define EA (for an Wikipedia entry for instance, assuming it might get the public vote of confidence demanded), I would adopt a synthetic and constructive style.

I would start with the object of discussion, the Enterprise, then define architecture, EA, the benefits, the know-how, frameworks and the reality on the ground.

The Enterprise is:

An organised group of people that, by employing various technologies, deliver products to customers.

This definition includes technology, people/organization and business process ("deliver"), the parts of an enterprise that will become the tiers of the architecture.

Architecture is

See ISO standard. But essentially, is components in interconnections seen through stakeholders views.

EA is

EA represents the structure of the enterprise and its representation, that is a blueprint describing the business functions and processes that deliver value/products, the information, people organisation and technology, all inter-linked.

In an extended view, EA depicts also the future states of the Enterprise and the transformation roadmap.

EA is also associated with the business function that practices and manages it.

Why EA?

For the architect, EA enables the Enterprise simplification (de-duplication, standardisation...), integration, alignment, improvement, agility, integrated roadmapping and cohesive strategy execution. In other words EA enhances the management of the Enterprise. It enables the reduction of the overall enterprise costs and higher returns from increased productivity and reduced time to market.

EA ultimately enables better enterprise change and complexity management. Once documented, implemented and managed, it becomes a key enterprise asset - that is, it is reusable and returns value constantly.

How is EA used in the Enterprise?

The resulting EA is employed by each and every stakeholder to analyse and resolve own work concerns. Each stakeholder may have its own View of the enterprise.

The IT/technology people document, analyse, optimise and roadmap the technology. Management takes investment decisions based on EA.

Business and IT experts align technology operation to business processes.

Business people analyse process bottlenecks.

Finance people document costs of EA functions and workflows. HR associates people, skills and remuneration to EA business functions, roles and streams.

All these views should be integrated in the EA representation, inter-linked and navigable. EA is ultimately composed of and decomposed in this unlimited number of views.

Who does EA?

The Enterprise Architect specifies the EA framework, coordinates its population and organises the EA work and make sure that the stakeholders' parts fit into the EA whole.

The Enterprise business experts model and document the EA Views of the processes and systems they own. EA is a collective modelling and implementation effort.

How do you document and design EA?

Typically by documenting the base business, technology and people architectures by gradually integrating the stakeholders' views in the EA. Future enterprise states must be specified, agreed, documented and implemented to achieve strategy and resolve tactical concerns.

Enterprise stakeholders develop their own capabilities guided by EA principles, process checkpoints and roadmap in the context of the overall EA.

Why an EA framework?

The core EA framework integrates the parts of the Enterprise, independently modelled and designed by stakeholders, in the whole. The resulting EA can be navigated as such for process effectiveness and cost analysis or for impacts of change on resources.

The framework offers to all EA developments a common reference, predictable results, reusability and repeatability.

An extended EA framework would include architecture principles, technology standards, maturity and value measurement framework, EA development process and governance.

Existing EA frameworks

- Zachman: a method of system analysis covering aspects like who, why and development value chain from concept to implementation. This, of specific interest to management, applies to any system. It is not practical for the EA development though. Filling in the Zachman framework will not result in an EA because the artefacts are not integrated.

- TOGAF: a transformation process plus a collection of requirements, risks, security... good practices that apply to a project. They are not specific though to the enterprise architecture development. Essential concepts for EA transformation like roadmap and strategy are missing. Filling in TOGAF phases outcomes does not result in an EA for the same reason as above, i.e. because the resulting artefacts do not fit into a whole but rather fill in the ADM phases deliverables.

- DoDAF: a method of describing structural and behavioural aspects of the

Enterprise. Good but too specific to the Defence field. Does not cover process like TOGAF or taxonomy of artefacts like Zachman.

- FEA: the US government best practice aimed to unify agencies approaches to IT. Too general, and as such interpreted in too many ways. Introduces the Performance view which is of interest to management.

There are other approaches but most consist of common development processes, a few tiers of IT architecture or simply abbreviations of a few aspects an EA has to cover. Most do not cover technology except IT and lump organisation into business.

What should EA also do?

EA should integrate and coordinate:

- The many fragmented or loose coupled Enterprise developments in IT such as SOA, IT Architecture, Application Integration (EAI), ITIL efforts...

- And the many independently performed activities such as organisation alignment to business strategy and goals, compliance to regulation, business process management, Six/Lean Sigma, Business Performance Management, Mergers and Acquisitions and Outsourcing.

What does EA, in reality

Since its typical scope is IT, EA is an effort to discover the IT systems landscape and specify its roadmapping in alignment to strategy. More often than not, the IT EA looks like a collection of isolated islands of systems automation, since it is devoid of the business architecture background. As such, its utility is limited to IT.

Hence, many business as usual EA efforts are reduced to solution architecture design & check-ups and Architecture Review Boards' activities, both of which being subjective, missing the foundation of a full EA.

EA FAQ short answers

Jul 15, 2010

http://it.toolbox.com/blogs/ea-matters/ea-faq-short-answers-39919

Here are my answers to a few frequently asked questions that frequently get wrong answers.

What is Enterprise Architecture (EA)?

EA is the Architecture i.e. the blueprint of the Enterprise. It describes its structure and the human and technology resources operating it. The EA structure and operation are embedded in the Enterprise.

Long definition: The EA is the Enterprise structure and operation blueprint, describing the current and future states of the Enterprise and its transformation roadmap in terms of process, information, technology and people architectures, all linked by an EA navigation framework.

Why EA?

Because EA is an (reusable) asset in the Enterprise competitive race, characterised by the growing pace of change and a soaring amount of information and complexity.

What is the purpose of EA?

The EA, as a blueprint, is employed by each and every stakeholder for own work purposes.

For instance, IT people document, analyse and roadmap the IT. Finance people document the budget and cost flows. HR associates people, skills and remuneration to business functions and operation. All these views would be linked and traversed on the EA representation.

Overall, EA enables the Enterprise simplification, integration, operational improvements, resource saving, assets management, enhanced agility through modular services, coherent roadmapping... and in general enables a superior management of the Enterprise and its growing complexity.

Who does EA?

The Enterprise Architect specifies the EA framework and coordinates the EA work.

The Enterprise domain experts model and document their own concerns in the Enterprise, the Views. EA is a collective effort.

What should EA do?

EA should also coordinate, be involved in and document the many fragmented or loose coupled Enterprise developments such as SOA, IT Architecture, Application Integration (EAI), ITIL efforts and many independently performed activities such as Enterprise alignment to Business Strategy and Goals, compliance to regulation, Business Process Improvement, Six/Lean Sigma, Mergers and Acquisitions and Outsourcing (such as BPO, SaaS...).

Ultimately, EA becomes the Enterprise Knowledge database.

What does EA in practice?

In practice, EA is used for the discovery of IT systems landscape and its roadmapping. Once this done, many business as usual EA efforts are reduced to Architecture Review Boards' solution architectures reviews which are seldom based on an existing EA since there is often none.

Why an EA framework?

The EA framework links together in the EA whole the parts of the Enterprise modelled and designed independently by owners so that the EA can be navigated for process analysis, impacts on resources, strategy mapping and so on. The framework offers predictability, repeatability to EA developments.

The EA is not the sum of the parts but the whole

January 26, 2012

http://www.ebizq.net/blogs/ea_matters/2012/01/thw-enterprise-architecture-we-do-today.php

In time it became rather clear to me that most EA architects usually labour at describing simple capabilities, design solution architectures, police the development of solutions, establish architecture principles - but not the full EA framework -, specify IT strategy and spend a lot of time justifying themselves and selling Enterprise Architecture. What is missing? The Enterprise Architecture itself.

Can you judge a solution architecture outside the context of an Enterprise Architecture? While we do it all the time, the EA big picture would still save time and reduce the costly errors of missing parts and connections.

Can you specify best strategy without the picture of the whole? A strategy not based on EA would most probably be incomplete and inconsistent and as such would be satisfactory only to parts of the enterprise.

The truth is that no two architects have the same understanding of EA, use the same methodology or achieve similar results. Still, why so many architects claim success and when asked to share the results shy away?

The answer may be as simple as that. We don't do anything new. We describe the enterprise in bits and shards, as we always did, which are not integrated.

That is because there is no Architecture framework in the sense of a frame where the EA parts fit in to render the whole. I often wondered how can we deliver an Enterprise Architecture without a proper EA framework.

TOGAF is effectively a process template plus lots of advice. Zachman a model of systemic thinking. DoDAF a method of description...

Nevertheless, they do not provide a framework to which you can fit the parts of the Enterprise to give the whole.

In the absence of this framework, what do we deliver then? Parts. But not integrated in the EA whole. We do this all the time. We do it now without an Enterprise Architecture. We have the bits of the puzzle but not the big picture. In the end, the implementation of the target enterprise state would not work properly as a whole since the parts/solutions are not integrated, the strategy covers just pieces...

A proper EA framework would enforce parts compliance to the whole and their interconnection enabling the proper discovery, design and implementation of a consistent and complete whole.

The EA is about describing, roadmapping and improving the Enterprise as a whole of parts rather than describing... parts in isolation as many architects did and do today claiming they do EA.

Enterprise Architecture, what do we do about it?

February 12, 2011

http://www.ebizq.net/blogs/ea_matters/2011/02/save-the-enterprise-architecture.php

Candid questions like " what is EA" or "how do I become an EA architect?" still asked nowadays prove that something is wrong with the EA profession.

The classical answer given today is stating EA purpose (strategy, reduce complexity...). There always is the self serving response "do our training course and you'll get an EA architect certificate as well". But is it right to define a concept solely by its purpose? And how many types of certifications are out there? Too many, too different.

A series of posts will try to discover how Enterprise Architecture fairs today.

The EA definition or is there a definition?

Enterprise Architecture has no agreed definition, that is no single definition or worse, too many of them. What is EA in fact? Is it a practice, a blueprint, a process, strategic planning...?

Often definitions narrow to much the EA scope. For instance, EA is limited to strategic planning or target architecture alone. That not only is misleading because proper strategic planning is one of many benefits EA can return, but it ignores the fact that EA describes first and foremost the current blueprint of the Enterprise. The architecture of your home is a blueprint rather than the plan to extend it in the future; isn't that so?

Interestingly, most of us are tempted to define EA in our own terms ignoring all other existing definitions. That is because either we haven't found the existing definitions satisfactory or those definitions do not match our job reality. We also feel we can add bits to them and sometimes, we need to competitively differentiate our view. But is it helpful? How many definitions can be out there for the same concept? Web 2.0 communications possibilities and the anonymity of the Internet seems to reduce the barriers of communication. Is that good? yes but one has to sift tones of soil to get to the gold.

With different definitions, are we talking then about the same thing?

The fuzziness of the situation also enables unqualified but self important entrants join in as experts, speculating on various loosely defined issues. They talk particularly about strategy and business issues because it sounds good and fuzzy.

What is the EA scope?

Is it IT alone? It mostly is today. Does it include business architecture? Mostly not. Does it include organization or people? No. Does it cover culture? Nope. How does it relate to Six/Lean Sigma or TQM, BPM...? No way. Can then EA reflect the reality of the Enterprise?

What is the EA purpose?

Is it strategy, change. alignment, complexity...? Is it about improving communications? There were more than 1500 answers for this question in a Linkedin discussion. No matter what it is, the purpose itself is just a small part of the definition. After all there are various ways to reach the same destination. But the purpose of EA varies with stakeholders' use. It may be operational improvements, automation, reduction in duplication... or/and strategic planning. There is no single purpose.

Enterprise Architecture and stakeholders' plans

Jan 16, 2010

http://it.toolbox.com/blogs/ea-matters/enterprise-architecture-and-stakeholders-plans-36425

EA was compared to city planning. One needs to plan infrastructure like roads, water and gas pipes tracts, electricity and telephone cables then shopping malls, official buildings, entertainment venues etc. There are blueprints for electricity wires, sewage pipes, road maps and tourist maps... They all together form the city map.

At the same time towns are the result of an organic evolution over centuries of spontaneous building in various fashionable architectural styles. US cities are planned to a degree few other cities are because the rectangular grid was planned early in the city lifecycle. But most cities build around old cities. Few are constructed from scratch. As such architecture is about managing the change from one state to another, in small increments of time and realizations.

What is EA about though? In an Enterprise, we have all these plans for the CRM, data warehouse, portal, printing and floor maps, networks, manufacturing band, building, locations... Every stakeholder with his own plan. But they are designed taking into account different components, different diagramming techniques, symbols, tools... Each and every map is useful to a small community.

EA relates all these architectures in a whole where one can navigate from one item to another in a logical manner. For instance, track the performance of a process from a step to another from one resource to another from one function to another.

Of course, to get that unique integrated set of views, one needs the frame that holds them together exposing placeholders when the components have not been represented yet. Do the current EA frameworks achieve that?

EA, as a practice, needs to roadmap to change in the Enterprise, facilitate the alignment of the structure to changing ends.

EA is used for many and various purposes, in fact as many as stakeholders. Each would see a part of EA, a plan of concern to own work, but integrated in the whole.

Enterprise architecture looks like an MRI scan

February 14, 2013

http://www.ebizq.net/blogs/ea_matters/2013/02/what-enterprise-architecture-is-about-yet-again.php

Architecture, in general, is about models and blueprints. Hence, enterprise architects have to devise models that describe the enterprise.

Based on these models many people in the enterprise visualize, analyze and solve their own issues, in context. Because you cannot properly solve an issue without looking at the environment it takes place in.

A wide variety of specialist doctors diagnose and treat health problems, using pictures like x-rays in the process the same way business professionals analyze and solve enterprise problems, using the EA description of the enterprise produced by the   architect.
The EA architect may be asked to assist the process, sometimes, just like the x-ray specialist, but the architect does not solve the problems of the enterprise. He is not qualified to do so. Moreover an EA architect working in IT is not tasked to solve enterprise wide issues.

X-raying simplifies matters though. EA is not just about snapping a picture. The EA "model" looks more like an MRI scan, a method to create an integrated set of views of a body, taken from different angles. The views depict virtual sections through the body. That is how the enterprise model, the EA, should look.

Nevertheless, the scan methods and technology have been developed for a long time now and with plenty of effort. EA has not reached this stage yet. I describe in my blogs and book an analogy between EA and the anatomy and physiology of a body.

If you are not doing models, then you are not doing architecture. And then you should not call enterprise architecture (EA) what you do and you should not call yourself an EA architect. It does not mean though that your work isn't valuable or strategic.

Anyway, who is going to model or describe the "anatomy" of the enterprise if not the EA architect?

In practice, many assume that EA is about strategy, policies... in fact anything but architecture.

Other EA efforts come with a few pictures of the EA that, in fact, have always existed in the enterprise. They are not useful to the stakeholders with enterprise wide concerns because they are disjoint.

The diagrams are and have always been disconnected because of the lack of a proper integrating modelling framework to link the models together in the bigger enterprise wide picture. Without this framework, the various models designed in separation with different aims tools and conventions in mind remain isolated, rendering the end to end analysis of the enterprise and its problem resolution rather difficult.

It is true though that few can properly and consistently do EA since most current frameworks do not support modelling. They are anything but enterprise modelling frameworks. They mostly describe the process of development of the target EA. Hence, each and every EA architect has to re-invent at some expense own modelling methods with known results.

For instance, frameworks like Zachman, TOGAF... are not meant to do enterprise modelling.

THE SCOPE OF EA

<u>**The scope of Enterprise Architecture**</u>

November 8, 2010

<u>http://www.ebizq.net/blogs/ea_matters/2010/11/the-scope-of-enterprise-architecture.php</u>

EA, extended to or over its limits, maybe about strategy, transformation and in general about all things related to an Enterprise, depending on whom you are talking to. In practice though, an architecture is a set of integrated blueprints.

Let's take an example: a city has an urban architecture described by blueprints illustrating residential and industrial areas, parks, public building, roads, transport, pipes and cable networks etc.

If you consider the city an Enterprise, that is include people, then you may add the operation of the city that is, how does it deliver medical services, how does it clean the streets etc.

Now, the town officials devise strategies to develop the city for the next 100 years and plan the tactics to improve it etc. But are these strategies, tactical plans and transformation programs part of the architecture?

They are definitely not part of the city architecture or map, as we know it. They are not part of a City Enterprise Architecture that describes the current city operation. They may be partly part of the future city architecture, if there is one.

But the strategic transformation execution, is it part of City Enterprise Architecture?

It depends on how you define EA and its scope. Who establishes the scope? It ultimately comes down to your definition, expectations and the EA lead level of authority (usually not at all).

To start with, I think that there will be quite a virulent reaction from the top enterprise management and business when if trying to include business transformation programs under EA. Strategy had also been in existence long before

EA was born. Business would expect the transformation to use an EA blueprint, but would not expect EA to take over the Enterprise transformation and install an Enterprise Architect as CEO.

What is the scope of an Enterprise Architecture?

Jun 23, 2009

http://it.toolbox.com/blogs/ea-matters/what-is-the-scope-of-an-enterprise-architecture-32287

To what extent an Enterprise Architecture effort, Strategy or a more common IT development can be applied Enterprise wide across geographies or business operations or to a Group of companies? The answer is essential for the scope specification of the development.

In this blog Gartner defines a few conditions that make up an Enterprise. I am not sure I agree but the question remains.

Java Enterprise Edition (JavaEE), Enterprise Applications Integration (EAI) ..., the Enterprise portal they all refer to the Enterprise. But what is that Enterprise?

Legally an Enterprise (Group) has an identity and a single governance. It is up to the management to define the Group Operating Model (unification..., see Enterprise Architecture as Strategy book). If any. An operating model is the degree of integration and standardisation of various companies within a group. Some companies are part of the financial group but otherwise are left to their own devices. Loosely coupled, I would say, by design.

In IT, the scope of the Enterprise may vary with every IT development.

In the absence of an Operating Model (the norm), it is ultimately up to an IT group to negotiate with stakeholders the scope of the "Enterprise" for the specific development, if not clearly defined by business. It depends upon the organisational remit of the IT department, culture, individuals, business requirements...

The scope of the Enterprise Architecture is frequently seen from an IT team point of view. As such, it may vary with every EA development.

EA is more than IT Architecture and Technology is more than IT

June 11, 2010

http://www.ebizq.net/blogs/ea_matters/2010/06/enterprise-architecture-is-more-than-it-architecture-and-technology-is-more-than-it.php

Enterprise Architecture (EA) has promised a thorough transformation of the business world by streamlining enterprise operations, aligning IT to business strategy and documenting the company blueprint to improve understanding, measurement and management of its operation.

Although EA has been around for some time, the value it promised to offer has not quite materialised - I hope you disagree! But what are the factors inhibiting adoption or its success?

I would discuss some of the deterring factors.

EA is frequently seen as an IT only architecture

not addressing the interests of business stakeholders

There is nothing wrong with an IT architecture. The issue is that the expectations promised by the Enterprise name and advertisement are not fulfilled. This spawns a noteworthy scope issue. Most importantly it prevents the involvement, funding and support of business people and firm's management. The EA is not visible to the business side and what is more relevant it does not cover business aspects. Such an EA fails to raise interest or ultimately induce usage outside the IT and is often associated to an IT only framework as ITIL.

In terms of EA implementation the IT EA team - the program is initiated by IT - has little authority to drive business architecture issues, influence corporate strategy or recommend organisational changes. Usually the EA team has little control of the business process documentation effort for instance even if successfully initiated. I have witnessed an EA development effort and a business process and best practices optimisation program, performed at the same time, in parallel and totally uncorrelated, by two different consultancies.

IT architecture is only a part of an EA architecture. To succeed an EA architecture needs address business concerns, to be sanctioned, supported and have visibility at the business and management board level. EA needs the wider scope to include and provide motivation to business teams and enable adoption and usage.

Technology is only seen as IT

for a wider adoption EA has to cover all technologies

No other kind of technology, mechanical for instance is considered. What about manufacturing technologies? 50 years ago there was no IT. Banks and factories still existed though. It is hardly an Enterprise wide Architecture a development which does not describe the manufacturing equipment for your products as cars, shoes etc.

The IT only view is restricting the sphere of interest to just a few types of IT intensive enterprises and, inside a company, to a few stakeholders. It is again a matter of scope, not only in design but in business users' involvement, support and usage.

EA approached as an IT only architecture, reduces the EA scope to IT and fails to involve business and other non-IT technology stakeholders.

Enterprise Architecture is really more than IT Architecture and Technology is more than IT.

EA, is it truly Enterprise wide or limited to IT only?

Oct 25, 2009

http://it.toolbox.com/blogs/ea-matters/enterprise-architecture-is-it-trully-enterprise-wide-or-limited-to-it-only-34952

It depends on viewpoint. But it is mostly IT today although, more and more people would like the EA to cover the whole Enterprise.

EA is an IT term. It initially came from Zachman. Then it was adopted by the IT community in branding their technologies Enterprise wide: Enterprise Java, EAI, ESB... So why not Enterprise (wide) Architecture? Well, there is no "IT" in the name because it looked evident to them.

The role called Enterprise (Java) Architect has also been introduced by IT to denote an expert programmer that was able to design SW on top of complex application packages and their many interfaces, like Java, .Net. But this adds to the confusion reigning today, about EA. Many still think of EA in terms of software.

It is likely that the term architecture, borrowed from the construction industry, came from IT system design, where the diagram of the logical system blocks and their interconnections was coined architecture.

The business vocabulary does not have an architecture term. There is no concept of architecture in the business domain, in my opinion. Business uses Value Chains, business models, process maps...

So the EA concept comes from IT. More, the design methods come from IT: structure analysis, OO... IT can do architecture work but it can hardly do EA without business knowledge and a business architecture. EA is mainly designed by IT for IT.

EA has a high penetration though; its potential was understood by business due to the promise in the name. Still, it delivers little, since most people have to work out first what that is, then its scope, what framework to use etc. The Enterprise specific work is only done after that.

So EA is an IT term, but with a great promise that does not escape the business people. As such it was also adopted in the larger business context of the Enterprise.

Business Architecture and BPM are part of the EA (taken in the context of the Enterprise rather than IT alone). Zachman's matrix proves this and I guess we all know it.

EA, as a term, is too good to be abandoned to IT, I believe. Anyway it would be hard to abandon the name in practice. "EA" is currently used without qualification and discussions always arise on the surrounding scope. We should qualify EA with: Enterprise IT architecture, Enterprise Business Architecture, Enterprise people architecture... Business, IT, People are in fact layers in most EA frameworks.

EA, ultimately, should become, from an IT centric activity, a coordinated set of various business activities: IT, BPM, Six Sigma, organization design... IT cannot really cover alone business processes for instance. Business knows them best and analysts do it. Six Sigma would look into processes IT would not care about because they are performed by humans. Organization design and alignment to business architecture should be another EA activity done by business.

The Chief EA architect should report high up and coordinate all EA related activities like BPM, Six Sigma, IT architecture, alignment of technology to business and strategy...

If the current Enterprise Architecture is IT...

Jan 9, 2010

http://it.toolbox.com/blogs/ea-matters/if-the-current-enterprise-architecture-is-it-34558

Enterprise Architecture currently and mostly equals IT. With a growing emphasis on business architecture, a question was raised in various fora: how to differentiate it from the existing EA profession and practitioners which mainly deliver IT architecture but promise the goods of, at least, a business architecture. As expectations are not met, the image of EA is tarnished.

IT does its best to provide an IT EA, given the fact that there is no business picture the IT systems can be aligned to. For IT, the business architecture is a departure from the IT job description.

The existing EA IT architects are keen though to move into the business architecture space. And that is not too difficult as long as there is demand, there is no specific body of BA knowledge and no selection criteria for a business architect. I've already seen ads for business architects requiring TOGAF certification, which is essentially IT. Many EArchitects are claiming the business domain by throwing around a few notions like capabilities, process and strategy.

The issue is that the rather new breed of Business Architects would like to differentiate themselves and call themselves otherwise from the existing EA (IT) architects and the current not quite flattering EA image which did not deliver on its promise, lessening its credibility.

But IT architecture is a part of Enterprise Architecture. So are the organization or people and the non-IT technology architecture, seldom covered today, if at all.

The business architecture is the top layer of the stack, as we know, and most important because it shapes them all. Without a business architecture current EA (IT) attempts fail because the IT systems picture does not convey the structure or operation of the Enterprise.

To me, the EA name is relevant. The EA must be seen in its whole, including business, IT, organization... If we change the name of Enterprise Business Architecture to anything new, and leave the EA name to IT, we severe the link to the complete EA framework and we create competition with the EA architects from the IT space attempting to cover the whole EA.

I don't think we need a new name for EA. We just need to qualify the architect title with the EA domain we work in, emphasize the specializations (Enterprise Business/Applications/Infrastructure... architect and also the generalist EArchitect or the Chief EArchitect, covering it all).

But how can one stop the flood of imposture without a decent body of knowledge and selection criteria for an EA business architect (or even for an Enterprise IT architect)? No matter the name, the profession can be easily hijacked. I don't think certification for the current frameworks is an answer, as many new organizations appear to propose, for the simple reason that certification has to be done against a body of knowledge.

The business architecture body of knowledge is scattered and architecture is not a term in the business vocabulary. Without an agreed framework, the BA will fail to produce the goods.

The E Business Architecture is also claimed by the BPM domain.

To defeat the current scepticism about EA, we have to produce though the overall Enterprise architecture so that the technology and organization align to business operation. For that we have to define what business architecture is, what are its artefacts...

EA versus Enterprise IT Architecture debate

Aug 15, 2012

http://it.toolbox.com/blogs/ea-matters/enterprise-architecture-ea-versus-enterprise-it-architecture-debate-52718

This is a LinkedIn discussion that stands at the origin of this post.

The link: "EA ≠ EITA is a myth that dinosaur EAs cling to."

Quote: "There was a time when the business stakeholders saw a difference between their business operations and the supporting/enabling ICT. That time has passed, enterprise business capabilities are enabled by and tightly coupled to ICT, when was the last time you wrote and send a memo and filed a paper copy in a filing cabinet. Architects who feel that EA does not equal EITA must move up to the times or be left behind."

For starters, this statement is meant to be controversial. But while I think the outcome is quite clear, it's still worth the challenge.

Here are my few brief points.

1. Today we do EITA but talk about EA

EA is aspirational today, as someone pointed out. But it returns few remarkable results.

EITA though is practical and doable now even if the results are seldom used outside IT. That is why the EA belongs to the IT department now.

The issue is that we often promise the EA benefits while we deliver the EITA's which are much less comprehensive. Hence the debates...

2. EA consists of Business (process), Technology and People while EITA consists solely of IT architecture.

EITA alone cannot fully describe the making of a product such as the production of a book or a car. It can only describe the architecture of the IT islands of automation.

As such EITA is solely an EA set of views, out of many.

3. The business architecture of EA should be decoupled as much as possible from the resources implementing them such as IT for instance, so that evolution and change should be readily possible

4. Many business such as restaurants, cleaners... (or even the banks of the forgotten past), are/were still IT devoid or almost.

Hence, EITA renders little value to these firms.

5. After all, it is still the case today that "the company is the people" rather than "the company is the IT" as in fact claimed.

6. Nevertheless, the IT is not only an expensive resource but it could radically affect the future of the enterprise in case of malfunction because of the key and massive role in storing data and processing information.

As such, EITA is a most important view of the enterprise, which even designed in isolation of EA, returns great value.

Besides EITA delivers now, while the EA still promises.

7. There are dinosaurs out there who pretend that they were doing enterprise architecture long before we were even talking about the notion. True, but too often now, the EA misleadingly invaded the territory of other business disciplines, making the dinos right in reacting to this invasion to state that they have been doing for a long time what EA claims now to do.

This discussion is a matter of semantics, as most EA discussions are indeed, since we have not agreed yet on a definition of EA, a scope or deliveries.

EA BENEFITS AND THE VALUE IT RETURNS

EA benefits evaluation

July 15, 2010

http://www.ebizq.net/blogs/ea_matters/2010/07/ea-benefits-evaluation.php

Every Enterprise improvement ultimately translates into profit or cost saving for the business. For top management and external stakeholders that is what principally matters, after all. Nonetheless, to assess the effect of an EA action directly at these financial indicators level is impossible. A benefit tree would show though, how an improvement is cascaded to a profit or saving. One should record, at the top of the tree first, the EA basic deliveries and observe how they generate down the tree the benefits for the Enterprise. What an architecture typically enables:

- reduction in duplicated platforms, projects, in Enterprise units

- elimination of hair ball connections through integration

- introduction of modular services/interfaces

- technology standards

- application processes alignment to business operational needs

- systems alignment to strategic demands...

Then the EA maturity should be estimated since the above benefits may be lost in translation because the architecture may not be properly communicated and as such used, or its deliveries may not be fit for purpose:

-   how many departments use EA, how many people (especially outside IT)

-   how many EA controls are embedded in stakeholders' processes

-   how much feedback and how many requests for Views (proving EA success) from stakeholders

- not least, the degree of coverage of the Enterprise with EA artefacts...

At some level of the tree, compound measures for assessment of the simplification realised (-duplication + reuse+ reduced connections...), reduction in time to market (faster processes + automation + improved productivity...), cost saving (from duplication + re-use + ...) can be estimated for overall business value assessment.

And once we have these we can estimate the profit and cost saving generated by the EA.

Nevertheless, the EA is mostly an enabler of benefits. By employing it, people in every workplace could bring in own specific benefits.

The EA architect could specify measures for EA progress, maturity and quality of EA deliveries. The overall EA benefits can be assessed though at the EA program level where every stakeholder adds the benefits enabled by EA in own department.

Measure the Value of EA

Oct 10, 2008

http://it.toolbox.com/blogs/ea-matters/measure-the-value-of-ea-22834

EA, like any architecture, represents the structure of an Enterprise and its documentation describing how the Enterprise operates. The better the architecture, the better the outcome, the returned value.

A good architecture structure reduces duplications and overlays in processes, platforms, projects and sometimes people and it consolidates the many interconnections.

A good documentation describes the structure, standardises best practices and technologies, maps strategies on architecture components and architecture layers such as process to people and technology. It makes understanding the operation and training people easy.

The Enterprise Architecture delivers value, as soon as it is designed and implemented. It does that, gradually, while it is implemented by increasing the effectiveness and efficiency of your Enterprise. EA soon becomes an asset in its own, returning value to your Enterprise.

Project justification is done at Business Case time, before the start of the development by enumerating and estimating a number of key benefits. Ideally, all these initial benefits should be tracked and measured at implementation time to prove the delivery of promises. Same applies to EA.

The EA scope is key though, since more scope should return more value. EA iterations may add scope and as such new value.

EA, is it an IT only architecture? Then you are looking only at the benefits of standardising technology and integrating applications. With business and people architecture the picture changes significantly. The Business, Organization and IT alignment and ensuing benefits can be only achieved if you include in scope a

Business Architecture.

Once the scope and deliverables are established, the benefits and business case of the development can be estimated. The EA success should be measured against the listed benefits and deliverables in scope rather than against an abstract EA that does not have an agreed definition but promises a lot, in vague terms.

A table of key business improvement benefits, the way to measure them, and their stakeholders should be defined from the beginning and measured at the end of an EA iteration. The key benefit indicators may be grouped in a few categories:

- Operational (those enhancing the operation): single customer view (master data management)

- Development (improving your innovation and product development process); NPD: time to market

- Governance (enabling understanding, communication and decision making in the organisation)

- Support (enabling creative people and technology support processes); single version of truth for reporting

The EA development success is measured at implementation time with project progress indicators.

An EA maturity framework will help you also measure progress in the development phase and compliance at exploitation, by measuring success from a process and extent of business participation points of view rather than from a business value view quantified in key improvement indicators.

Value sometimes comes down to how do I justify my job as an EA architect!

Firstly, many "EA architects" are not really doing an EA design work. They are Enterprise level technology and applications integration experts and IT veterans.

But if you are really doing EA work, using the business benefits stated in the business case, measured by key improvement indicators correlated with a maturity framework evaluating the EA development progress and compliance to EA, can save your job.

The EA Value

Jul 5, 2010

http://it.toolbox.com/blogs/ea-matters/ea-value-39783

Presently, the EA term is conveniently defined by each and everyone to do whatever an (s)he does or prefers to do. Still EA lives in the IT space, even though some people would prefer otherwise.

In any case, the EA value should be measured per iteration in terms of

- overall Value delivered (from reduced costs of duplication, overlaps in activities, time-to-market...),

- its specific deliveries and as such value delivered to stakeholders (saved so much, improved efficiency by 10%...)

The results of an EA project are measurable if iterations deliverables are established upfront. Often though, the outcomes are not really relevant to other EA developments since EA outcomes are different from case to case (after all, there is no agreed EA definition or framework). People will tell you that this is because no problem or Enterprise is the same. True, but no two football games are the same, but they are still football, played according to the same rules. What makes them the same?

Few frameworks come with a list of artefacts or deliveries. As such that makes EAs even less comparable in terms of Value delivered. Even so, many deliveries look like matrices, so uninspiring.

In practice, EA is used for the discovery of IT systems landscape and technology roadmapping. Then many ongoing, business as usual EA efforts also are reduced to solution architectures reviews, since the ARBs (Architecture Review Boards) are their central activity. And the reviews are seldom based on an existing EA since there is none.

Careful though about EA costs. I have a feeling that most EAs cost more than they return, that is, their return is negative.

The Enterprise Architecture Return of Investment

April 29, 2010

http://www.ebizq.net/blogs/ea_matters/2010/04/the-enterprise-architecture-would-enable.php

The Enterprise Architecture would document your Enterprise and enable the alignment of technology to the operation it supports. The Enterprise operation would be streamlined, duplications reduced, projects grouped in a portfolio with dependencies and priorities, the strategy effectively mapped for execution... In the end, EA facilitates a better understanding of your Enterprise workings.

I classified the principal advantages of the EA in four categories:

- Operational (improved operations, technology resources aligned to business needs),
- Governance (improved governance structures, decision making...)
- Strategic (vision mapped and executed)
- Communications and Collaboration (having same EA vocabulary...).

An Off-the-Shelves framework enables the construction of an EA with all the benefits at a fraction of the cost, since it is saving you the effort of developing one which effort, if unsuccessful, will inhibit any further EA development, as it is so often the case. Furthermore a framework guarantees predictable and repeatable deliveries. What you want to do is describe your Enterprise, mend issues, align technology, map your goals... not re-invent and develop EA frameworks.

EA benefits in each category can be classified in a table of key benefit indicators that can be used to justify and guess/estimate the value of the EA development.

To be representative, the benefits have to be expressed as relative values to the no-EA case, in percentages, that is point to advantages to be had compared to the case you don't build the EA.

While the EA is implemented, the table can be also used to measure the actual value of each indicator and as such, in the end, an overall relative figure for benefits that suggest the real value added by the EA as it is implemented. That will please the management indeed. This is what they need to support your effort.

One can change, add or weight these key benefit indicators. Thus, this is a method rather than a prescriptive procedure. The benefits can be refined and improved.

Overall, assuming the simplification that the key indicators equally contribute to benefits, the relative revenue/costs ratio of the architecture versus the revenue/costs for the non architecture case will give you the relative return on the EA. In truth, EA becomes an asset, once developed. The better the framework, the better the EA and better the return that increases with the EA deployment progress.

Because the business thinks in financial terms, considering the EA a competitive asset, an NPV can be calculated, taking into account the investment costs over the development time plus the relative revenue/costs of the architecture vs. non architecture case, calculated as stated before. I build a conceptual model in a spreadsheet so that I can play with key parameters like investment size, assumed benefits, initial EA development time. It was a mild surprise to discover that if done properly and in time the costs may out-weight the savings and increases in efficiencies.

Why do you need this? Because you have to justify the costs of your project to build an EA, like any other project, in other words you need to build a business case. Then you may want to quantify progress in delivering the business benefits rather than the EA.

Benefits are enabled by the EA but realised by stakeholders

July 20, 2010

http://www.ebizq.net/blogs/ea_matters/2010/07/benefits-are-enabled-by-the-enterprise-architecture-but-realised-by-stakeholders-and-solely.php

It's worth pointing out again that EA is not in itself about business improvement, technology alignment, strategic planning and portfolio management; EA **enables** them all though, if properly modelled.

As such, to measure Enterprise Architecture value as an EA architect, one needs to evaluate what EA delivers to Enterprise stakeholders, taking into account their views.

These stakeholders, not the architects, are in charge of strategic planning, process improvement, technology alignment to business, decision making etc and thus they will eventually materialise the benefits if properly supplied with the EA artefacts they need. The EA architect does not do strategy, portfolio management... but works to support these efforts.

Nevertheless, when top management asks though what are the EA benefits, they indeed talk about the whole Enterprise. Then the EA architect needs to pull together all benefits realised at all Stakeholders for the good of the Enterprise.

Overall and in the end, assuming EA is mature enough (has a proper EA development and utilisation process), the EA benefits may be translated in Enterprise Simplification, Integration, Alignment, Agility and Strategic planning.

A note. EA has strong roots in IT. It consists though not only of business and IT but also of non-IT and organization architectures. Without the business view the IT picture alone cannot offer the touted benefits. As such the business and organisation architectures become essential in returning benefits to all people rather than IT alone as is the case today.

Enterprise Architecture in times of economic downturn

July 27, 2010

http://www.ebizq.net/blogs/ea_matters/2010/07/enterprise-architecture-in-times-of-economic-downturn.php

In times of economic crisis and after, but not only, to survive, a company needs to

- increase effectiveness (i.e. produce more with less)

by discovering, documenting, improving and streamlining its processes. This requires alignment of BPM, Lean/Six-Sigma, CMM efforts...

- enhance organization efficiency

by aligning roles and responsibilities in the organization chart to systems & processes in the EA

- reduce costs

by standardization and elimination of duplications in products, platforms, processes ...

- execute properly the strategy to achieve business objectives by mapping strategies to organizational units and EA capability projects

 - rationalize resource consuming projects

by prioritising all tactical and strategic projects in a Project Portfolio

What is the value of a Sigma effort if the systems described in EA are not properly supporting the improved processes?

How can one properly execute strategy if this is not mapped to business capabilities for lack of an EA blueprint?

Only a full Enterprise Architecture alone will support all these developments through coordination rather than replacement of existing developments. An EA that is not confined to IT. And there is no need for additional investments but for a better correlation of existing Enterprise initiatives.

EA DELIVERABLES AND ITS PURPOSE

The Enterprise Architecture purpose and definition

February 21, 2013

http://www.ebizq.net/blogs/ea_matters/2013/02/the.php

EA, as the name states, is the architecture that is the integrated blueprint of the enterprise. It, simply put, describes the enterprise from the many angles that serve its various stakeholders.

Hence, EA, as an architecture, is to be employed to

- simplify the enterprise

- operation improvement,

- cost reduction

- align of technology operation to the business wants

- align of the enterprise components evolution to strategy

- analyse business models

- create an enterprise wide transformation project portfolio

- guide decisions and investment

In more general terms, EA is employed to ease complexity and change management. The EA may be asked to do strategy but only for IT but this not necessarily an EA task.

The purpose of an EA framework is to enable the delivery of the EA, that is the architecture of the enterprise, rather than solving the problems of the enterprise.

The EA itself, once created, would be employed by stakeholders (clients) to achieve their specific goals such as fixing process issues, enterprise standardisation, integration, technology alignment to business operation, investment decisions, strategy implementation... in which activities, the EA architect may not be called to assist at all.

Once the architect delivers a proper EA framework and EA, he succeeds, more or less, to make own self redundant.

EA is successful if it delivers the integrated EA architecture with views for most of its stakeholders (for example top management, finance, IT development, Quality improvement etc) enabling them to achieve their own work objectives in alignment with the enterprise strategy.

If the EA team engages only in policing efforts around the enterprise, without delivering a reference EA, then the EA team failed. The EA blueprint should be used by stakeholders, as much as possible, without the engagement of the architects. The architects are not the factotum of the enterprise.

But the definition of the EA states more than its purpose. It has to answer the What then other W like questions such as Why, Who, How...

It denotes the EA practice that should collaborate and coordinate the many other activities in an enterprise to discover, design and implement the EA and the enterprise target state.

EA also means the EA team that manages the enterprise.

And the EA body of knowledge, the discipline that could be studied and taught.

Enterprise Architecture, cui bono?

Aug 12, 2010

http://it.toolbox.com/blogs/ea-matters/enterprise-architecture-cui-bono-40547

- CEOs and in general top management, to perform the decision making process and to optimize the Enterprise to achieve higher growth through reduced time to market and increased customer satisfaction and cost efficiency through streamlined operations.

- CTOs and Line-Of-Business executives to align technology investment to business objectives

- CIOs and Chief IT Architects to transform business strategy into IT programmes and technology roadmaps, integrate Enterprise applications, streamline infrastructure, optimise IT governance and ultimately improve the return on IT

- IT Solution Architects, Software Architects and Quality Engineers responsible for IT architecture guidelines and standards, from the use of a common Framework, vocabulary, and methodology provided by the EA

- Programme Management Team and Business and Technology Strategists to build a strategy put it into action so that it is traceable to the Enterprise functions, processes

- Owners and shareholders to understand how he Enterprise returns value to them by looking at the business models mapped on the EA blueprints

- Stakeholders that deal with regulation to position compliance (TO SOX, Basel III...) in the context of the enterprise structure and processes,

- every stakeholder in an enterprise to understand and improve operation in own domain

EA like Strategy, is about long term thinking. It is the way an Enterprise can survive the furious rate of change and competition, the increasing acquisitions and outsourcing trends and the exponential increase in complexity and amount of information.

Imagine you chose Not to develop an Enterprise Architecture, while your competitors do it; your investments maybe misplaced, products will reach the market later, will be less reliable and your investors will lack confidence because your strategy is poorly executed. Where does this leave you?

Ultimately EA is promising you a Competitive Advantage by streamlining your Enterprise, enabling faster product delivery at lower costs, handling the exploding amount of information and providing greater Enterprise agility to cope with change.

EA is an essential Asset, the knowledge DB of your Enterprise and the basis for all change.

Does the EA function run without an EA?

Dec 31, 2010

http://it.toolbox.com/blogs/ea-matters/does-the-enterprise-architecture-function-run-without-an-ea-41642

What happens when the EA function does not produce an EA and it runs without an EA, without a blueprint...?

In the absence of the EA blueprint, the EA function can only run arbitrarily. And that's happening so often today.

EA work mainly validates solution architectures and technology investments against a few experienced IT minds. But there is no reference EA.

EA results depend on the EA architect skills as such. Too much so. The EA architect becomes the main risk, factor of success or lack of it.

The EA team, without an EA, does typically solution architecture reviews work and eventually IT roadmapping.

It does not coordinate the production of an EA against which solutions should be verified, technology should be selected, processes could be improved...

Thus EA team skills are thus focused on general IT and knowledge of the enterprise and domain rather than architecture.

That is why so often EA is defined as a function alone, as a practice and governance rather than as an Enterprise blueprint and structure, in the first place. But EA requires both.

What happens when the EA function does not produce an EA?

December 31, 2010

http://www.ebizq.net/blogs/ea_matters/2010/12/what-happens-when-the-ea-function-does-not-produce-an-ea.php

What happens when the EA function does not produce an EA and it runs without an EA, without a blueprint...?

In the absence of the EA blueprint, the EA function can only run arbitrarily. And that's happening so often today.

EA work mainly validates solution architectures and technology investments against a few experienced IT minds. But there is no reference EA.

EA results depend on the EA architect skills as such. Too much so. The EA architect becomes the main risk, factor of success or lack of it.

The EA team, without an EA, does typically solution architecture reviews work and eventually IT roadmapping.

It does not coordinate the production of an EA against which solutions should be verified, technology should be selected, processes could be improved...

Thus EA team skills are thus focused on general IT and knowledge of the enterprise and domain rather than architecture.

That is why so often EA is defined as a function alone, as a practice and governance rather than as an Enterprise blueprint and structure, in the first place. But EA requires both.

EA is not aimed at creating models. Is that so?

 Jan 26, 2013

http://it.toolbox.com/blogs/ea-matters/enterprise-architecture-is-not-aimed-at-creating-models-is-that-so-54747

Here is a link to a post by Sunil Duttjha on the "Biggest myth – "Enterprise Architecture is a discipline aimed at creating models". And here are my comments.

Quote:

"*Biggest myth – "Enterprise Architecture is a discipline aimed at creating models".* Unfortunately, most of the Enterprise Architecture practitioners and several branded consulting organizations are caught in this trap. The situation has worsened as several architects & business process experts are building "composite models" (multi variable model) and calling it "architecture" model...

... a doctor (surgeon) is not about creating a physical "X-ray", but use the "x-ray" to do the proper "diagnosis" and prescribe necessary "treatment.

Architecture, in general, is about models, blueprints. Hence, enterprise architects have to devise models that describe the enterprise. Based on these models many people in the enterprise visualise, analyse and solve their own issues, in context. You cannot properly solve an issue without looking at the environment it takes place in.

If you are not doing that, then you are not doing architecture. And then you should not call EA what you do and you should not call yourself an EA architect.

And who is going to model or describe the "anatomy" of the enterprise if not the EA architects?

A wide variety of specialised doctors, rather than the x-ray specialist, do diagnose and treat the problems, using the x-ray in the process.

Similarly, business professionals analyse and solve the enterprise problems, using the EA description of the enterprise produced by the architect.

The EA architect may be asked to assist the process, sometimes, just like the x-ray specialist, but the architect does not solve the problems of the enterprise. He is not even qualified to do so. Moreover an EA architect working in IT is not tasked to solve the enterprise issues.

X-raying, like EA modelling, is made look simple though. But it's not just about snapping a picture. The EA "model" looks more like an MRI scan, a method to create an integrated set of views of a body, taken from different perspectives amongst which even virtual sections through the body as if you cut it to see what's inside. That is how the enterprise model, the EA, should look like.

Still, the scan methods and technology have been developed for a long time now and with plenty of effort. EA has not reached this stage yet.

This kind of EA positioning creates unnecessary friction in the enterprise because the architect claims to resolve problems that are normally the job of business experts and management. They have been doing that long before we even talked about EA.

To paraphrase Sunil, "this ignorance has serious ramification, as several Enterprises are making considerable investments in this area without significant gain". And it contributes to the rejection and failure of EA.

Because of such views that EA is not about modelling, EA loses its credibility with the business especially in the context in which it fails.

And EA fails because the pictures the EA produces now are not useful. In fact, these diagrams have since long existed in the enterprise. The problem is that they are and have always been disjoint, disconnected and that because of the lack of a proper integrating modelling framework that links the models together to give the bigger enterprise wide picture. Without this framework, the end to end analysis of the enterprise and its problem resolution is made rather impossible, the result of guess work alone.

It is true that few can properly and consistently do EA since most current frameworks do not help modelling. They are anything but enterprise modelling frameworks. Mostly they describe the process of development of the target EA. Hence, each and every EA architect has to re-invent own modelling methods which give the known results.

Zachman's framework was used by people for modelling but it constantly fails because it is not meant to do that as Sunil cites and reckons: "...the concept Enterprise Architecture. It is not about building models"; "all the frameworks (except the Zachman Framework) are about creating models..."

The purpose of Enterprise Architecture

Nov 21, 2009

http://it.toolbox.com/blogs/ea-matters/the-purpose-of-enterprise-architecture-35139

There was a challenge to describe the EA purpose in 160 chars on Linkedin EA Network discussion group. There were more than 300 responses. It looks like the challenge was taken as to define the purpose of EA for the first time, since seldom were posted definitions coming from well known fora or from Zachman, for instance, who is well known for his discourses on EA justification.

What pushed us to create new definitions? Isn't this originality coming from the lack of agreed standards?

Obviously, there is division in our ranks on what we do and for what purpose. As such, do we perform the same job? Having seen this, what would be the expectations of our customers? Could customers expect consistent results?

No wonder then we have so many Enterprise Architects and so few Enterprise Architectures.

An analysis of such responses should conclude, not on the purpose of EA, but rather on the state of our profession, surviving without an agreed EA body of knowledge that is definition, scope, method, framework... What governance do we need to agree on these basic assumptions?

Even architects' certification would not help without a reference body of knowledge because there is no basis to assess a professional against.

But in the end the answer is simple. EA means architecture (after all it's in the name), i.e. a blueprint. As such, each and every stakeholder uses the blueprints for own purpose: discover a system, improve a process, map strategy... There is no single purpose.

Or, were I to classify them, I would say EA enables Enterprise streamlining, alignment, agility and strategic planning.

The Business and IT alignment issue

Sep 25, 2009

http://it.toolbox.com/blogs/ea-matters/the-business-and-it-alignment-issue-34379

The alignment between business and IT has three dimensions.

From an operational viewpoint, IT needs to implement the processes and interfaces that business people need. Often the IT systems are inflexible, with hard coded processes and information. They resist change and hinder the business effort to deliver the service/product in time and quality.

Systems cost a lot to maintain only and IT expertise is dear. Often because systems are designed in isolation, for a large number of customers, they are too complex to master, have overlapping functionality and do not integrate well with other systems in terms of processes and information exchange. How do business and IT people make business processes work well, end to end on such weakly integrated systems? EA is a potential solution.

From a strategic point of view, IT has to align its capabilities and strategy to implement the business roadmap. As such, the IT systems have to evolve in line with the business plans. But sometimes this happens the other way around. And this is the strategic alignment issue.

Partly, the alignment problem is caused by the IT systems state of art. They have not been designed with an overall Enterprise view in mind, from the beginning.

An Enterprise Architecture is, amongst other, a late attempt to fix business and IT alignment issues caused by a lack of an overall Enterprise Architectural view in the design phase of each Enterprise system. Frameworks like NGOSS of TM forum attempt to remedy this. And SOA makes things easier.

One has also to align people responsibilities. A separate large IT department that serves the Enterprise is too slow to respond to business needs. It has a life of its own. Segregated to/in IT business units, it responds better and faster but costs more due to duplication.

Is complexity a problem for the enterprise?

Feb 11 2013

http://www.ebizq.net/blogs/ea_matters/2013/02/is-complexity-a-problem-for-the-enterprise.php

Richard Veryard states that "*Complexity is not a problem*". Let me see.

Complexity is growing rapidly today. And that is as it should be.

Should we not control complexity, the management of our systems and enterprises, of their issues and their aligned evolution, would require greater and greater efforts and costs.

Architecture helps us manage complexity though since it documents, breaks, groups and encapsulates it in blocks which can be independently managed like computer chips.

This is what the architect typically does and architecture comes with.

Besides how could one be able to convincingly say what an enterprise looks like without an architectural description? How would one be able to isolate a defect in time? How would one make the strategy happen without gross gaps?

The EA architect documents the complex enterprise (otherwise described by many pictures in many drawers), establishes principles and guidelines of evolution and creates the target architecture so that complexity would grow in a controlled manner rather than feeding on itself to result in even more complexity in more diversity.
The architect also standardizes to reduce complexity.

Complexity creates for the human enterprise a problem that grows. Unmanaged, it alters the capability of the enterprise to deliver and respond to market change. The knowledge in various domains is increasing too quickly. How do we cope with this? People specialise. But in the process, they lose the big picture, the overall architecture.
Hence, somebody in the enterprise has to hold this synoptic picture. This would be the EA architect.

The amount of information is growing. The Information architects then come to create and manage the information and its map, as part of an enterprise architecture

Architects document enterprises, guide their service based modular transformation. In general, they are the keepers of the big picture.

Unmanaged complexity amplifies problems and slows down opportunity realisation.

Managing complexity diminishes problems and their solving cost and amplifies opportunities.

Complexity becomes one of the biggest problems of an enterprise when not properly managed.

The architect stalls not the growth in complexity since it is inevitable. Firms can add new functionality which. as a rule, adds complexity. They ought to manage it, since otherwise it may turn against them in terms of operation stability, reliability, integration, response time, cost etc.

At similar complexity, competing firms are differentiated, by their capabilities to manage complexity.

That's how EA becomes a competitive advantage.

The EA architects have the task to guide the enterprise evolution to avoid unnecessary complexity. To do that, they employ the EA blueprint, principles, service orientation, roadmaps etc. For example, if the business suggests to procure a new application, of which the enterprise already as a few of the kind, the architect has to analyse and, if the proposal does not have enough business merit, suggest a solution for re-use. In fact, the architect has to automate that decision for others to do, by creating upfront principles, standards... that are agreed by and enforced by all business stakeholders.

WHAT EA DOES OR SHOULD DO

Is EA about "architecting" the Enterprise?

Feb 26, 2007

http://it.toolbox.com/blogs/ea-matters/is-ea-about-architecting-the-enterprise-14764

Responding to a challenge from John Wu about "what is EA" here. I think this discussion is of significance to the EA understanding and proper development. I will focus on two questions: Does EA include "architecting" the Enterprise? And is EA an IT only development?

Looking at the name alone, you would conclude that EA describes the structure and operation of an Enterprise. That being said, Enterprise Architecture (EA) has different meanings for different people. The proof resides in the diversity of approach in the available EA frameworks.

EA appears to have its roots in IT - interestingly enough Zachman drew comparisons with the aircraft industry in designing his framework. EA, for most IT people, means an Enterprise wide IT architecture. For this reason I would call it "Enterprise IT Architecture" to allow "Enterprise Architecture" alone cover what it is entitled to, the Enterprise wide business processes, information, organization and technology. IT is not the only or even the most important technology in an Enterprise, take for example the manufacturing cases.

To fully describe an Enterprise one needs to consider, to begin with, the business mission, stakeholders, products, processes, organization and governance and All technology (not only IT); not to mention financial aspects, real estate and other views of real interest to internal or external stakeholders.

Once the current Enterprise blueprint is documented and understood to your satisfaction, a next logical step would be to attempt to enhance the Enterprise operation by using the EA to reduce duplication in platforms, projects and people

(!), align Enterprise Entities performance to business objectives and provide agility to change by re-engineering the Enterprise in a SOA manner (let's say). In other words you may anticipate the future shape of your Enterprise, "architect" it accordingly to attain the competitive advantage and then proceed on the business transformation path. But you may choose not to do it.

There are a few large EA developments in institutions which are based almost entirely on IT technology. Governments for one. A key objective for these is to co-ordinate IT investment and re-use between the many departments. But "architecting" the Enterprise for the future would enable e-government with interactive Web 2.0 technologies for public benefit.

In the end it all comes down to the scope of and specific priorities of the EA development once you consider the whole spectrum. EA is about the Enterprise not only IT and "architecting" the Enterprise will convey you a competitive advantage.

Enterprise Architecture, how does it look like?

March 12, 2011

http://www.ebizq.net/blogs/ea_matters/2011/03/enterprise-architecture.php

Why do we do EA, the everlasting question.

Companies have lived without an EA for a long time now and they would continue to do so. Is there an EA business case after all? Yes, but touted benefits can be realised only for the enterprise scope rather than for IT alone.

EA, as it is, would continue though to survive in the enterprise even if not returning the advertised benefits. The EA concept is resilient since intuitively, stakeholders perceive good value in having the architecture of their enterprise documented.

How does an EA look like in fact?

There are few published or publicly available case studies to describe a full EA that includes business architecture, organization, non-IT technology....

Books about EA are so oddly different that you wonder if they treat the same concept. But, in truth, many are about IT architecture and strategy or describe known frameworks.

Are there reference models available?

That is templates, generic business and IT architectures. Not really. TOGAF speaks about the Architecture Continuum but does not offer any model.

Is there an agreed body of knowledge?

There are at least a few rather independent schools of thought: Zachman, TOGAF, FEA, DODAF... They neither cover the same ground nor the whole EA territory. FEA and DODAF are too specialized for general use.

TOGAF is essentially a development method, rather lush and unstructured. A process alone - like TOGAF ADM - cannot lead to an EA without Enterprise specific reference models and frameworks describing structure and behaviour.

Zachman is simple a structured method of thinking asking basic questions like why, what...

None of these approaches are enterprise specific except FEA which is composed of a few government specific sub-frameworks.

There is no over arching professional authority but many EA associations. There is no single organization or personality to steer the field. Reputed consultancies and schools seem not to have an opinion, agree or they come with apocalyptic visions about new EA paradigms that will emerge soon... Mind the business architecture! Or EA is about strategy and future states alone!

There are too many different training courses and certifications.

Multiple independent training and certifications and bodies that ignoring each other, compete for you. They make little difference in practice in the delivery of EA but they can obviously aid you in getting an EA job.

The Enterprise Architect naming and the EA profession

Aug 31, 2010

http://www.ebizq.net/blogs/ea_matters/2010/08/the-enterprise-architect-name-and-ea-profession.php

Jeff Scott of Forrester blogged about the Enterprise Architect in "What's in a name". I replied but I would further like to expand on this.

Were we to look at the name alone, we would conclude that Enterprise Architect is someone performing the role of an architect of the Enterprise.

And architecture produces blueprints typically for buildings, bridges; and now the Enterprise.

Including Zachman in the assessment we would note that the EA architect would have to ask "w" questions from a number of perspectives to discover how the Enterprise works and what is its structure.

DODAF, the oldest EA framework, architects the way the whole DoD and its operations work.

But there is nothing much about strategy and even less about IT in this. Solely the Why question reminds us vaguely of strategy.

How can one determine that EA is about strategy alone? Even TOGAF says different.

You may do strategy, business or IT, and call yourself accordingly a strategist... and not an EA architect. This will be fair. But it would not be fair to attempt to change the Enterprise Architect name for there are true EA professionals.

It is true that, in practice, EA was somehow hijacked by IT and strategists that call themselves Enterprise Architects. And it is true that everyone in IT seems to be an architect today. It probably all started with the grand Enterprise name in technologies such as EAI, ERP, JavaEE... to denote the capability of technology to serve the whole Enterprise.

And it is also true that most EA architects do IT solution architecture and reviews and IT strategy according to an own Forrester's survey (see recent post).

But the EA profession survives because it is clear to us that it holds great promise in describing the Enterprise and enabling its transformation.

Survey proves that EA does only IT strategy, solution architecture...

August 4, 2010

http://www.ebizq.net/blogs/ea_matters/2010/08/ea-survey-proves-that-enterprise-architecture-does-it-strategy-solution-architecture-and-project-rev.php

Here is a Forrester survey from 2009 on what IT professionals part of an EA group, typically do. I add my source and the picture for convenience.

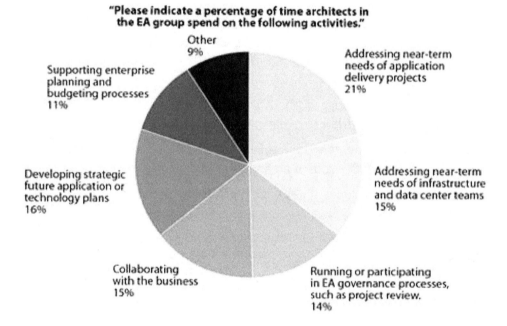

"Please indicate a percentage of time architects in the EA group spend on the following activities."

- Other 9%
- Addressing near-term needs of application delivery projects 21%
- Supporting enterprise planning and budgeting processes 11%
- Developing strategic future application or technology plans 16%
- Addressing near-term needs of infrastructure and data center teams 15%
- Collaborating with the business 15%
- Running or participating in EA governance processes, such as project review. 14%

Base: 416 IT professionals familiar with EA
(percentages may not add to 100 due to rounding)
Source: September 2009 Global Annual State of Enterprise Architecture Online Survey

"Addressing near-term needs of applications... " (21%) and Addressing near-term needs of infrastructure" (15%) suggest, at first sight, application or solution architecture work. This a substantial amount of their time NOT spent on Enterprise Architecture.

"Collaboration with business"(15%). Most IT professionals collaborate with business to gather requirements, deliver services, check satisfaction etc. Nothing suggests that this is time spent on Business or Enterprise Architecture.

Overall, the time spent by EA architects on business as usual IT solutions architecture activity amounts to 60% of their time (21%+15%+15% +9%other)!

There remain a few key EA group work items:

- Project reviews - "Running or participating in EA governance processes"- 14%

- IT strategic planning and support - "Developing future applications or technology plans - 16% and "Supporting Enterprise planning and budgeting" (11%): I assume the activity is limited to IT and is related to new applications and systems roadmaps and strategy.

Overall amounting to 41% of the time of the architect.

A first conclusion is that the work is nearly All IT. Then that EA architects, or member of the EA group mostly do Solution Architecture work.

I can see no hint of architecture modelling work, that, I would have said, it's a key component of the EA, that is if we still want to call it EA. Also there is no EA definition work, that is work like framework selection, repository design, specification of principles and measures for EA maturity and value delivered etc. There is no mention of EA work done by business stakeholders or IT professionals not part of the EA team.

Looking again at the graph, the end deliveries of the EA group appear to be applications and technology planning. No wonder EA is so often confused with IT strategy.

To recap, currently, EA seems to be all about IT, focused on solution architecture, project reviews and IT strategy.

That may explain why EA is of so little consequence in the Enterprise today and TOGAF, consisting mainly of the ADM process, is the development method of choice. There are no business or IT architecture blueprints whatsoever which we may naturally associate with EA.

This is not really EA work and the professionals in the group are IT rather than EA architects.

THE EA DESIGN AND VISUALISATION

The Enterprise Architecture Socratic approach

May 3, 2009

http://it.toolbox.com/blogs/ea-matters/the-enterprise-architecture-socratic-approach-31339

The first approach to Enterprise Architecture, the Socratic one (see previous blogs), is an application of the wisdom of old. Kipling, in 1902, wrote for our little ones (and us, later) "The Elephant's Child" of "Just So Stories". I quote:

"I Keep six honest serving-men:

(They taught me all I knew)

Their names are What and Where and When

And How and Why and Who..."

The method served us since infancy so why not use it now for Enterprise Architecture, which is in its own infancy. It's true that this time we address the questions to ourselves, that is, we have to come with the answers. After this "questioning" phase we have to clarify for ourselves what "What" means (data, objects, nodes, systems, functions etc) or "When"... mean, and so on.

Nevertheless the "six honest serving-men" (What, Where, When, How...) serve us to check the scope of the EA. Have we covered the how, the why...? The approach establishes the bare bones of an EA. Unfortunately that's where it stops supporting our efforts.

As these questions apply to any system, the framework would do equally well for a barn or an Enterprise Architecture design. That would leave us to define or find and use a reference structure of the type we need.

But no EA framework currently provides Enterprise reference maps or templates to show the structure of the Enterprise, the typical parts in interconnection. It is like you start designing or modifying a building without understanding its purpose, the actual or future blueprint. It is only our relative experience that tells us that we need.

For the Enterprise, what are the typical components?

Here the business academy should help us more otherwise, how can we align our systems to an EA business architecture/map that does not exist?

Unfortunately, the big names in business management do not show much interest in Enterprise Architecture, at least, not yet. No sign that they grasped the problem of the business architecture vacuum. I wonder, sometimes, how can they avoid using an architecture or business map in their work.

The Enterprise Architecture discipline is itself condemned without a business architecture.

An IT architecture would show only applications and technology in a myriad of interconnections without showing the business functions they perform, how the business processes work or what information is exchanged over the wires. The Business Architecture would respond to all questions starting with How and Why.

EA is about how to fit the parts in the whole rather...

Jan 30, 2012

http://it.toolbox.com/blogs/ea-matters/enterprise-architecture-is-about-how-to-fit-the-parts-in-the-whole-rather-50203

In time it became rather clear to me that most EA architects usually labour at describing simple capabilities, design solution architectures, police the development of solutions, establish architecture principles - but not the full EA framework -, specify IT strategy and spend a lot of time justifying themselves and selling Enterprise Architecture. What is missing? The Enterprise Architecture itself.

Can you judge a solution architecture outside the context of an Enterprise Architecture? While we do it all the time, the EA big picture would still save time and reduce the costly errors of missing parts and connections.

Can you specify best strategy without the picture of the whole? A strategy not based on EA would most probably be incomplete and inconsistent and as such would be satisfactory only to parts of the enterprise.

The truth is that no two architects have the same understanding of EA, use the same methodology or achieve similar results. Still, why so many architects claim success and when asked to share the results shy away?

The answer may be as simple as that. We don't do anything new. We describe the enterprise in bits and shards, as we always did. But the bits are neither consistent nor integrated.

That is because there is no Architecture framework in the sense of a frame where the EA parts fit in to render the whole. I often wondered how can we implement an

Enterprise Architecture without a proper EA framework.

TOGAF is effectively a process template plus lots of advice. Zachman a model of systemic thinking. DoDAF a method of description... Nevertheless, they do not provide a framework to which you can fit the parts of the Enterprise to give the whole.

In the absence of this framework, what do we deliver then? Parts. But not integrated in the EA whole. We do this all the time. We do it now without an Enterprise Architecture. We have the bits of the puzzle but not the big picture. In the end, the implementation of the target enterprise state would not work as desired since the parts/solutions are not integrated, the transformation strategy covers just pieces...

A proper EA framework would enforce parts compliance to the whole and their interconnection enabling the proper discovery, design and implementation of a consistent and complete whole.

The EA is about describing, roadmapping and improving the Enterprise as a whole of parts rather than describing... the parts in separation as many architects do today claiming they do EA. We did that for many years now. But is that collection of parts description an EA? Do the parts work seamlessly as a whole?

The EA design has to begin with the whole rather than the parts

October 8, 2012

http://www.ebizq.net/blogs/ea_matters/2012/10/what-the-stakeholders-need-from-ea.php

Not unexpectedly, one of the key business stakeholders from finance asked - while I was in the process of "selling" him the EA - "why do we need EA, since you, in IT, surely have an architecture, don't you, otherwise how can the technology properly function and be maintained today?".

Good question, how does the technology keeps working without an architecture to describe its layout that would facilitate our understanding, defect fixing, improvements and evolution?

Well, I did not dare alienate him by responding that it works the same way as the business works today without having a coherent picture of the overall business operation.

But we, EAs, have to explain ourselves a lot, unlike other professionals. And patience is king.

What I said in exchange, is that indeed, IT has currently have quite a few architecture diagrams. In fact, everybody seems to have a model in his drawer. But this is also the problem since these models don't add up to give the big picture. And they don't, since they were not produced to that purpose, but in isolation, with different tools, conventions, naming, scope and purpose in mind.

I proposed an architecture on a table exercise where all diagrams in existence would be exhibited on a table. Did they form the bigger picture? Obviously not, because the glue and rules that connected the parts and made them look consistent was missing. The artefacts were often overlapping and parts were missing.

This is what EA aims to do, I continued: rather than providing the partial architectures designed in separation, we start from the EA big picture that can be decomposed in these architectures for each and every stakeholder. These diagrams, unlike the existing ones, interconnect to each other and are consistent in terms of components, terminology, drawing tools... and so on. And they can be put back in whole, in the Enterprise picture.

As such you can navigate from one artefact to another in order to analyse an end to end process or navigate to the executing technology resources and people so that you can come out with costs, impacts of change and propose fixes.

What do you, the EA team, have to do for that? You'll provide the EA framework that everyone should use in designing own part, so that every artefact would have the same look and feel and refer to the same components and links. (see the FFLV-GODS framework).

You'll provide the principles, constraints, tools, repository and support for the stakeholders to produce the bit of architecture they are concerned with. You'll make sure that the bits would fit back into the EA.

Today, the technology up-keep depends too much, for anyone's liking, on the people who manned it, on their expensive skills and experience. In the absence of architecture, the process is marred by guessing and debate, by trials and errors and as such, delays that cost the enterprise much more. EA will come with the enterprise layout and with the up-keep process that would help optimise this process.

EA would enable the logical identification of a defect using the business architecture and afterward, its quick fix using the corresponding technology architecture.

You also need EA for the process of keeping update the existing designs to fit the picture of the consistent whole.

Therefore, rather than coming bottom up to discover the enterprise with isolated parts, you come top down as well, to make sure that the parts fit the whole, that gives us the end to end picture. Again FFLV-GODS provides this big picture and framework.

Imagine now that the enterprise is a real tri-dimensional system. We can take out a part, document and fix it. And then put it back. But how could you put the parts back in the whole if there is no whole to begin with?

You as EA architects do not improve the enterprise, but produce the EA framework and the governance that guides the enterprise stakeholders in consistently producing the EA artefacts of their concern.

Then, based on the resulting EA, and with the guidance of the architect and EA method, stakeholders implement fixes and changes in their parts of the enterprise, in synergy but according to the EA roadmap.

EA methods today do not support the top-down design starting from the whole because they simply do not supply a framework in which the parts fit back. Also they do not have a concept of one page enterprise architecture that would be the EA artefact used by all stakeholders.

EA, the anatomy and physiology of the Enterprise

March 21, 2012

http://www.ebizq.net/blogs/ea_matters/2012/03/enterprise-architecture-the-anatomy-and-physiology-of-the-enterprise.php

How do we describe an Enterprise? Let me give you an well known example, the human body and illustrate the way the enterprise should be described, by comparison.

The description of the structure and operation of the Enterprise is shown here by analogy with the anatomy and physiology of the body.

The structure is illustrated by anatomy while the operation by physiology. Anatomy illustrates the body by depicting its

- parts: the head, torso, neck, limbs and organs like lungs, heart, liver...
- systems in separation: circulatory, nervous, skeletal, muscular systems...

These reflect two points of categorisation, two taxonomies. Systems look like cross body sections in a CT (computer tomography) scan.

Physiology describes how the vital flows such as breathing, digestion etc operate over these various systems and parts. The digestive process, for instance, depicts the food ingestion, distribution and transformation into energy from mouth to stomach and beyond. The respiratory process shows how the body processes and transports oxygen to organs.

Comparison:

- A body part (organ) implements a few of the body vital processes. For an Enterprise Architecture, the term "Function" (or Capability) plays the same role, grouping related business processes.

- A body system depicts the assembly of a few parts of a body with similar functionality. In EA, a View is an abstract cross-section in the Enterprise, looking like a virtual cut or a CT (computer tomography) picture. A layer is a physical View consisting of elements of same type, such a layer of muscles in the body or applications in EA.

- The organs or body parts, are interconnected by nerves, arteries... In EA, the interconnections between business functions are Lines that are implemented by connections.

A vital flow is a sequence of activities performed in organs (body parts). Like breathing. In EA, a "Flow" (aka value stream) is defined as a sequence of processes (in Functions) delivering the service/product.

A body interacts with the environment i.e. eats , breathes, feels... In the Enterprise, Use Case scenarios describe the interaction with the environment and stakeholders.

A doctor, a surgeon cannot diagnose or operate without being familiar with all the body parts, systems and vital processes. If he cuts the wrong link (read artery, nerve...) the operation will be successful but the patient probably dead.

Similarly, an Enterprise Architect, or those who need to operate the enterprise and implement strategy, cannot properly do so without knowledge of the business Functions, Flows, Layers and Views (FFLV) e.g. the anatomy and physiology of the enterprise.

Without anatomy and physiology medicine could not progress. We are at a stage now where we able to roughly describe what happens in a human body.

But we don't have a clue how an enterprise operates, end to end. We are at the beginning of the journey to understand, fix and improve the Enterprise.

We have first to understand the enterprise anatomy and physiology.

The FFLV (Functions-Flows-Layers-Views) EA framework, described in my book, blogs and site, can be used to describe the anatomy and physiology of the enterprise.

Enterprise Architecture visualisation

Sep 7, 2012

http://it.toolbox.com/blogs/ea-matters/enterprise-architecture-visualisation-52879

In this post, I will show how architecture visualisation methods used by architects for centuries (see Drew Skau's post Visualization Architect at Visual.ly) are relevant to an EA. I'll exemplify the procedures on the FFLV-GODS, a full EA framework.

- Begin quote from visual.ly

"...drawing techniques, developed very early in the history of architecture, were so successful at communicating and recording the ideas, processes, and concepts that go into a building that they are still used widely today.

... Even the advent of digital 3D modelling has not changed the necessity of having a basic set of plans, sections, elevations, details, and site plans...

Plan drawings:

Think of them as a map of the building, as they provide a view of the layout from above. Imagine cutting horizontally through a building at about three feet (or approximately 100cm) above the floor level and drawing everything that was sliced through"... Some plan view drawings happen at other levels in a building.

Section drawings

Section drawings involve the same cutting technique as plans, although the cutting plane is vertical instead of horizontal...

Details

Detail Sections show cuts through a portion of a building in order to describe the construction technique and material use.

Site Plans

In addition to the building itself, it is important for architects to provide context for a building.

- End quote

Typically, an architecture describes an entity by using visualisation techniques which have been used as well to describe the anatomy of human body.

The problem though with our EA frameworks is that they don't show the enterprise as a single entity as it is usual the case for classical architecture, but mostly as a list of separate views, selected rather at random, that do not link to each other or fit into a whole simply because there is no whole. It's like trying to reconstruct a body from a few partial remains or plans.

To sum it up, classical architecture (and FFLV) first shows the whole then the views which look like cuts into the whole. The current EA frameworks illustrate the views with no whole at all. How do even know that the views are part of or what part they cover from the EA whole?

The FFLV framework though is built as a cube (details on the web site or kindle book). Hence, the FFLV cube can be dissected using the classical architecture methods: plans, sections, details... as described above.

Assuming that EA is a single body has also the advantage that we make sure that all possible and potential aspects of an enterprise are implicitly part of the EA body even if they are not described yet. As such the EA framework is Open for the addition of any other architectural view.

We can cut the EA cube horizontally to obtain "plan drawings", vertically to get "section drawings", delve and zoom in to produce "detail drawings" or look at the enterprise context to describe the "site plans".

The three horizontal layers of the FFLV are the business, technology and people (see picture). Every layer can be cut (or CT scanned) by many views.

We can cut horizontally through

- the Business layer to see various functions and flows (workflows) and the information they use. For instance we can see in a view or plane only the Create Demand flows. Or we can see all the ERP functions and connections.

- the Technology layer to describe or get to all the technology views we need to observe, such as servers, networks, applications, productions bands.... The applications views would have the elements mapped on the elements in the servers view.

- the People to see organization charts, roles, salary, recruitment views.

People and technology views would show how business functions and flows are executed.

All these views/cuts can be seen as transparencies that overlaid would give the whole. The resulting whole would eventually look unreadable, since there is too much detail. That is why we need the separation on views.

We can manage complexity as well by managing aspects in isolation. Experts can analyse views separately and then put them back into the whole.

We can cut the EA Vertically to show

- a specific Function or a Flow along with all its resources, the people and technology that execute it.

For instance we can see the make of a product Flow from end to finish.

We can cut partially both vertically and horizontally to inspect a Detail plan of a certain EA aspect as well.

The FFLV cube representation may become the EA navigation User Interface. In the

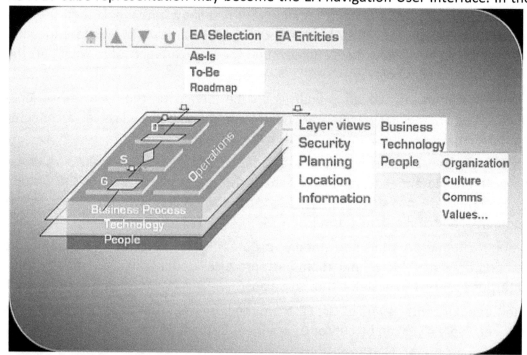

picture you can see the Views as transparencies cutting the cube horizontally.

Ultimately any aspect, such as Function, Flows... of the architecture, can be seen as a View.

The Functions, Flows and Layers Views (FFLV) would represent entry points into the EA navigation framework.

You may pick a Flow or a Function view to navigate for instance: up and down (through layers business, technology, people) a Function, to inspect the resources executing a business process

horizontally, to follow outputs/interconnections and inspect an end to end Flow

This is the FFLV Framework Navigation Screen.

For navigation one needs to select the architecture stage, current,... target, from the menu.

Then select the Function, Flow, Layer Views from the Drop-Down Menu or click directly on a Function, Flow or Layer View on the cube representation.

One can select one of the Governance, Operations, Development and Support (GODS) top level Functions of the enterprise to narrow down to a specific sub-function.

Navigation can also be performed with Up/Down, Back and Home buttons; you may also select a different level of business function detail or granularity (zoom in/out).

One can see top level Views such as Location, Security that would filter only the specs of interest such as location or security.

In the picture we have selected the organisation chart of the Layer People. The chart would appear on the next screen.

Here are a few descriptions of the FFLV-GODS EA framework [1], [2], [3].

The FFLV-GODS framework was used and implemented in practice. It comes with a transformation process, of the shelves models (templates), recommended design techniques/diagrams and metamodel indeed.

The book also describes a strategy design framework and many other techniques, such as patterns, maturity evaluation, SOA design etc

Enterprise Architecture as a blueprint

Nov 22, 2009

http://it.toolbox.com/blogs/ea-matters/enterprise-architecture-as-a-blueprint-35483

From http://science.howstuffworks.com/question321.htm.

"If you have ever watched a house being built, or if you have ever had an addition put onto an existing house, you know that the standard method of communication is a big piece of paper called a blueprint. Blueprinting is the standard method used to copy large architectural and construction drawings. A blueprint used to consist of white lines on a blue background. A more recent process uses blue lines on a white background."

It is designed by the architect and used by the plumber, electrician, owner, potential buyer...

The blueprint comes with guidance materials, when necessary. A plan of transformation is the result of strategy executed as (a portfolio of) projects transforming the Blueprint components.

The blueprint reflects the structure that changes in time with its purpose. The architecture could be classic or baroque, depending on the architectural style. The relationship between structure and its purpose is shaped by the architectural style.

The blueprint is not static. It should be constantly updated to reflect the change in structure result of all on-going projects in an Enterprise. That may not always happen but this is the role of the EA architect.

The EA blueprint is the base of all conversations on changing the structure to fit the purpose or fitness for purpose, maintenance, renovation and transformation. It should be the basis of change in the Enterprise, be it operational, tactical or strategic. Without a blueprint, the transformation cannot be properly managed; the Enterprise would grow organically until a point when nothing works properly any longer and its decay starts.

But it is not the task of the Enterprise Architect to do strategy. That is more related to markets, customers, financials, environment and regulatory concerns. The architect does not do planning but roadmaps.

The EA, as a blueprint, should be seen as the cornerstone of any Enterprise transformation, as a strategy, as in the title of a well known EA book.

What happens when the EA function does not produce an EA?

December 31, 2010

http://www.ebizq.net/blogs/ea_matters/2010/12/what-happens-when-the-ea-function-does-not-produce-an-ea.php

What happens when the EA function does not produce an EA and it runs without an EA, without a blueprint...?

In the absence of the EA blueprint, the EA function can only run arbitrarily. And that's happening so often today.

EA work mainly validates solution architectures and technology investments against a few experienced IT minds. But there is no reference EA.

EA results depend on the EA architect skills as such. Too much so. The EA architect becomes the main risk, factor of success or lack of it.

The EA team, without an EA, does typically solution architecture reviews work and eventually IT roadmapping.

It does not coordinate the production of an EA against which solutions should be verified, technology should be selected, processes could be improved...

Thus EA team skills are thus focused on general IT and knowledge of the enterprise and domain rather than architecture.

That is why so often EA is defined as a function alone, as a practice and governance rather than as an Enterprise blueprint and structure, in the first place. But EA requires both.

EA BUSINESS ARCHITECTURE, CAPABILITIES, VALUE CHAINS & STREAMS

Do Enterprise Architects do Business Architecture?

May 23, 2008

http://it.toolbox.com/blogs/ea-matters/do-enterprise-architects-do-business-architecture-24663

Business architects, when they exist, usually occupy business analyst roles, mostly belonging to the "business" community, not the IT; they have the task to look into requirements and model the business processes but typically out of the Enterprise Architecture context.

Still the business architecture is the key to the whole Enterprise Architecture. One cannot understand what applications do without a picture of what business wants to do and how it does it. In fact I would go so far to say that, without a business architecture, the EA (or SOA for that matter) means little: loose diagrams of a patchy collection of systems without the unifying picture of the business delivery flows.

The lack of a proper business architecture may be the ground for failure of Enterprise Architecture developments (and SOA - which is based on it -) to deliver the touted benefits and the subsequent management scepticism.

The problem with Enterprise Architects is that they do not cover business architecture since it is not part of their curriculum. Similarly, business people and analysts do not cover technology or even architecture as a discipline. The division between business and IT does the rest of the damage to the EA.

Hence, while there are "Enterprise Architects" in place doing IT integration, inventories... more often than not there is no one to do the business architecture i.e. business functional decomposition, process documentation...

The Enterprise Business Architecture and Architect's role

Jun 7, 2008

http://it.toolbox.com/blogs/ea-matters/the-enterprise-business-architecture-and-architects-role-24859

The problem with Enterprise Architecture and existing frameworks is that they are IT oriented, designed by IT, for IT ignoring the business views and architecture. That is why in most cases Enterprise Architects are selected from the ranks of IT Solution and Java Architects... While existing EA architects are eminent IT people there is no guarantee they understand or are even interested in the business methods and theory since they generally find employment on IT skills. In its current technology only approach, EA does not help much the Enterprise except for IT standardization purposes.

Business Architecture is often mentioned in the EA context. Fact is that reference business architectures and development methodologies barely exist, with exceptions. In fact they are called Value or/and Supply Chains (they are not the same) in business theory. Examples are VRM (Value Reference Model), SCOR (Supply Chain Organization Model), APQC, NGOSS (eTOM) in telecommunications... A warning: they all have slightly different approaches, not dissimilar to the EA frameworks   situation.
The architecture discipline does not exist in the business domain that deals with practical issues rather than organization design, value chains analysis, business models... Hence, the Enterprise Business Architect, while sometimes mentioned, does not really exist or the role is often allocated to a business analyst, not adequately equipped for the job.

The EA business architect should design the business architecture, the model on which you can base your IT architecture, and be knowledgeable of business operation, value chain analysis, supply chains, business models, BPM, business process design, Six/Lean Sigma, strategy, and eventually governance, organization design, business cases, management financials... and have an understanding of IT as well. This job description is not that of a business analyst that is most often found playing this role.

Many of these business architecture related topics are taught in an MBA program and as such it could be a route for an IT Architect to rise to an Enterprise Business Architect position. On the other hand, a business consultant skilled in IT might be a candidate for the role.

Architectural skills, typically acquired during a long career, are so important since structuring systems is the main activity of an Enterprise Architect. Business people and consultancies are not very much into Enterprise Architecture because, in the first place, they seldom cover the whole spectrum of business issues and they are not cultivating architectural skills that are more typically grown in a technology environment.

In the computer technology domain there is a long tradition of designing architecture represented in diagrams of electronic components and connections, systems and networks. The architecture was adopted afterwards in IT, at applications level, to depict integration, control and data flows. But applications alone hardly paint a picture of how the business works. To truly do Enterprise Architecture one needs to elevate the architecture discipline in the business domain, taking into account the already existing business concepts.

How to do Business Architecture

Sep 29, 2009

http://it.toolbox.com/blogs/ea-matters/how-to-do-business-architecture-34452

I posted this because I noticed an increased concern for business architecture in the EA community and many questions. EA architecture narrowed to IT fails to reveal the structure or operation of the Enterprise i.e. the Enterprise Architecture.

What would a picture with an ERP, CRM, Portal, DW and an e-commerce application... tell you? Little. Most companies have that. You wouldn't know your company from another. We'd all end up with the same picture.

You would not be able to align IT to business, because there is no business picture, never mind the organization and other technologies.

Your company is better described by its products, the company structure and business processes, the flow of your transactions.

How would we build a real business picture?

1. describe the products, stakeholders and environment. I use UML.

2. Map the business structure

I break the Enterprise in four business functions areas called collectively GODS: Governance (e.g. Board, CEO office...), Operations (e.g. Sourcing, Production, Sales), Development (R&D, Product Development) and Support (e.g. HR, IT...). Any Enterprise has this complete set of functions. Then I use Value Chains. In fact I produced a template business reference map to get anyone started. This is the business process map.

3. Depict processes

Use a business process framework (some call them Value Streams). I put together a simple generic one that will get the process documentation started. It is clearly describing key processes you have to model. It's not the same as the business reference map. This work can stretch over years and it is not in the IT scope. But EA is about coordination and collaboration.

4. Map Strategy and sketch future EA state, agree roadmap

I describe a strategy design and mapping process. That applies also to the IT architecture layers. Objectives are here cascaded to EA components, processes...

5. Then map the organization to business; need your CEO backing or back off; an organization design template is given with its alignment to architecture.

But there is more to that: what is the difference between a function and a process? In fact I use the term flow instead of process to eliminate confusion. This small issue may stop a good architecture in its tracks.

How do function, process and information link together? An EA framework shows the EA layers and views. A metamodel explains all EA entities and their relationships. The metamodel does not make you lose sleep by requiring modelling of services and contracts, as some do, because simply they don't really exist at this stage in most companies.

There always is an architecture design method recommending artefacts, design sequence... based on the old structured and OO SW design methodologies. Only DODAF has it. But key artefacts need to be standardised. When do we do activity or state diagrams? It is simpler than DODAF though.

Zachman and TOGAF would not help you with business architecture. Zachman asks the questions at the business layer but goes no further. You have to come with all the answers. TOGAF mostly lists business artefacts.

You would also see the difference between business modelling, business model and operating model in one place, one book and how to use them.

The most important EA artefact is the Single Page Architecture, or the business architecture on a page with entities, links and legend illustrated in the book.

The whole framework enables stakeholders to navigate the graphical EA framework representation from business entities to technology and organization, to trace processes, discover resources and impacts, analyse performance and eventually unearth faults.

This is cutting edge material for Business Architecture. BA materials are few since neither Business is trained in architecture nor IT in business theory. The book URL can be found in the footer of the blog. It is available on Amazon and other sites.

... defining what is an Enterprise capability?

October 29, 2011

http://www.ebizq.net/blogs/ea_matters/2011/10/what-if-we-start-from-ground-up-defining-what-is-an-enterprise-capability.php

Given the fact that we can hardly get an agreement on what the Enterprise capability is, that is from an Enterprise Architecture point of view.

The term Capability seems to come from the EA field rather than from the business process management discipline. Being often associated with the function or process, it raises questions in the BPM world. The fact BPM and EA don't intersect may explain why the term appeared in the first place and why it overlaps with the BPM terminology.

This is a follow-up of a discussion on Capabilities versus Processes that takes place on BP Trends LinkedIn. But as usual, these discussions on definitions lead nowhere, sliding from the initial purpose of answering a question or resolving an issue to prolonged monologues on ourselves.

I would describe first an entity that ties a functional process group to the people and technology that execute them. This functional process grouping consists of related processes (such as recruiting, for instance). The associated people would have the skills to execute the processes (to recruit). A (recruitment) application would perform the automated part of the process.

The entity would consist of the process, the skilled people and the application performing the activity. A process alone is an abstract concept; it cannot deliver without the people and systems.

Let's call this entity a Capability.

The capability can be performed repeatedly or on demand and it can provide services to the enterprise or to other parties. It can be roadmapped and strategies would cascade to capabilities for implementation.

Most companies would need to rely on a set of fundamental capabilities. Some capabilities would become differentiators or core to the enterprise, some would be outsourced.

At a large granularity, (capabilities may be decomposed), firms would need Sales, Marketing, Development, Support (HR, IT...)... These can be described in capability maps.

Capability maps may look different though from process frameworks because their definition depends also on the existing system designs. This is why EA does not typically re-use the existing process frameworks.

This capability concept, or whatever we may decide to call it, may help bridge the EA with the BPM world.

In my book I describe the term Function as a related process grouping, at its basics. Processes in functions are executed by the systems in the Technology Layer of the FFLV EA framework and by the resources in the People Layer. As such a function with its associated resources in layers looks like a Function Stack. As such a Capability is a function stack. It is not abstract. It can deliver as an independent entity, almost.

But Capability alone is not sufficient to describe a business architecture. Processes are still necessary to describe the end to end delivery of a product or in general of value.

Architectural views must be representative of EA... framework

November 17, 2010

http://www.ebizq.net/blogs/ea_matters/2010/11/architectural-views-must-be-representative-of-business-architecture-and-ea-framework.php

An EA architect does not have to provide business views. This is the business of business professionals. The architect should supply though the EA framework, the component repository, guidelines... for all stakeholders to use in producing their own views so that they fit back in the whole.

Views are unlimited in number. After all, every Enterprise stakeholder has its own View. So what we need is not a list of perspectives but an EA framework (like FFLV see my site) that allows for a View to be added at any time without breaking the integrity of the EA.

Views are any aspects of the Enterprise of concern to a stakeholder, representations of which can be linked to EA as long as they comply with the enterprise structure and EA framework.

Views are not designed in isolation. They must be consistent, linked and navigable across the EA. The problem I perceived is that the Views we have in the Enterprise today are not integrated; they keep re-defining, re-naming, re-interpreting, duplicating and reinventing the enterprise components and their relationships. They are not useful to other parties either. That is why Views must be designed taking into account the business architecture components and EA framework.

Indeed, a full BA would add many views at relevant detail but useful to the business professional though rather than the business architect. Still, a top level BA stays in one page, no views.

The generic BA (see previous posts) would become the template for the one page BA, your Views in effect, and the documentation of the current and the target BAs.

The generic business architecture was built with technology systems mapping in mind. In the generic business architecture

(http://www.enterprise-architecture-matters.co.uk/gods-business-architecture) mapping of your IT systems is pretty straightforward (Portal, Campaign, User Authorization systems, Shop equipment...).

Business customers would also be pleased since they can recognize their key business flows and systems.

Business and IT can talk about it now without division.

Organization improvement can easily map their functional organization to it.

Even the business academia can talk about Value Chains which are extended by the GODS architecture model.

And top management would recognize their own Governance functions, eventually.

Business Model Canvas is neither ontology, nor BA, but a...

Dec 31, 2012

http://www.ebizq.net/blogs/ea_matters/2012/12/the-business-model-canvas-is-neither-a-business-architectur-nor-an-ontology-it-is-a-value-chain.php

Is Alex Osterwalder's Business Model Canvas, BMC, an ontology or a (business) architecture as it is sometimes claimed or... something else?

To start with, BMC cannot be both a (business) architecture and an ontology. That is, assuming that an architecture is a model then and ontology is a metamodel of the architecture domain under scrutiny. BMC is either one or the other.

Whatis.com states that "an ontology is the working model of entities and interactions in some particular domain of knowledge or practices."

A first question is then, what is the domain which the BMC is an ontology for? Without that, we cannot proceed with the ontology assumption. It does not seem to be the enterprise since there too are many missing elements.

But let's take the Customer and Supplier, parts of the BMC canvas, are they elements of an enterprise domain?

Imagine only an enterprise like Microsoft whose customers represent a generous section of the individuals and companies of the world. Had the enterprise included customers, then it has to include the customers of the customer enterprises, and so on. Not to mention that a Customer is a Supplier too, which another element of the BMC. What would the final enterprise footprint look like then? If it could be ever drawn, it would appear like a giant picture of all the companies in the world.

Well then, we have to eliminate Customers and Suppliers as part of an Enterprise ontology.

I can continue to argue for each element of the BMC but I won't do that here and now.

There are a number of other BMC versions that exhibit different elements and even links. But the links have not been ever specified. They have loose meanings. In any case, the BMC model in use looks like the Windows 8 start screen, that is a number of boxes without interconnections. That might have been the reason it was called a canvas in the first place rather than an ontology or an architecture which exhibit meaningful interconnections. In practice, one just fills in the boxes of the canvas. Links are not necessary.

Also we do not fill in ontologies, or metamodels for that matter, like we do fill in the BMC.

Some BMC representations feature connections in a kind of general boxes and lines diagram that could denote any diagram, for example a flow one rather than an ontology which might look more like an entity relationship diagram.

Rather than continue on this path, let me state what BMC does represent in my view. It is a basic product value chain. Take for instance SCOR's (Supply Chain...) Source - Make - Deliver.

The BMC shows the flow

- beginning with Sourcing from Suppliers

- to Making activities and resources

- and Delivering to Customers through channels

Now this a thing I can work with. I can see how the Business Models are implemented on an enterprise value chain. I can map a business model on an enterprise architecture that describes its processes and resources. I can calculate then the costs, the revenue and as such the value proposition of the Business Model. Moreover, Porter's Value Chain exhibits an element called margin. This would be the profit of the BMC value proposition.

Could the BMC illustrate then some kind of a basic value chain flow diagram then? It could and it does in my view.

But then, is it a business architecture?

No, because there are more value chains in an enterprise. Resources are not part of a business architecture but of an enterprise architecture that includes technology and people.

But you can map the BMC on an EA described by GODS-FFLV for instance which exhibits both a generic business architecture and an EA framework. The BMC elements can be easily identified then on the EA, the path through the EA drawn and the costs and revenue calculated.

Business Models versus business modelling

Dec 20, 2010

http://www.ebizq.net/blogs/ea_matters/2010/12/business-models-versus-business-modelling.php

A business model is neither a business architecture nor the result of "business modelling", even though they sound related. The result of business modelling is not a business model but a business architecture.

A business model describes the elements to consider in order to deliver a profitable product. For example, Osterwalder's view, summarised in a canvas template, consists of nine elements: from key processes, resources, channels and partners to cost and value proposition.

A business model does not depict the components of the Enterprise and their relationships as an architecture does.

The business model though would benefit from a business architecture (or better enterprise architecture) that illustrates the enterprise functions, flows, channels and human and technology resources.

As such, a business model cannot be used instead of a business architecture; a BA though would enable the business model evaluation and implementation.

When you fill in the business model canvas you need to work out processes, resources, channels and costs, at least. That is easily and consistently done with a BA/EA.

An automated BA blueprint can enact, automate a business model, make it easy to play with various versions of business models since the BA can quickly exhibit the key processes, resources, channels, costs and partners.

The Business Process journey in IT

Mar 20, 2008

http://it.toolbox.com/blogs/ea-matters/the-business-process-journey-in-it-22301

A process exists in whatever we do. Sometimes, it is documented. A cook book is a good example of a process manual: boil the fish, fry the onions, add salt and garlic, bake for half an hour, serve the outcome and hope for the best or add salt (why don't they do it in BPMN?). This looks like a Value Chain too: plan, source, make, deliver.

With regard to IT, processes were first coded in the mainframe software and in those punched cards or perforated paper band. Later the Enterprise processes were embedded in various applications in the Enterprise. There was no end to end flow and one could only change and recompile the whole application to change the process.

Then distributed applications based on Remote Procedure Calls using CORBA for instance attempted to integrate the isolate applications but one had to know the inner objects of an application and use the same language and technology. With messaging middleware, the EAI, that changed. The processes could be expanded outside and across systems in some overall process. The end processes were still hard to modify although they could exchange information.

A higher level of coordination was later added on top of the EAI integration middleware to introduce intelligent message routing to exchange information between various IT applications. Applications adapters were still expensive and the whole process was rigid. Workflow was treated like a different proposition altogether: application sending documents between humans to achieve an end state of approval, for instance. But Business Process Management becomes gradually a separate engine, above the distributed middleware, to coordinate execution of an end to end process built over a few applications.

Lately, SOA introduced the modularisation and encapsulation of applications as Business Services. SOA standardised the adaptors; more, applications began coming with standard interfaces (Web Services, SOAP/UDDI/WSDL). People can now apply a top down MDA (Model Driven Architecture) approach to the IT processes driven by the business expert.

Drag and drop GUI BP design appeared and process languages such as BPMN were standardised. At the same time Web Services paradigm takes off and with it, BPEL, a business process execution language orchestrating Web Services and later on Human Interactions, thus uniting the two worlds of process and workflow. Vendors are now selling to you: ESB distributed middleware for integration, GUI design environment, business rules engine to separate routing and decision making from processes, MDM hubs to integrate data, Portals for User interaction, Business Analytics modules for reporting, SOA services UDDI/WSDL repositories and service management and governance applications.

In the end Business Process Management already a process design tool, execution engine and routing engine, becomes an enabler of the decision making process by extracting and providing access to rules for the automation of decision making and process. Moreover business people are becoming close now to that dream time where they could directly change their business processes implemented as an orchestration of services.

EA IT ARCHITECTURE

The role of IT in the enterprise and EA

Jan 18, 2008

http://it.toolbox.com/blogs/ea-matters/the-role-of-it-and-enterprise-architecture-21866

It is hard to conceive a business without IT in some form these days. Overall IT supports the UI, distribution channels, customer service and call centre technology, marketing, business logic execution and workflow, business automation, B2B, complex calculations, communications and collaboration, data storage, archiving, document creation and management, decision making, infrastructure management, office automation and their security. Let me list some of the today's Enterprise IT capabilities:

- business and support activities execution (ERP, CRM, SCM, service specific... IT applications)

- business automation through business process & rules engines and workflow replacing repetitive human activities

- storage of structured customer, product, supplier... information

- content management processes such as creation, transformation (paper to digital and vice versa...), storage, archiving, search, publishing and presentation for document, web, media, records...

- identification of customers, partners and employees

- User Interface for documents and processes

- customer distribution channels: web, email, chat

- automated B2B exchange services with partners

- distribution and collaboration services

- communications and mobility: data, voice, video

- data and process integration middleware

- powerful calculations tools for complex algorithms or financial applications

- DW/BI/Dashboards/Risk Management and Roadmapping tools

- decision making tools

- remote access to business processes and data

- office tools for typing, printing, faxing (Office suites)

- drawing and design tools: SDK, RAD, CAD...

- management of all other IT infrastructure

- security (encryption, digital signatures, firewalling...), load balancing

- the infrastructure to support all above: processing servers, disks, RAID..., archiving tapes ...

The list is still open.

Often not recognised as IT, since there is no human intervention, SW/HW powers real time appliances and machines in the Enterprise manufacturing equipment, robots, SCADA technology, mobile phones...

Since IT has such a high innovation rate, IT may represent a major source of innovation and competitive advantage in the enterprise or, alternatively, when poorly managed, a source of pain and costs. As the IT complexity and usage grows, Enterprise Architecture, SOA, ITIL frameworks and outsourcing will help you manage the complexity of IT in alignment with the business needs and strategy.

Outsourced, IT will reduce the concern of business people and leave them focus on their own objectives while IT people have the freedom to innovate, architect at will ... with the condition to deliver on time, cost and quality. Both parties are happy as long as the contractual SLA is convenient for both.

IT doesn't matter, EA does

Dec 21, 2007

http://it.toolbox.com/blogs/ea-matters/it-doesnt-matter-ea-does-21385

A traditional business consists of a group of people executing activities aimed to deliver a product by using tools and technologies. Nonetheless, human activities and decisions are increasingly performed by IT systems. Could a business survive without IT these days? What is role of IT now? How much does a business depend on it? This discussion might help explain why typically, it is IT to lead in the development of an Enterprise Architecture.

Nicolas Carr of Harvard, in 2003, has promoted the idea (a very truncated meaning rendered here) that IT, having become a commodity, like electricity, represents no longer a competitive advantage for a business and as such IT investment should be carefully and selectively done - which, for that matter, is not a bad advice for any investment -. Naturally, this was quite debated at the time.

I was and am against it since IT is not a single technology but a complex set in which each technology lives at a different point in its lifecycle, with some IT technologies commoditised and some not yet. And a second argument is that it is not enough to have a technology; one has to master the art or science of management of the technology for best results - like cooking, for instance.

On the other hand we have the privilege of living in the future and as such thinking wisely about the past. These days we can see how everybody tends to outsource everything remotely connected to IT. So far, so good.

But we outsource the day to day IT routine operations, that is precisely the commoditised IT Nicolas Carr was talking about; we do not outsource IT architecture, strategy, innovation or emerging technologies.

What we remain with is the IT Architecture and Strategy, e.g. in two words, Enterprise Architecture. And this is where I intended to lead you.

IT obsolescence criteria

Dec 7, 2007

http://it.toolbox.com/blogs/ea-matters/it-obsolescence-criteria-21090

I define obsolescence in IT as the state of a system in its lifecycle when it becomes... obsolete - that is old, outmoded, falling into disuse - from a both functional and technological point of view. Given a few years more it becomes an antique and were the system sufficiently rare it will pay you off more than new.

In the business world, there already are a few concepts that help with obsolescence: depreciation of an asset and even amortization in accounting terms. An EA architecture repository and tool should support the obsolescence analysis by adding specific attributes to the metadata of the entity. The EA applications and infrastructure assets may have different obsolescence criteria.

The obsolescence discussion should be had with the business owners using of the application and the IT maintenance teams. All IT assets should have recommended obsolescence periods for planning their replacement. And here I remind you of the concept of value of replacement in the insurance industry.

Obsolescence from a business perspective:

- the service (delivered by IT systems) is not competitive or not making profit any longer

- the service logic needs significant updates (legislation changes, compliance ...)
- the User Interface has to be significantly upgraded
- competitors grabbed an edge with new technology features, need to offer similar or better

Technology obsolescence causes:

- technical skills no longer available or becoming too expensive
- the scalability has reached its limits
- the architecture is harder and harder to maintain, too many patches
- asset already depreciated

...

As a result of an obsolescence analysis a number of "standard" measures can be adopted. The analysis should also document the cost of replacement in an attribute and time frame of obsolescence.

- remove, no replacement
- replace with newer technology
- upgrade
- wrap application, virtualise technology to extend life...

Obsolescence should be included in your Enterprise transformation roadmap and projects portfolio.

Enterprise Architecture and solution architecture projects

Apr 11, 2008

http://it.toolbox.com/blogs/ea-matters/enterprise-architecture-and-solution-architecture-projects-22341

Most key projects change your Enterprise structure. The Enterprise Architecture (EA) itself, reflecting the Enterprise structure, evolves, changes with each successful project, even if not documented.

Every project has a timeline delivering at various implementation milestones, starting from an As-Is state of a few systems in the Enterprise towards a Vision state through a few transition states. Frequently, a project has to take into account all concurrent changes, outcome of all other on-going or even future implementation projects, through many communication channels.

With an Enterprise Architecture in place, every project would document changes and update the EA. Hence, EA records all changes in the Enterprise and becomes the single source of updated information for all developments. By consulting this single reference, the EA, all other projects can take stock of changes in the current architecture as soon as planned or implemented.

The target state of the Enterprise is sketched, dictated by your Strategy. This target Enterprise state will have to be equally recorded in the EA so that the end project design would take into account the changes in your end goals.

PEOPLE ARCHITECTURE, THE EA ORGANIZATION LAYER AND CULTURE

EA should consider people and organization

June 24, 2010

http://www.ebizq.net/blogs/ea_matters/2010/06/enterprise-architecture-should-consider-people-and-organization.php

Not long ago I felt that Enterprise Architecture (EA) had not been growing at the pace I, at least, thought it should. I asked myself why and came up with a couple of issues. I never thought though the list would expand but it did. This being the case, no wonder that people are reluctant about the EA development: it may be costly, takes time and resources, its business case is not proved and the outcome may not live to expectations.

What I found is that

- EA is seen mainly as an IT discipline

- All other technologies beside IT seem to be ignored

- EA is overly simplified to four architectural layers with no other "views" to respond to non-IT stakeholders' concerns

- Good practices from system design like logical architecture, use cases are not really adopted

- There is seldom a link to the enterprise Value Chain or business model that business people understand and not least

- People and organization are not included in the EA scope, my topic now.

Typically business processes or parts of them are still performed by people rather than applications. These processes, in fact more accurately workflows, are still relying on human interventions for data input, validation, phase approval... In other words they are not automated. Processes lag too because people taking decisions are away or technology fails at the hands of poorly trained personnel. More often than not the human intervention is not portrayed in business workflows for the simple reason that people are not part of the framework. If human performance is not accounted for the overall processes will perform as well as their weakest link, the people.

EA looks like an unfinished business without people manning processes and technology.

Organization (people) design is often the object of an entirely separate and non-correlated initiative. I witnessed in the same company

 - a process and best practices optimization effort,

 - an organization re-design process and

 - an Enterprise Architecture program

performed by three different groups, in parallel. That is process, people and the EA activities were executed in isolation, without correlation.

I believe that the organization chart should be aligned to your Enterprise Architecture so that people take ownership of EA functions, processes and technology.

Culture and people communications also affect your Enterprise performance, but this is quite a topic for another time. Also process improvement activities that should be correlated to the EA development.

After all, "the Company is the People" who govern, plan and operate the Enterprise.

Organization and Enterprise Architecture

Feb 1, 2011

http://it.toolbox.com/blogs/ea-matters/organization-and-enterprise-architecture-44045

Here is Nick Gall's post in a discussion with Tom Graves on the role of organization in EA.

I agree with this Nick's stand, or what I made of it:

"why don't enterprise architects draw their insights and examples from and base their practices on fields like organizational studies?"

Yes, an Enterprise Architect should understand organization design and theory to enable alignment between people organization, business and technology architecture. After all, they are all layers of a full Enterprise Architecture. Processes are executed by people not only technology.

The alignment would enable people roles & responsibilities be clearly set against processes and technology. Anyway, for top management, the working architecture seems to be the organization chart.

I don't think though that motivating people is the job of an architect or that it can be achieved by an architect, for that matter, except when convincing people to adopt EA practices, i.e. selling EA.

The architect does not make decisions and does not motivate people to make them, but documents enterprise operation and target states as set by stakeholders. It does not make technology choices or specifies strategy. The architect can propose though choices to relevant fora for decision making.

But as any leader in an enterprise the architect has the responsibility to motivate, to a degree.

A problem is that, in reality, the Enterprise Architect is a small cog in IT, and quite complacent with that, at times. As it is, the EA function seldom liaises with other process improvement efforts in the Enterprise not to mention the organization design and improvement that would seldom be on the EA IT agenda anyway. We all seem to have at times an idealised, almost heroic EA role in mind.

The people organization architecture and social aspects of an EA

Feb 2, 2011

http://www.ebizq.net/blogs/ea_matters/2011/02/the-organization-and-social-point-of-view-of-an-enterprise-architecture.php

Nick Gall's post speaks about organization and motivating people as part of an EA workday. The organization architecture, the 3rd architecture tier of an EA as I call it, is invaluable, since it brings all enterprise stakeholders around the table. In practice though, when I suggested slight adjustments to the chart to align the organization and EA, the feedback was less than thrilling. After all, we are all hired to serve in IT.

Nevertheless, the point is that when you compare the organization chart with the enterprise blueprint you will observe differences that could be ironed out. That is, in case you have a blue print or a capability map at least.

I realise though that an organization works poorly, if mechanically partitioned alone, without taking into account its soul as well, the human culture, relationships and motivation as pointed out.

As an architect I enable as such the EA, by adding to the framework a social architecture point of view that permits the description of the collaboration and communication patterns that once analysed and acted upon, may enhance the usage of enterprise human resources in conjunction with technology.

Business Architecture in support of organization re-design

November 4, 2010

http://www.ebizq.net/blogs/ea_matters/2010/11/business-architecture-in-support-of-organization-re-design.php

Let's say you have the task to improve the sales department workings in the context of the Enterprise. Use business architecture. This has nothing to do with IT or technology though.

 To align Sales and Services operation with the organization one has to understand the interactions with other functions and indeed the key activities in Sales and Services, current roles and organization, products, customer types and segments.

Begin by sketching such an interaction diagram starting from the customer and considering all other functions. Sales and Services have various internal functions that must be illustrated in exchanges. Then qualify these exchanges in terms of importance, frequency... to find out with whom you interact most. This is the current picture.

Then streamline these exchanges and try different organizations designs. Use swimlanes diagrams. Come with a target functional architecture and proposed organization design that implements it.

The organization may not be optimal because of existing silos with different management and objectives that make those exchanges more difficult.

Organization design is based on a mixture of business units, product lines, functional and geographical criteria. Consider these if you propose a different organization.

Consider too describing current and future organization roles in terms of tasks that contribute to the function.

Then consider how to move from the current organization to the future one with minimum disruption and plan the move. Work with all concerned to make it happen.

Ideally one should understand the key sales and business workflows and the functional organization of the Enterprise.

You may start from the reference architecture to describe own processes at a relevant level of detail. Group related activities in a function to enhance exchanges.

Common performance indicators may help align sales to other departments without re-organization.

You may also create horizontal (besides vertical organization) business responsibilities and (like in a matrix organization) to oversee products flow along the value chain, from production, distribution to sales. Similar to process managers in business process improvement approaches.

The Organization Culture and EA

Nov 26, 2008

http://it.toolbox.com/blogs/ea-matters/the-organization-culture-and-enterprise-architecture-24930

The Enterprise Architecture development must be supported by the organization and culture. People are the company; they can make or break the EA. To succeed one has to adapt the organization and subtly sniff and influence the culture. SOA for instance requires a new distributed governance. People are accountable for the service they deliver, its roadmap, business, IT technology, usage, defects, service continuity and for acquiring internal or even external customers. Here are a few definitions for culture, from the web:

- "The set of learned beliefs, attitudes, values and behaviour that are characteristic of a particular social group or organization."

- "A set of shared norms and values which establish a sense of identity for those who share them".

- "A specific set of social, educational, religious and professional behaviours, practices and values that individuals learn and adhere to while participating in or out of groups they usually interact with."

- "The sum total of the ways of life of a people; includes norms, learned behaviour patterns, attitudes, and artefacts; also involves traditions, habits or customs; how people behave, feel and interact; the means by which they order and interpret the world; ways of perceiving, relating ... "

And my attempt at a definition: culture is an assemble of unwritten rules and values that drive the behaviour of a group living or working together; culture ultimately shapes how people respond to events and the way things are done beyond established procedures. It consists of and is transmitted by rites (ceremonials), traditions (established ways of doing things), legends (people and deeds people treasure) and education (training).

It is reflected in the way people solve issues, communicate, celebrate, approach management (direct phone call/email, kick the door open, or other protocols of engagement...).

Well known organization cultures:

- "Meritocracy" is the culture of reward and recognition associated with rapid progress and pride in the organization

- The "can do" as opposed to the "can talk" culture of people sitting in meetings or on the phone all day, with the obvious results

- "Blame culture" where if anything goes wrong a scapegoat is found; the consequence is that people rarely assume accountability

- "Innovative" culture where invention is rewarded and praised

- "Agile" where formalism is replaced by people empowered to act

- "silo " where the departments don't care about the greater, collective good.

How can one change culture? That is, change it in a positive sense since it often done otherwise. The cultural change starts at the top. It requires honesty (as opposed to political spin), justification, communication, openness (information available to anyone concerned) that is, all in all, transparency (information available to anyone), enforced by a Freedom of Information like act.

Accountability (be able to associate people performance to task accomplishment) and recognition of merit are essential to enforce a successful culture.

The culture is the collective soul of the organization, of a group of people. It is influenced by type of governance, internal regulation, empowerment policies (liberty to act in some limits), recognition policies, height of the organization tree (bureaucracy), clarity of accountabilities and roles, freedom of communications, rights of opinion. Recognition makes employees happy which in turn make the company successful.

EA GOVERNANCE, PRINCIPLES AND BUDGETING

Essential Enterprise Architecture governance

May 8, 2012

http://www.ebizq.net/blogs/ea_matters/2012/05/essential-enterprise-architecture-governance.php

A governance framework establishes who makes what decisions and based on what.

The EA architects shall propose a governance framework that regulates the EA development itself and its employment in the enterprise.

The development governance is the instrument to control the EA efforts, solutions design and changes in the enterprise so that they are all aligned to realising the goals and strategy while achieving simplicity, agility and lower costs.

The governance is embodied in people tasks, architecture principles, technology guidelines, security policies, roadmaps and the bodies (such as the Architecture Review Board) that make decisions about them.

The EA governance for the EA employment in the enterprise regulates that and how stakeholders shall use the EA in their activities. It is implemented in checkpoints in business processes and boards that supervise operations and investment activities.

The governance shall be approved by a higher enterprise wide fora - the Architecture Review, Investments and Operations boards - and it shall be used by all stakeholders for decision making in their own work.

The EA architects will Police - someone has to do it - EA developments that fall into scope; they will check compliance and submit exceptions to the Architecture Review Board.

The EA architects are not judge, jury and executioner; they are not making the Law (even if they propose it) and they should not be executing the solutions (they often do though).

Currently though the architects are playing Police without a Law (the EA...). Decisions are arbitrary and raise legitimate questions on Governance.

Enterprise Architecture principles, let's talk about them

November 15, 2011

http://www.ebizq.net/blogs/ea_matters/2011/11/enterprise-architecture-principles-lets-talk-about-them.php

EA professionals often specify architecture principles but rarely use them, if at all. In fact, are you using architecture principles in practice? And how, as an afterthought tick list or actively during the decision process?

We all have principles that guide our ways in life. They are essentially rules guiding our decision making. Useful indeed. Principles make the hard decision taking process less agonising than it is. They direct you to select an option or follow the order of choice. That saves you time and provides consistency across time and the Enterprise.

Principles may be expressed as commands/imperative statements, something like the Ten Commandments or Seven Commands ("You shall not steal"). Sometimes they exclude options. Principles are valid though only in a certain context that must be specified. That is, if the conditions are different the principles would not apply.

For principles to work, a governance framework must be defined: the definition of a principle should specify the decision that has to be made, the choices (eventually), the body (role)that makes the decision and the typical use case (when to use it).

To justify usage, the definition of the principle must state the expected benefits returned by the application of the principle (the why, rationale).

Enterprise Architecture (EA) principles though are more than Architecture principles. But this distinction is seldom made.

EA principles could be roughly categorised around EA development phases - *architecture*, design, implementation, deployment... - or non-technology EA domains such as Information Management or Security.

Architecture principles, a subset of EA, aim to provide simplification, rationalisation, re-use and standardisation of the current "organically grown" architectures (any system has one). That is architecture principles are about designing a "clean" architecture. They are employed by architects and should be applied at a solution design phase. The benefits are coming from the simplicity of the design: managed complexity, reduced duplication, increased reliability, easy to build on and change...

Here are a few Architecture principles (and sub-principles):

• Group functionality in components/modules -

- Employ high cohesion and loose coupling
- Hide implementation behind interfaces
- Use SOA paradigm
  - Define services around business functions
  - Describe services in catalogue
- Group components in layers
  - Do not traverse layers
  - A layer shall provide services only to the layer above

or for the EA Design & Implementation phase

- Use web services technology
- Investigate first solution in the Cloud, Buy it or, at last resort, Build it. (Rent/Buy/Build)

"Data is an Asset", is this a principle judged through the above norms? The context is not specified. Data is sometimes an asset but at other times it is a liability. For instance, personal data not destroyed after usage, unnecessarily duplicated or existing in obsolete versions.

In any case, more than a handful of principles would be hard to employ in the real time thinking process unless you use them as a post-thinking tick list, which is not what we normally do.

To ease usage, reduce principles number, make them snappy and group them in categories of application. Care should be taken to avoid overlaps and conflicts of resolution - principles should be orthogonal.

Budgeting Enterprise Architecture

Nov 18, 2010

http://www.ebizq.net/blogs/ea_matters/2010/11/ea-budgeting.php

EA budgeting depends how the EA activity is conducted at a point in time: is it a project or a Business As Usual activity (BAU)?

Companies sometimes rely on short burst of activities (projects) to establish the EA foundations. And then continue with BAU. Or establish directly an EA practice.

Projects not followed by an EA practice establishment happen sometimes. But without a continuous EA governance, EA becomes quickly obsolete. On the other hand, EA practices established without the support of an initial project face the prospect of developing their own or at least customizing an EA framework and process.

The EA practice charter depends on the initial project and the quality of its output.

I will not consider the results of EA here but only the cost and funding of the EA practice - which may return on investment or not.

What can incur costs? The EA team and their expenses. The tools they use. The time they impose on others' input and the work others do for them. One has to remember that EA does coordination work but the bulk of work should be done by domain experts.

EA budgeting depends also on the scope of EA. For instance, if it is an IT activity alone as it typically is. If it is considered a strategy exercise or a to-be state effort alone as it often is. Typically an EA team reviews IT architecture solutions and roadmaps. This is the work it is paid for. Still a true EA practice would have to coordinate and integrate the work done by many other teams, in an EA.

For the project part, the funding should be approved and extracted from IT project funds, pending the business case approval.

For the BAU practice, the budget should be allocated, as for any other IT function, annually. But because it spills over in other domains, there is a need for the budget to support the EA related work in other functions. Since EA enables decision making, roadmapping, strategy, governance and so on, it should come from a management fund that could cover all these activities in other IT functions. This budget should be estimated at the beginning of a business cycle.

As typically, both project and BAU EA report to IT, funding comes from IT.

There is a distinction between the EA and the Solution Architecture functions even if both are about architecture. And there are different ways of funding them. Still if the EA team does mostly solution review work, it can be part of and funded by the architecture team.

In the end, if the EA is truly about the Enterprise, the funding should come from the CXO office to be able to cover all other enterprise wide required activities. The team should report to one of the top executives who could sponsor major decisions.

The EA team would have a hard time to get the necessary budget or the collaboration it requires, if it has to employ influencing, so touted in some circles; influencing is just another word for trying to sell the value of EA to every stakeholder, again and again. This happens when the EA team has no authority, the EA has not been communicated properly, results are little convincing or benefits are claimed beyond the means of the current EA.

HOW TO CREATE, MARKET AND COMMUNICATE EA

On starting a new EA group

November 4, 2012

www.ebizq.net/blogs/ea_matters/2012/11/on-starting-a-new-ea-group.php

Plan to fulfil the expectations of those who created or sponsored the EA group. After all, they pay the bill. So ask them what they expect.

In my experience, they would want to know how to select technology, what are the options, how to justify choices in order to minimise the cost and risk of IT. For that, they want you to come with principles and technology guidelines.

They would also want you to create a board to review solution architectures employing the principles. They would want you to provide an integrated IT view and standardisation. They would like an IT roadmap and strategy. But not least they would like you to come with a reference EA. Here is a Linkedin discussion on this topic.

Still, in practice, most EAs do solution architecture work and reviews. That is because most current frameworks do not help much.

They do also IT strategy and roadmapping. They usually come with a few principles which seldom pass the practice test.

But they seldom come that with an EA reference model which is in fact the prime task of an EA without which no one should call himself an EA architect. Without the EA any solution review is subjective and roadmapping and strategy are patchy. Without EA in fact, this work is performed as it was before the advent of EA.

That is, at best, EAs come bottom up with too many diagrams designed in isolation, that do not fit the enterprise architecture whole, in form, shape or content.

The problem is how to do the modelling in an integrated manner. You need a framework that integrates the parts. Today's frameworks seldom do that, if any. The design should also start from the big picture, top-down, from a single page architecture cascading down to detailed domain architectures. I, personally, have seen no such architecture model till now.

Nevertheless, without the big picture of the business architecture, the technology architecture has little meaning since there is no indication of how it serves the business purpose, of how it delivers the products, how the business strategy maps to IT etc. As such, there is a small audience for the IT architecture alone. Not to mention that it is patchy failing to cover many business domains and end to end processes, which normally would be described by a business architecture. To realise a proper EA, I use own framework. I also found that most EA frameworks look like EA development processes, which describe common and known good practices, rather than coming with frameworks that enable

- your architecture models to fit in the integrated and coherent EA whole

- a generic business architecture that supports the IT architecture design

- architecture templates that helps you jump start the EA modelling.

In the first 100 days, an EA should come up with the EA framework and an one page architecture (covering both business and technology).

The EA should also plan the next steps, so that the stakeholders know what to expect.

At the six months milestone, a strategy and roadmap should be proposed. Tasks to be accomplished in the 100 days should be

- organise EA team

- establish EA governance (including principles)

- create EA site

- propose tool, if any (for EA repository)

- liaise with stakeholders to discover expectations and sell EA

I would procure and use the cheapest EA tool available, a free open source one, or none in the beginning, because they are taking your focus away from the EA.

Tools may be a hindrance if you don't know what you are doing yet. They need training, they look like coming from another IT era more often than not. Besides, the internal metamodel is seldom complete or right. You have to come with your own which may be hard, costly or impossible to implement in the tool. Tools are hard to maintain, upgrade and costly to annually license, in particular when you use them little, as it is the case much too often.

Archimate, for instance, is counter intuitive. It jumps directly to detail. It does not come with an intuitive framework so you can see the parts and the whole. The diagrams discourage the business audience.

How to sell the EA

Dec 3, 2007

http://it.toolbox.com/blogs/ea-matters/how-to-sell-the-ea-20921

Selling the EA seems to be one of the issues continually confronting us in the EA arena. To sell it, start by identifying the interested and affected parties, the stakeholders. Ask the old question "what's in it for them?" and "what is the impact on them" since they would be asked to support or even contribute to it!

Top management, what is in it for them? The representation of the Enterprise governance, the roles and responsibilities, governance bodies and principles of decision making, the business models - how the business makes a profit -, financial P&L centres mapping on business functions, strategy alignment to the Enterprise organization, regulatory compliance... There is quite a lot to sell.

For Enterprise shared services organization: support functions as HR, Payrollï¿½ have to be described in terms of services, costs and effectiveness. For business people you should be providing information on other technologies like the SCADA and GIS for utility companies for instance. Or you should cover all business processes not only a few. If you provide this information the business organization would become your supporters.

To satisfy the interests of most potential stakeholders, the concept of architectural viewpoint/view is crucial: a view satisfies the concerns or needs of a stakeholder group. There are as many views as stakeholder types.

If you define your architecture in terms of applications, information and technology architecture you address an audience in IT for the most part, which audience is not too large. The potential audience depends entirely on the scope of your EA development which can vary a lot. Is your EA an IT only architecture? For IT, do you intend though to include content management, knowledge management, BI, DW, integration architectures? That will considerably enlarge your IT audience.

To sell EA I would put together, upfront, an EA drivers and benefits pack and a business case based on financial terms. Business management thinks in terms of Payback, ROI, NPV which are measures of profit vs. costs, typically applied to projects. A table of benefits, such as time to market, agilityï, and the estimated EA contribution to them at each EA iteration will do a lot of good to the sales process of EA.

The EA has to be planned to deliver first what the business needs (for instance a Single Customer View architecture).

A natural progression to EA with obsolete systems and technologies replaced when the time has come and not before would reinforce the EA sell effort.

Communicating Enterprise Architecture

Feb 11, 2012

http://it.toolbox.com/blogs/ea-matters/communicating-enterprise-architecture-50368

A few recent popular posts from Serge Thorn followed by Todd Biske's and Leo de Sousa's stirred my interest. About EA communications. Everybody wants or needs to do communications. Communications are never enough or so it seems, at least with regard to EA. Why so?

What are communications for? For one, to gather support. Forewarn stakeholders about requests to come. To advertise realizations or simply show progress.

I do communications because I think EA is difficult to achieve. It requires stakeholder support, which I aim to rally through communications. Then I want them use the outcomes.

Right at the start, an EA program or function should make the wider audiences aware of its intentions and the benefits of doing so in what they are concerned. Be prepared to answer the question on what EA is, in one short sentence.

Throughout the EA documentation, design and implementation phases results should be constantly communicated to keep people appraised and enable them to use the results.

Beware though that most stakeholders would like to know what's in it for them, and what and when you will deliver. You have to manage deliveries to expectations from then on.

EA practices that limit their scope to IT should rather refrain from selling the wider benefits of an EA that may never be achieved. It sounds good to market the advantages of an ideal EA but since you are held accountable, you must sell with care solely what you can and will deliver. Programs that do not deliver on the EA benefits they promise, add to the infamous reputation of EA within the business circles.

Communications have to be rooted in substance, that is deliver first, communicate after. Communications should not become self serving. The outcome should be of worth to stakeholders not only to yourself. Don't satiate your stakeholders with unnecessary comms. Know when to stop even if you are too engrossed in your work. If you have nothing to communicate just don't comm.

As EA has limited resources don't make your communications program too extensive. You'll end up doing communications about EA rather than EA.

Most of us know how to communicate. We just don't how much is necessary, through what channel and how often in order to reinforce our messages. Direct channels like one 2 one and presentations are best for the initial stage. Later, dashboards and web for communicating results. And discussions forums for interactivity with stakeholders.

Still, while important, I don't think though that communications is a top level EA service (see Bruce's of Gartner blog) for the simple reason that any reasonably complex work we do, does require communications. That is it is not specific to EA. As such, it is just a normal and necessary support activity. You'll do communications for any large program. I believe that Bruce is addressing the issue of services for Gartner's EA customers rather than the services that an EA function should provide to the enterprise stakeholders. No enterprise stakeholder would be interested in EA Research or Consulting services. This is a rather Gartner centric point of view to the problem.

THE EA ROLE IN THE ENTERPRISE AND ITS TRANSFORMATION

The EA role to coordinate Enterprise developments

December 12, 2010

http://www.ebizq.net/blogs/ea_matters/2010/12/organic-ea-governance-to-align-of-all-enterprise-developments.php

The concept of EA is self selling but the current results turn its appeal down. In any case, it would be a benefit for business to have a set of Enterprise blueprints they can all refer to, debate upon and navigate end to end flows to inspect performance and the technology and people resources involved.

Moreover, the EA can be used for process improvement, resource alignment, streamlining the Enterprise and so on. To really succeed in transforming the Enterprise, EA needs not only to act on its own, but to support, correlate or organically coordinate the efforts and teams in business, technology and organization, such as:

- Business efforts of process and quality improvement like BPM/xSigma/TQM, strategy teams in business strategy formulation, mapping and execution, projects alignment in an Enterprise portfolio

- Technology developments in IT/non-IT technology architecture design, roadmapping and strategy

- People/Organization optimisation, business management and investment decisions, projects organization improvement and alignment to the business needs

EA is not about IT alone but about aligning all these efforts in an Enterprise. It is about establishing a governance structure to enable synchronization of these efforts.

In the end, all stakeholders would become involved, having a view of interest, a stake in the EA. The EA architect would provide such a navigable framework where all the artefacts, designed and owned by stakeholders, would fit in framework placeholders, subject to constraints and guidance imposed by it.

As such an EA architect must have an understanding of all EA layers: business, technology and people organization. The E Architect should have a high enough position in the hierarchy to have access to top management and authority to act rather than advise or influence alone. Solely at that level an E Architect would have visibility of the whole Enterprise and be able to discover and propose common functions, eliminate duplication between business silos, improve end to end processes...

An Enterprise Architecture board, a governance structure close to the top management level, would make the key decisions.

To be relevant, EA needs organic maintenance, that is performed in the course of normal job tasks. For that

- solution architectures have to be integrated in the EA

- business stakeholders must be given ownership and responsibility of their own "architectural views"

- EA work should be delegated to those in the know and with a legitimate stake and accountability for it.

How to make the Enterprise Architecture relevant

Dec 3, 2009

http://it.toolbox.com/blogs/ea-matters/how-to-make-the-enterprise-architecture-relevant-34987

The concept of EA is self selling but the current results turn its appeal down. In any case, it would be a benefit for business to have a set of Enterprise blueprints they can all refer to and debate upon, and a framework enabling navigation and performance analysis of an end to end process illustrating its technology resources and people responsibilities involved.

I believe that to succeed EA needs to correlate and coordinate the activities and teams in EA layers like business, technology and organization. For instance:

- Business: efforts for process improvement like BPM/xSigma/TQM and Business Architecture in general (Business Models, process frameworks, business maps)

- Technology: in IT and non-IT Architecture design, roadmapping and strategy

- People/Organization: business management responsible for organization improvement and alignment to the business needs

But in the end, all stakeholders would become involved, having a view of interest, a stake in the EA. The EA architect would provide such a navigable framework where all the artefacts, designed and owned by stakeholders, would fit in framework placeholders, subject to constraints and guidance imposed by it.

EA needs to be lead by an overall EA architect having an understanding of all EA layers: business, technology and people organization. The E Architect should have a high enough position in the hierarchy to have access to top management and authority to act rather than advise. Solely at that level an E Architect would have visibility over the whole Enterprise and be able to discover and propose common functions, eliminate duplication between business silos, improve end to end processes...

An Enterprise Architecture board, a governance structure close to the top management level, would still make the key decisions.

The maintain the EA always updated and relevant,

 - the solution architectures have to be integrated in the EA

 - the business stakeholders must be given ownership and responsibility of their own "architectural views"

 - the EA work should be delegated to those in the know and with a legitimate stake and accountability for it.

EA supports business methods application rather than replaces them

Apr 22, 2012

http://it.toolbox.com/blogs/ea-matters/enterprise-architecture-supports-business-methods-application-rather-than-replaces-them-51030

EA is the discipline that consistently describes the entire enterprise structure and operation.

Business methods address, from various points of view, the analysis and ways to improve the business operation. They have been created in time, by various professionals, for solving different aspects of the enterprise equation. But they have been little integrated today, if at all.

Professionals pick one or another or a set of them they feel comfortable with and employ them for a specific purpose.

But these methods, even grouped, were not designed to complement each other and work as a whole.

They overlay, start from different assumptions and expose conflicts at times.

Business academia never entertained the concept of architecture to describe the enterprise as a whole. Porter's Value Chains is the closest concept business uses for an EA.

EA brings new the concept of architecture in the business domain, concept which is well defined in the technology domain.

EA, as the description of the enterprise, represents the underlying fact base, for other business methods.

EA does not replace the existing business methods but it supports them and offers them the perspective of the whole.

Take for instance the Balanced Score Card, business or operating models or business process improvement and quality management initiatives. EA represents the context on which to apply them for analysis and/or implementation.

Hence, business stakeholders could use their preferred business analysis and improvement methods in conjunction with the EA in order to enhance the operation of their areas of concern in the enterprise.

Nevertheless, EA architects are not really supposed to use the business methods, even if they do that when demanded by a customer.

The job of the EA architect is develop, to coordinate and provide the EA rather than employ it to improve the enterprise. That is the task of the business stakeholders. But the architect can, evidently, support the process.

Architecture should come with design principles and the frameworks that support the structuring, documentation and evolution of architecture.

An EA framework is a methodology to develop the EA.

Unfortunately the current EA frameworks don't support this, but rather describe process and governance aspects which are similar in nature and compete with other business methods.

In practice, since EA depicts only the IT landscape, it really fails to provide support to business practices, fails to deliver the touted overall enterprise level benefits and fails to reach a sizable audience.

EA, a collaborative... transformation effort

Sep 1, 2009

http://it.toolbox.com/blogs/ea-matters/ea-a-collaborative-business-process-organization-and-it-architecture-design-and-transformation-effort-33870

What is EA all about in these times and era? Good question after so many years of "doing" EA. But people seem to ask this question again. Gartner appears to redefine its approach to revive interest in EA. Forrester stresses the business architecture revolution in EA.

For sure, there is more emphasis on business architecture. With the advent of the cloud, lots of businesses will move some IT into the cloud. If all the technology is moved into the cloud there would not be much point for an EA defined as an IT architecture. Nobody clearly defines business architecture though.

The EA currently addresses only IT and not very well since there is hardly a mapping to business (no business architecture!).

Definitely the EA concept promises a lot. But, as it is, the EA hasn't returned the touted benefits to the business or, for that matter, even an architectural blueprint as the name implies.

EA comes, typically, with a few applications, servers and networks diagrams in a wide variety of forms and shapes. No navigation, little idea of what is missing, usually the artefacts satisfying just a few owners in IT. Few people use them. The main occupation of the EA Architects is to review solution architectures, to provide soon to be forgotten technology standards, lead architecture governance boards to make decisions on applications and technology with very little guidance from the existing EA, if any.

Currently, the EA work fails to deliver because is done in isolation by IT for IT without the business insight in how the firm works.

There are more books, more conferences, more dialogs, papers... But EA aspects are taken and analysed in isolation. The EA is about the whole.

Everybody seems to be waiting for a new direction, a wagon to jump on to make the EA really deliver.

So what do I suggest? A collective EA effort sponsored from the top.

Let the experts do the work at each layer: the business people (6 Sigma for instance) do the business process map work. Let them own the process improvement as they currently do, but integrate their work in the EA effort.

Let the IT people do what they call today EA. But link to the process work for mapping.

Let then the business improvement and management teams do the organization design work, redefine the chart in alignment to the business process and EA technology responsibilities.

There is the EA documentation work belonging to the EA architects and involved parties. Then there is the EA transformation work, according to strategy, that does not belong to the EA architect alone but to the top management and business teams.

The EA team must chiefly coordinate the process improvement and documentation (Lean/Six Sigma, BPM..., TQM) effort, the organization alignment work and, not least, the technology blueprint design, mapped to the business view.

The EA lead team needs to spell the work streams which should be lead by EA/domain architects, process and project managers and the organization design team.

Let us work together: the EA architect, the business experts, the business analyst, the organization design team, the management and business consultant and the top management sponsors. As such, independent efforts like BPM, Lean Sigma, organization design, IT architecture, strategy mapping come together under a single

EA umbrella effort and Enterprise project portfolio.

The EA architect was compared with a CEO. The EA job descriptions, mentioning strategy, roadmaps, blueprints, business models surely look very impressive. In practice an EA architect has no budget and no authority to implement anything. He is perched on a low branch in the hierarchy. How could one fulfil the expectations then?

The EA chief architect role needs to be higher to achieve anything, positioned to be able to have influence in process, organization design, strategy mapping, resourcing and budgeting decisions.

The EA function role is not of enterprise factotum

August 12, 2012

http://www.ebizq.net/blogs/ea_matters/2012/08/strategy.php

It is often assumed the enterprise architecture function includes planning and strategy. While this may be the case in practice, given the specifics of a job description, in theory, at least, they are separate disciplines.

The delineation of enterprise strategy, planning and architecture is rather straightforward.

The architecture is a snap in time of the enterprise state, a blueprint to which is associated information.

Planning maps in time the evolution of the enterprise state. It adds the time dimension of the enterprise transformation.

Strategy supplies the directions that guide the transformation in achieving the vision and goals.

The EA function should not really do strategy or planning but it would enable their proper formulation and consistency by providing information on all enterprise components and their relationships.

The EA team should work with planning and strategy though to make sure that Goals, Strategies and Projects are properly mapped to the architectural components and the dependencies are all counted in.

Also EA does not create, for instance, business models (in the Osterwalder sense) but EA will assist the business with the proper architectural information to develop them.

Essentially, EA is a tool used by the many existing enterprise functions to realise their own goals in harmony with the rest of the enterprise.

The EA team has a role in relating and coordinating the many such activities in the enterprise. They would certainly work with the planning and strategy teams.

The EA team itself would not have the resources to do the whole EA blueprinting at various detail levels. The enterprise stakeholders would have to do produce the EA blueprints for their own domain, designed though to fit in the EA framework, principles,... governance and tools established by the EA team.

That is why the EA function should have a governing role in the enterprise much more important than the IT role it plays today.

But for that, the EA function need a framework that enable the provision of the right EA architectural blueprint, a framework like FFLV GODS.

EA function in the organization hierarchy

Feb 2, 2010

http://it.toolbox.com/blogs/ea-matters/ea-function-in-the-organization-hierarchy-35304

An Enterprise Architect, whose scope of work is the whole Enterprise rather than IT, should coordinate and integrate the BPM effort with the rest of EA workstreams since (1) BPM is part of the EA business architecture layer and (2) the BPM CoE is already responsible and best qualified to do it.

Currently BPM/xSigma and EA developments are working in parallel, to my knowledge, because too frequently the EA is IT centric.

More, a BPM effort in isolation may not lead to expected results because processes are often implemented in IT, take for instance ERPs, CRMs...

Equally so, an IT EA devised in separation would lack the big picture of the business flows and aims.

For this to happen the role of the Enterprise Architect should be elevated at the business management level, indeed. How do we ever achieve this?

I would argue that EA should be logically at the level immediately above the organizational functions it coordinates (IT, business improvement, BPM...). But that depends on the scope of the EA in that specific organization. Ideally it would be reporting to the CEO for broadest scope and benefits. In practice it often reports to the Head of IT Architecture, with all the consequences related to scope, visibility and authority.

The Enterprise transformation blueprint based on EA

Mar 12, 2010

http://www.ebizq.net/blogs/ea_matters/2010/03/the-enterprise-transformation-blueprint-the-ea.php

A house blueprint is designed by the architect and used by the plumber, electrician, owner, potential buyer... It comes with guidance documentation, sometimes.

"If you have ever watched a house being built, or if you have ever had an addition put onto an existing house, you know that the standard method of communication is a big piece of paper called a blueprint. Blueprinting is the standard method used to copy large architectural and construction drawings. A blueprint used to consist of white lines on a blue background. A more recent process uses blue lines on a white background." (see blog).

A house transformation plan is executed first on the blueprint. Then, as a portfolio of projects changing the blueprint components (rooms, loft, garden...). The transformation plan implements your intent (I want a new floor, a study...), according to your strategy (do it on your own).

Quite similarly, the Enterprise Architecture blueprint is not static. It should be constantly updated to reflect the change in Enterprise structure, result of all on-going projects in an Enterprise. That may not always happen but this is the task of the EA architect. The blueprint should reflect the Enterprise changes and its evolving goals. For instance, your Enterprise adopts an online business model i.e. e-commerce, besides the traditional town shops. That demands automation of processes and introduction of new systems.

The relationship between structure and its purpose is shaped by the architectural style, take for instance SOA. For your house, a very simple analogy to SOA would be a house where all rooms open into a hall.

The EA blueprint should be the base of all conversations on maintenance, renovation and transformation of the Enterprise. Otherwise we wouldn't be sure that we talk about same things. It should be the basis of change in the Enterprise, be it operational, tactical or strategic. Without a blueprint, the transformation cannot be properly managed; the Enterprise would grow organically until a point where nothing works any longer and its decay starts.

Each and every stakeholder should also have an own blueprint of the small part of concern, which like a car part would fit into a whole that works.

Today, can you design or repair a car without a blueprint? We do that for our Enterprise. We succeed, more or less, because we all have in mind a picture of how our part works, but not the big picture. And then we interact, discuss, meet... to put it together, i.e. the end picture for each and every transformation. The cost of this approach may become prohibitively expensive. Too much re-iteration, interaction, too many misunderstandings, too much trial and error.

Then, should the EA blueprint be the cornerstone of the Enterprise transformation?

Transformations demand an integrated framework and process

Jul 1, 2010

http://www.tmforum.org/community/groups/frameworx/blog/archive/2010/01/15
/enterprise-soa-success-factors.aspx

Piggybacking on Martin's Four Transformation Myths blog. Well, I do that too often. After all, why do we need to transform our business? The world is revolving faster and faster. Too fast perhaps. And it's becoming ever more complex and organically so but not like the food, more like an organism; hard to tell how it really works.

There is another reason for transformation. The fear of becoming the infamous "pipe". There is neither prestige nor yield in that. Who wants to become an utility? It's unavoidable though if not climbing that Value Chain ladder towards where the real customer value lies.

Still how do we transform our business? Can we perform two or more transformations at a time? Like for instance transformations to reduce costs, replace legacy, introduce 4G (or 3G for the late), introduce a new business model... Well, we have to ; but we still need to avoid duplication in efforts, platforms, processes, applications or information coming with each.

The TM Forum solution frameworks are a way out. They standardize business process, information and applications. They represent a reference for change and aid you re-engineer your processes and information.

We need to look at the whole though, at the big picture, to make sure these transformations are synchronized and alter a component only once and not one after another and each in its turn. In other words a single coordinated transformation process and a common enterprise view would help. This would be provided by the integrated solution frameworks incorporated in an overall enterprise wide development method and view. What does this mean in practice? Probably, more work to do to find out.

The EA Architect, a leader in the enterprise transformation (i)

Sep 13, 2007

http://it.toolbox.com/blogs/ea-matters/the-ea-architect-a-leader-in-the-enterprise-
transformation-i-19023

Another outcome of the Enterprise Architecture conference in Sydney I recently participated to, was the positioning of the Enterprise architect as a leader in the transformation of the Enterprise and a participant in the business decision making process. All good news. Right now, this is not really the case although the trend may point in that direction.

But what is a leader or leadership for that matter? Let me point you to a recent discussion on HBS on this matter. What an interest this topic has raised! Latest thinking there points out that leaders must have theatrical qualities. I would say that actors becoming leaders are not rare, these days, especially in politics. But is it what leadership needs? I really believe that what is called theatre is in fact another term for excellent communication skills, being able to hold an inspiring speech in front of your people or at a conference.

What is a leader? My take: An individual who leads a group's activity to a specific purpose. But these individuals could be selected, nominated, self-nominated or inheriting a leading position, a position of authority. In this case, a group may not even respect or agree with these individuals. The authority of this leader comes from the power of the position and political games. This is not what we mean by leadership in general.

What is leadership then? Leadership is the quality of an individual to attract followers for a specific purpose. For that a leader must inspire trust and respect coming from natural personal qualities, learned from experience or taught knowledge and skills. Leadership requires self confidence and emotional control.

But it is possible to have a leading position without having leadership capabilities or the other way around. From here onwards, I would prefer to discuss the case of leaders capable of leadership only for keeping a simple and healthy tone of debate.

What are the qualities of leadership? Inspiring trust and respect is tantamount, even if the leader has a position of power, since there is little he/she can achieve otherwise. How to inspire trust and respect? In the first place, the individual has to be credible and lead by example; that will require top competence in that field of activity, a basic sine qua non condition for the leader. So the leader bases his confidence on knowledge and experience. How could confidence come otherwise?

The EA Architect, a leader in the enterprise transformation (ii)

Sep 27, 2007

http://it.toolbox.com/blogs/ea-matters/the-enterprise-architect-a-leader-in-the-enterprise-transformation-ii-19341

The leader will have a vision, an ideal that inspires people and determines them to follow. He would be finding solutions where few can. A leader does the "right things" some say, but also should do the "things right", a good manager/administrator does.

A leader should be emotionally stable having a degree of Emotional Intelligence (EQ as opposed to IQ), so that he could understand, interpret and control emotion in others. But the leader is in control of himself first. A leader, alternatively, could be passionate to inspire his followers with his energy and enthusiasm. Which alternative do you think is right? (believe it depends on culture: EQ is cool for the Anglo-American culture while passion may be the norm for Latin cultures.

It is said that another way to inspire a followership is to act, as in theatre, i.e. play the role of a leader to inspire people. I do not believe this really works to the end although, nobody can deny, acting may have, sometimes, charming results, offering an alternative dimension to the grim reality. But in the long term the one who benefits is the actor, the "leader" and not the group. There is the difference between the role and the reality, the personage and the person. An actor is at his best when plays naturally since he is authentic i.e. there is match between substance and form. A mismatch is decoded by primitive but efficient detectors within ourselves: the eyes which do not smile or avoid looking you into your eyes, the gesture that does not confirm the words, the intonation gone the other way.

Leadership needs authenticity to succeed, that is the image shown should fit the substance and competence. Authenticity means "you do what you say" and "you say what you think"

There are archetypes or worse stereotypes of leader types. The hero in films is a typical example. People are moulding themselves on heroes since early childhood. We struggle to imitate the best, their behaviour, we learn from them. There is also the stereotype of the business manager played by many, unfortunately. Someone who looks confident, decided, sure of success, looking the part but without the depth to deliver.

The problem is that without the underlying professional ability, the confidence is wrong footed and the results average. The surrogate leader fails without knowing why since he is playing the role well and moreover believes in himself. Acting alone will not deliver professional results.

In a culture driven by acting leaders the real work would not be prized any longer; meritocracy would be applied in terms of acting skills. An acting leader can empower, delegate but the immediate ranks feel the competence void and are tempted to step up the ladder. Then leadership will be maintained not by respect inspired by competence but through power, minute control and politics.

The style of leadership depends on field: a warrior leader would be bold and ready to fight, a president would be a decision maker, and a conductor would orchestrate the individuals in the orchestra. This would require different qualities

Leadership depends on situation. A company in difficult times for instance. In normal times leadership is welcome but not in demand.

Leadership does not necessarily means moral "good"; the proposed ideal appeals to followers good or evil. It is still leadership. There are evil leaders having their followers. Usually, they take on the good cause leaders. Why people follow? Because trust, belief, the lack of doubt it is said to make people content, if not happy. Following is easier than leading. Too many choices or decisions makes us unhappy, it was discovered. People follow because of fear as well in order to get protection.

Finally, leadership comes from will or desire to lead, since it is not solely a blessing but a very consuming activity, requiring sacrifice and dedication to the cause.

The leadership of the enterprise architect

Apr 23, 2010

http://www.ebizq.net/blogs/ea_matters/2010/04/leadership-and-enterprise-architecture.php

"There is an argument that the Enterprise Architect is a leader in the transformation of the Enterprise and a participant in the business decision making process. Right now, this is not the case but the trend points in that direction.

But what is a leader or leadership for that matter? And what is it compared to management? Management is about organization, control, planning and budgeting. Leadership is about motivation, mobilization, creating the vision and establishing the culture and relationships. To succeed, an Enterprise Architect has to act as a leader to motivate people, mobilize resources and create the EA vision while as a manager has to manage the complexity of the Enterprise Architecture development, documentation and day to day running." (quote from my EA book).

Now, what HBR has discovered is surprising:

"We've found that contrary to what many CEOs assume, leadership is not really about delegating tasks and monitoring results; it is about imbuing the entire workforce with a sense of responsibility for the business. This applies mainly to knowledge organizations, but even production-oriented companies can benefit from having employees who feel more empowered and engaged." Read here.

"In chaotic times, an executive's instinct may be to strive for greater efficiency by tightening control. But the truth is that relinquishing authority and giving employees considerable autonomy can boost innovation and success at knowledge firms, even during crises. Our research provides hard evidence that leaders who give in to the urge to clamp down can end up doing their companies a serious disservice. Although business thinkers have long proposed that companies can engage workers and stimulate innovation by abdicating control--establishing non-hierarchical teams that focus on various issues and allowing those teams to make most of the company's decisions--guidance on implementing such a policy is lacking. So is evidence of its consequences. Indeed, companies that actually practice abdication of control are rare. Two of them, however, compellingly demonstrate that if it's implemented properly, this counter-intuitive idea can dramatically improve results."

EA RELATION TO INNOVATION, STRATEGY AND TRANSFORMATION

EA relation to Strategy, Innovation, Risk, Investment...

August 20, 2010

http://www.ebizq.net/blogs/ea_matters/2010/08/enterprise-architecture-and-strategy-innovation-risk-investment-and-transformation.php

1. Strategy formulation is not an EA discipline. The EA would enable though the strategy mapping on the functions, processes and organizational units so that it can be executed.

Also the Enterprise transformation process that executes the strategy is guided by the EA

You'll find a whole chapter in my book about strategy formulation and a clear diagram summarising the whole process for business or IT strategists.

2. Emerging technologies and innovation are similarly not in the scope EA; but are essential to the Enterprise survival. EA plays a key role though in standardising the technology of the future and establishing principles that may promote innovation. It's upon you ultimately to include this far seeing aspects.

3. Technology risk and impacts are part of the EA gap analysis. The EA blueprint would also enable visualisation of issues and hot areas that may present risks and need investment (valid for 4).

4. Investment oversight; by establishing technology selection guidelines and architecture principles the EA would render the investment decision making consistent and fast.

5. Transformation is the major potential benefit of architecture. The blueprint, the current situation documentation, the gap analysis would enable you to plan the transformation of the Enterprise in synch, without losing parts, and ultimately effect change for tactical or strategic purposes.

Enterprise Architecture, how does it relate to strategy

August 26, 2010

http://www.ebizq.net/blogs/ea_matters/2010/08/enterprise-architecture-how-does-it-relate-to-strategy.php

The Enterprise Architecture relationship to strategy, ontology, design (thinking)... is debated yet again in the EA communities. Perhaps, that will still happen till we get that EA definition hammered down and agreed, somehow. Still, EA looks like a honey pot around which other rather equally well defined disciplines rotate or attempt to land and feed from it.

It certainly looks like these debates never steer to a conclusion; a reason could be that any valuable input could be easily appropriated. As long as peers' contribution is not somehow acknowledged that may change little.

It is also interesting to note that many participants listen or talk to their own echo alone. And uttering nonsense comes at no cost since anonymity in a larger crowd helps.

Debates are not really focused, they branch a lot, lacking the direction they need to stay on track. The person initiating the discussion should be in charge of steering the debate to a conclusion and emphasise the good bits, but seldom is. That's a suggestion. That would be good schooling for many of us to get to the point, precisely what I am not doing here.

In this post, I'll discuss the EA relationship to strategy. Please chip in.

Strategy has four phases: formulation, mapping, planning and execution.

My book describes these aspects in a few concise diagrams and then in some detail.

EA has little impact on Strategy formulation except that it makes clear, for the first time and to some's surprise, that the Enterprise strategy is a composite of many business, technology and people strategies.

The business or I would call it management strategy (aiming at more profit, more markets...), is only a part of the whole Enterprise strategy, mind you. As an example, the Business Intelligence strategy has to be integrated in the business and then in the Enterprise strategy. That may not happen, since that management "more profit" strategy is the only Strategy that counts and as such, the BI strategy is sometimes implemented by stealth, if at all.

No wonder people are complaining the strategy is seldom implemented. But it's not because of poor execution but because strategies are not integrated in the overall Enterprise strategy, in the first place and as such left out in the execution phase.

Technology has its own strategies that have to be aligned with the business ones. For example, you need to plan the upgrade to a new product, servers, platforms or networks because the current are not supported any longer. And technology is more than IT.

Higher level strategies, such as management's, should be cascaded and blended at lower EA layers in a strategy alignment process aided by an EA framework..

Enterprise Architecture and Strategy

September 30, 2010

http://www.ebizq.net/blogs/ea_matters/2010/09/enterprise-architecture-and-strategy.php

EA as the architecture of the Enterprise, i.e. integrated blueprint and associated information, offers a solid base for roadmapping, planning and strategy specification and execution because EA describes the components of the Enterprise and their relationships.

Strategic Planning is based on programs changing EA components, executed as part of the EA process of transforming the Enterprise from the current to future states.

EA does not do strategic planning for you. But with a proper EA you should have a all the components of the Enterprise and their relationships to consider in strategy design and execution. You would be able to take into consideration all systems, technology, organizational units and their dependencies. Ideally nothing would be left out, and there would be no conflicts for resources in execution.

Strategy execution would be implemented as an Enterprise Project Portfolio transforming all components in synchronization, according to vision.

With the EA you have an idea of how your strategy to reduce costs is supported by a reduction in duplication of such components as IT platforms, projects, people and processes.

In my book I describe an one page strategy specification process, its mapping mechanism and how to assemble the overall Enterprise strategy which is more than business strategy.

An issue creating confusion is that EA definitions, usually associated to an EA purpose, identify EA only with strategy. People associate EA only with strategic planning for instance. But alignment, simplification, understanding documentation are equal goals for an EA.

It is also true that the EA transformation is typically called strategy (execution) or IT strategy sometimes and as such EA is associated only with the Enterprise transformation process, ignoring the as-is state discovery for example.

You don't need EA to do the strategic planning but EA, through that intimate knowledge of elements and dependencies, enables a holistic view and application of methods such Enterprise Project Portfolio Management.

How EA doesn't do the work of strategy and planning functions

October 8, 2010

http://www.ebizq.net/blogs/ea_matters/2010/10/how-strategy-planning-and-ea-functions-work-together.php

Most, if not all, organizations already have strategy and planning functions. So why do enterprise architecture pundits and reputable firms stress that EA architects do strategy? What is the relationship between these functions--that is, strategy, planning and EA? I would like to invite you to debate here on this so that we can shelve the issue once for all.

You may have heard about the book "Enterprise Architecture as Strategy." It emphasizes that the "strategy" needed to succeed in the continuous transformation of today's enterprise is building and exploiting an EA to guide the transformation. that's something that Zachman has said for a long time. But that does not mean that EA architects do strategy themselves.

At its narrowest definition, EA means the enterprise blueprint. It may be used for managing complexity and enabling change--be it operational, tactical or strategic--since it describes the functions, systems, technology and organizational units that the change applies to.

As such, EA may assist strategy formulation and mapping by describing the enterprise parts to which the strategy applies.

 The strategy function specifies the overall business strategy. Nevertheless every key department specifies its own strategy in alignment to business strategy. IT has its own strategy, for example. Enterprise Architecture enables the alignment of these strategies under one single enterprise strategy--but still it does not formulate the business strategy.

EA, in its wider definition, is the process of enterprise transformation from a current to a future state, enabling strategy planning from the EA gap analysis and roadmaps. Thus, EA assists strategy planning by providing gaps analysis and roadmaps but EA itself, does not do it, at least because the planning function did this work long before and independent of EA.

The enterprise transformation according to strategy is achieved by programs coordinated by the PM office and executed by development people. EA assists the strategy execution process by enabling an enterprise program portfolio approach, but it does not execute the Enterprise transformation itself.

Therefore, the EA function does not formulate, plan or execute strategies; thus, it does not have a conflict of interest with strategists, planners or development teams, as may often appear to be the case in contemporary debates and various opinions on EA.

The strategy, EA, program office and development organizational functions should work in harmony, though, to achieve strategy formulation, mapping, alignment, planning and execution.

But if the EA scope is IT alone, as it currently happens, EA will have a diminutive role in the strategic transformation process, if any role at all.

Requirements, Strategy and Enterprise Architecture

April 18, 2012

http://www.ebizq.net/blogs/ea_matters/2012/04/are-requirements-necessary-for-ea.php

Requirements apply to projects rather than to Enterprise Architecture. It is the strategy concept that applies to the EA, rather than the requirements one.

The strategy team (which usually, is not the same as the EA team), is responsible for putting together the goals and the directions of enterprise transformation in order to realise the desired enterprise state and vision.

These strategic directions are then analysed and implemented by Programs/Projects, executed by transformation teams, which will collect their own Requirements.

The EA would not collect the requirements for these individual programs, at least because it will not be able to.

The EA could be seen though as implementing the requirements of all the individual programs gathered under the enterprise transformation portfolio that executes the strategy.

Hence, the requirements concept does not apply to EA.

From this point of view, TOGAF ADM represents a project delivery rather than an EA development process. In TOGAF, strategy is seldom mentioned, if at all.

Strategy, Planning, EA functions, roles and relationships

Oct 7, 2010

http://it.toolbox.com/blogs/ea-matters/strategy-planning-and-enterprise-architecture-functions-roles-and-relationships-41709

Most if not every organization already have Strategy and Planning functions. So why do Enterprise Architecture pundits and reputed firms stress that EA architects do strategy? What is the relationship between these functions i.e. Strategy, Planning and EA? I would like to invite you to debate here on this so that we can shelve the issue once for all.

The book "Enterprise Architecture as Strategy", you may have heard about. emphasizes that the "strategy" to succeed in the continuous transformation of today's Enterprise is to build and exploit an EA to guide the transformation. Something that Zachman has said for a long time.

But that does not mean that EA architects do themselves strategy.

At its narrowest definition, EA means the Enterprise blueprint. It may be used for managing complexity and enable change, be it operational, tactical or strategically since it describes the functions, systems, technology, organizational units... the change applies to.

As such, EA may assist strategy formulation and mapping by describing the Enterprise parts to which the strategy applies.

The Business Strategy function specifies the overall business strategy. Nevertheless every key department specifies its own strategy in alignment (?) to business strategy. IT has its own strategy, for example.

Enterprise Architecture enables the alignment of these strategies under one single Enterprise strategy but EA does not formulate business strategy.

EA, in its wider definition, as the process of Enterprise transformation from a current to a future state (like TOGAF ADM suggests), enables strategy planning from the EA gap analysis and roadmaps.

Thus, EA assists strategy planning by providing gaps analysis and roadmaps but EA itself, does not do it, at least because strategic planning existed long before and independent of EA.

The Enterprise transformation according to strategy, is achieved by programs coordinated by the PM office and executed by development people.

EA assists the strategy execution process by enabling an Enterprise Program Portfolio approach but it does not execute the Enterprise transformation itself

Therefore, the EA function does not formulate, plan or execute strategies; as such it does not have a conflict of interest with strategists, planners or development teams as it may often appear to be the case in contemporary debates and various opinions on EA.

The Strategy, EA, Program Office and Development org functions should work in harmony though to achieve strategy formulation, mapping & alignment, planning and execution, respectively.

But if the EA scope is IT alone, as it currently happens, EA will have a diminutive role in the strategic transformation process, if at all.

WHO DOES EA, THE ARCHITECT ROLE, SKILLS AND RECRUITMENT

The type of work an Enterprise Architect does

Oct 10, 2009

http://it.toolbox.com/blogs/ea-matters/the-type-of-work-an-enterprise-architect-does-34283

I realize that many of us, Enterprise Architects, our pay masters, and recruiters emphasize at times different aspects of EA. But they are all part of an Enterprise Architect's work day.

Here are the types:

 - EA Sell, justify (build business case) and sell EA

 - EA Design Architecture discovery and modelling

 - EA Roadmapping, planning

 - EA Maintenance and compliance work

And, in a way, each type requests a specific set of skills:

Justification and sell use skills like the knowledge of the enterprise workings (KPIs), what makes them effective, how costs could be reduced... Also the business case specification implies some financials. Selling and communications require soft skills.

Architecture modelling assumes methodologies like structured and OO analysis and design, a structured mind and disposition... Also a wide knowledge of technologies and architecture principles.

Roadmapping and strategy skills are still an art form demanding an understanding of trends, business and IT strategy skills, planning...

EA Maintenance demands project and solution architecture knowledge, change management, governance and organization skills, influencing, discipline, organized mind etc.

Enterprise Architecture value is delivered by its stakeholders

Jul 22, 2010

http://it.toolbox.com/blogs/ea-matters/the-enterprise-architecture-values-is-delivered-by-its-stakeholders-40107

EA is not in itself about business improvement, technology alignment, strategic planning and portfolio management; EA enables them all though, if properly modelled. As such, to measure Enterprise Architecture value as an EA architect, one needs to evaluate what EA delivers to Enterprise stakeholders, taking into account their views.

These stakeholders, not the architects, are in charge of strategic planning, process improvement, technology alignment to business, decision making etc and thus they will eventually materialise the benefits if properly supplied with the EA artefacts they need. The EA architect does not do strategy, portfolio management... but works to support these efforts.

Nevertheless, when top management asks though what are the EA benefits, they indeed talk about the whole Enterprise. Then the EA architect needs to pull together all benefits realised at all Stakeholders for the good of the Enterprise.

Overall and in the end, assuming EA is mature enough (has a proper EA development and utilisation process), the EA benefits may be translated in Enterprise Simplification, Integration, Alignment, Agility and Strategic planning.

A note. EA has strong roots in IT. It consists though not only of business and IT but also of non-IT and organization architectures. Without the business view the IT picture alone cannot offer the touted benefits. As such the business and organisation architectures become essential in returning benefits to all people rather than IT alone as is the case today.

Is the Enterprise Architect leading the enterprise development?

Nov 20, 2012

http://it.toolbox.com/blogs/ea-matters/is-the-enterprise-architect-leading-the-enterprise-development-53983

This comes as a result of this post from Gartner on "Enterprise architects, creationism and absolutism". I posted an opinion but I believe that the issue is relevant enough to be included in my blog.

While it raises the blood pressure a tad, the opinion is right. It is true that (quote from Mark of Gartner) "the idea that enterprise architects are the only ones with the breadth of knowledge, intellectual horsepower and perspective to design how an enterprise works is a business equivalent to divine intervention."

Is this just an honest mistake? I think it's rather hypocritical self advertising in a chaotic market that has little criteria of evaluation for the EA end product and the frameworks that would help deliver it. It works though.

Enterprises have been born today without an EA. Even documented after the fact, EA would provide an edge to the enterprise in this utterly competitive world. At least because it improves the understanding and provides a common vocabulary and plan for the enterprise.

At the end of the day, EA still is the blueprint of the enterprise. It can and should be equally used by all stakeholders (CxO, strategy, operations, programmes, architects. sourcing...) to document the enterprise, fix its operation, improve, roadmap it, implement its strategy and govern it. That is still mighty impressive if it is executed properly which is mostly not.

The main task of the EA is to deliver that blueprint for the stakeholders to be able to achieve the above outcomes, unless a job description specifically states differently.

The EA architect does not replace though the strategist, the business process man, the quality team... The architect just provide the tool, the context, the principles and the advice necessary for them to better their jobs.

Still the EA can be used, after sorting out its vagaries, in building up the enterprise from inception. A target EA view could be included in the initial business plan.

The reality is also that today EA happens and serves the IT alone. The dream is that the EA would serve the whole enterprise. But the these two are often confounded.

It is odd though that this post comes from the organisation which, for what it matters, is not far from stating that EA is "leading enterprise responses to disruptive forces...".

See this quote from Gartner's glossary:

"Enterprise architecture (EA) is a discipline for proactively and holistically leading enterprise responses to disruptive forces by identifying and analyzing the execution of change toward desired business vision and outcomes. EA delivers value by presenting business and IT leaders with signature-ready recommendations for adjusting policies and projects to achieve target business outcomes that capitalize on relevant business disruptions..."

Enterprise Architects and Enterprise Architecture

Nov 3, 2009

http://it.toolbox.com/blogs/ea-matters/enterprise-architects-and-enterprise-architecture-35119

I often wondered how does a recruiter recognize an Enterprise Architect. I concluded he/she does not. Too hard a job if the architects, those occupying EA positions or employers have different views of what EA is, its purpose and what they do.

While I watched an EA purpose discussion (> 200 entries) on Linkedin, I realised that few quoted definitions from known sources. As most entries were different, I concluded that the EA body of knowledge is fragmented, not agreed upon. That is most likely because there are too many schools, definitions and frameworks. The intriguing thought, given the creativity of these responses, is that the architects themselves seem content with this state of art that gives them freedom to define as EA whatever they do. As a result, E architects most likely, do different jobs. The beneficiaries of EA would never know what they get, in particular because, they don't know what to ask.

There is a category of Enterprise wide IT Architects for domain like infrastructure, applications... They are professionals able to see and draw a big picture, for a few functions of an Enterprise, in the domain there are in. They are not really Enterprise architects but they are called so when they are part of an EA team.

EA is not about SW architecture either. SW architects, Enterprise Java Architects are in fact developers.

IT solution architects design the block diagram of an application, its components and its context.

IT Architects are not Enterprise Architects for the simple reason that they don't know and are not even interested in how the Enterprise works. They are often called E Architects, when having accumulate experience, they review all IT solution architectures in the Enterprise in order to make recommendation to reduce duplication, standardise etc but seldom having a common framework or EA blueprint as reference for decision making.

In fact, there are too many Enterprise Architects and too few Enterprise Architectures.

The confusion between EA architects and IT architects bothers because the "wrong architects" as Gartner calls them in "10 pitfalls...", are employed with results for firms and EA discipline we already know.

What an Enterprise Architect needs to know

Oct 6, 2007

http://it.toolbox.com/blogs/ea-matters/what-an-enterprise-architect-needs-to-know-19555

The difficulty is to manage the vast knowledge required by an EA, spanning all business, technology and organization domains. To develop an EA, an Enterprise Architect and a well-oiled EA team needs to cover expertise that stretches across fields such diverse as:

- Enterprise Value Chains, Business Models and Strategy, Operations
- Business Process Frameworks, BPM, Rules, orchestration, BAM, B2B
- EA frameworks (Zachman, TOGAF, FEA, TEAF, IAF...), architecture design methodology, best practices
- UML and other modelling and tools
- IT Applications and ITIL, DW/BI, MDM, Identity Management
- IT Infrastructure, servers, networks, storage, application servers based, JavaEE, .NET
- All other technologies involved (production band, telecom networks, SCADA ...)
- Applications and suites - ERP, CRM, SCM, CM, KM, Portals...
- SOA, Web Services - SOAP, UDDI, WSDL, ESB, Web2.0
- Project management, Change management, Business Case specification
- Maturity models (CMM), Balanced Score Cards
- M&A, outsourcing, BPO, SaaS...
- Organization design and Human Performance, governance, politics

These are some of the challenges Enterprise Architects and all involved face. Without an Enterprise Architect, to know the parts and the moves, everything can derail quickly in terms of quality cost or schedule.

That calls for leadership. Often employing the wrong EA team can hamper the whole project. Select a quality, politically astute EA team, since it is a major risk. Soft skills for negotiation, extracting the knowledge distributed in human heads, selling the benefits of EA are in high demand.

After the architecture phase, the Enterprise transformation requires many other resources be involved. The governance is key to the whole process.

Business Model Canvas is neither ontology, nor BA, but a...

Dec 31, 2012

http://www.ebizq.net/blogs/ea_matters/2012/12/the-business-model-canvas-is-neither-a-business-architectur-nor-an-ontology-it-is-a-value-chain.php

Is Alex Osterwalder's Business Model Canvas, BMC, an ontology or a (business) architecture as it is sometimes claimed or... something else?

To start with, BMC cannot be both a (business) architecture and an ontology. That is, assuming that an architecture is a model then and ontology is a metamodel of the architecture domain under scrutiny. BMC is either one or the other.

Whatis.com states that "an ontology is the working model of entities and interactions in some particular domain of knowledge or practices."

A first question is then, what is the domain which the BMC is an ontology for? Without that, we cannot proceed with the ontology assumption. It does not seem to be the enterprise since there too are many missing elements.

But let's take the Customer and Supplier, parts of the BMC canvas, are they elements of an enterprise domain?

Imagine only an enterprise like Microsoft whose customers represent a generous section of the individuals and companies of the world. Had the enterprise included customers, then it has to include the customers of the customer enterprises, and so on. Not to mention that a Customer is a Supplier too, which another element of the BMC. What would the final enterprise footprint look like then? If it could be ever drawn, it would appear like a giant picture of all the companies in the world.

Well then, we have to eliminate Customers and Suppliers as part of an Enterprise ontology.

I can continue to argue for each element of the BMC but I won't do that here and now.

There are a number of other BMC versions that exhibit different elements and even links. But the links have not been ever specified. They have loose meanings. In any case, the BMC model in use looks like the Windows 8 start screen, that is a number of boxes without interconnections. That might have been the reason it was called a canvas in the first place rather than an ontology or an architecture which exhibit meaningful interconnections. In practice, one just fills in the boxes of the canvas. Links are not necessary.

Also we do not fill in ontologies, or metamodels for that matter, like we do fill in the BMC.

Some BMC representations feature connections in a kind of general boxes and lines diagram that could denote any diagram, for example a flow one rather than an ontology which might look more like an entity relationship diagram.

Rather than continue on this path, let me state what BMC does represent in my view. It is a basic product value chain. Take for instance SCOR's (Supply Chain...) Source - Make - Deliver.

The BMC shows the flow

- beginning with Sourcing from Suppliers

- to Making activities and resources

- and Delivering to Customers through channels

Now this a thing I can work with. I can see how the Business Models are implemented on an enterprise value chain. I can map a business model on an enterprise architecture that describes its processes and resources. I can calculate then the costs, the revenue and as such the value proposition of the Business Model. Moreover, Porter's Value Chain exhibits an element called margin. This would be the profit of the BMC value proposition.

Could the BMC illustrate then some kind of a basic value chain flow diagram then? It could and it does in my view.

But then, is it a business architecture?

No, because there are more value chains in an enterprise. Resources are not part of a business architecture but of an enterprise architecture that includes technology and people.

But you can map the BMC on an EA described by GODS-FFLV for instance which exhibits both a generic business architecture and an EA framework. The BMC elements can be easily identified then on the EA, the path through the EA drawn and the costs and revenue calculated.

The role and responsibilities of an Enterprise Architect

Oct 11, 2007

http://it.toolbox.com/blogs/ea-matters/the-role-and-responsibilities-of-an-enterprise-architect-19651

Following the post on architect's knowledge and skills I list here few of the Enterprise Architect's responsibilities (not exhaustive):

- Prepares EA business case, exposes benefits and drivers, financial merits
- Presents, justifies communicates to all stakeholders in business and IT
- Specifies EA framework, best practices and tools
- Establishes architecture, design and technology principles and guidelines
- Participates in EA design and development
- Coordinates works done by domain architects
- Controls the consistency and compliancy of artefacts
- Owns the EA repository and decides access rights
- Recommends transformation roadmap and works with Program Management
- Controls EA iterations deliveries
- Establishes compliance checkpoints in major capability development processes
- Assesses EA maturity
- Measures returned value at each iteration

The Authority of an Enterprise Architect:

- Makes decisions with regard to EA artefacts design, principles and implementation
- Proposes and enforces EA check points in main capability delivery processes
- Drives the virtual team of solution, domain, applications and infrastructure architects

- Resolves architecture disputes

From a social viewpoint, the Enterprise Architect should be able to communicate, influence, negotiate, motivate, facilitate and inspire, in other words, get the human interaction right. It should be able to guide the EA development process and get support from all levels:

- The Enterprise Architect should be politically savvy
- Able to present and argue at all levels of management

SOA architects have a subset of these responsibilities. Additionally they manage the services catalogue.

Is the Enterprise Architect's job about influencing?

Oct 24, 2010

http://it.toolbox.com/blogs/ea-matters/is-the-enterprise-architects-job-about-influencing-42075

To start with, the fact is that the current EA architect role does not typically have the authority to make decisions. As such, pundits have suggested that "influencing" is the way the EA architect should do the job. It would be much clearer though had the kind of decisions been illustrated. After all, there are too many kinds of EA architects out there (see ads), from infrastructure, applications, Java, SAP, BI... to strategy and business architects.

In practice, EA work consists of solution reviews, integration and IT strategy, see this. Even if the architect would have the mandate to make decisions, they would be limited to IT. There is little scope for business decisions making even if the architect would be qualified for that since the role more often than not reports to the Head of IT Strategy and Architecture which has limited authority anyway.

For decisions making there is an organization and governance structure in place in which the EA architect does not really sit. Moreover, as EA trespasses so many domains that any attempt at influencing or unauthorised decision making would meet politics.

More the EA role should only provide the information for decision making. The analysis and decisions are made by other bodies not the EA architect. Because of the knowledge span, the EA architect can be invited at the decision table, sometimes.

... In the current role the architect is not a leader. Moreover, leadership comes usually with authority.

But I believe we all have to influence in our jobs. In general it's a time consuming and risky avenue to get somewhere. Petty politics can halt your good intentions and what's good for the Enterprise.

What is the meaning of influencing though? I assume that it means convincing people through various methods, passion and professionalism, to take the decisions you could only suggest. What are the chances that influencing succeeds though? 50-50%? It depends on personal skills. Would the management leave the future of the company at the mercy of an architect's skills and meagre pay?

If Enterprise Architecture is so important to a company why not empower the EA function to shape the Enterprise?

The problem is that top managements do not really think that current EA architects and EA bring value. So it is not about the EA professional having to influence but about having to convince everybody else that EA returns business value which has not been too often the case. What the EA architect has to do is to sell the EA based on real achievements. If that is what is meant by "influencing" then I agree. But you still needs practical results. How many good EA blueprints have you seen today?

Mike Rollings of Gartner wrote at "An EA program typically requires a massive amount of influence and communication because it includes the implementation of organizational change. It includes changes to governance, changes to processes, new decision-making responsibilities, and a wide-range of other changes to how an organization does planning and implementation."

In reality an Enterprise Transformation and change program, if any, would not be lead by the EA architect but by Program Management as an Enterprise Project Portfolio, controlled by a high up governance body. The EA architect does not plan the change either. The EA architect only produces the architecture and I agree here, collaborates and with all key efforts in the Enterprise.

The was also discussion about a hypothetical and idealised executive EA position that shapes the Enterprise; but this does not really exist, and it won't until there will be a proper body of knowledge to arm the EA architect with and guarantee the EA value return. This position sits much higher in the organization, is empowered and no longer an IT role alone.

How to select an Enterprise Architect?

Jun 21, 2008

http://it.toolbox.com/blogs/ea-matters/how-to-select-an-enterprise-architect-25288

How does one select an Enterprise Architect (EAs)? So many around these days. No wonder because the title and pay are attractive. Since there are few distinctive qualifications or selection criteria for an Enterprise Architect, how do you recognize an Enterprise Architect? Is it intuition? Is it the good old boys network?

 Most EAs have studied TOGAF, Zachman, FEA and quickly gave up on DoDAF. These appear to be the universal requirements for an Enterprise Architect. Nothing earth shuttering though, no mathematics, almost marketing like material.

Zachman it's quite straightforward to read and understand by all. It is common sense. Long before that, Rudyard Kipling's poem "Elephant's child" from "Just so stories" beautifully suggested, an everyday life discovery process based on the "w" questions.

(Zachman 2 is coming, I hear, surely adding some substance to the Mendeleev's elements table, the framework was likened to) All of us browsed TOGAF (hard to go through otherwise due to its richness).

FEA is a bit of a read, in fact there are quite a number of documents, but what remains in one's mind is the simple framework (consisting of performance,... business, services, technology reference layers) which is not quite rocket science. But if you read specific agency frameworks you discover they differ in many ways, fact that may baffle you a bit.

DODAF, not bad at all, formalizing descriptions in diagrams types connected by a metamodel, complementing FEA models in many ways, has its own vocabulary that departs too much from the EA accepted modelling. Hence it is hardly usable except in defence.

As such, it is not too hard to tick the methodology boxes for an Enterprise Architecture job: Zachman, TOGAF, FEA and other (IAF, EAP, E2AF...). But unfortunately this is not too distinctive, in fact it provides no differentiation since most architects can claim this.

That is why the Enterprise Architect's curriculum must be backed by a long IT experience and references. Good social skills proving that he/she is articulate as well to communicate with stakeholders and "C" level management (sounds catchy!) is a must, they say. In any case, you must keep your nerve explaining to everybody again and again what it is, why, how you are going to do it. As soon as you leave, people start asking anew, what was that for?

How to select an Enterprise Architect? (ii)

Jun 27, 2008

http://it.toolbox.com/blogs/ea-matters/how-to-select-an-enterprise-architect-ii-25519

Counting the selection criteria (the previous blog), is it possible to narrow down the candidates to a short list? Currently, Zachman, TOGAF and the soft skills tick boxes decimate the number of candidates; but is that enough? By the way, has anyone been asked at an EA interview, what are Zachman or TOGAF about? I find it difficult to find questions with answers relevant to the framework since knowledge about, is either straightforward or common to other disciplines.

Typically, technology criteria are further employed for selection: experience with Java frameworks, .Net platforms... although software programming is not a basic requirement, strictly speaking, for an Enterprise Architect, but some experience of it, perhaps. An Enterprise Java architect knows more about programming in JEE than the development of an Enterprise Architecture, which is natural. The real need for an Enterprise Java Architect is in Enterprise Applications Integration and patching.

You will often find the Enterprise Solution Architect role as well, where the chosen one ought to do whatever work comes that way, Enterprise wide, from Java to TOGAF. This is quite an one man band requirement but would attract a Solution rather than an Enterprise Architect. A solution architect is someone who, starting from business requirements, selects an IT application most suitable from a functional viewpoint and for integration in the existing IT landscape. The role is less hands on than the Enterprise Java Architect, working more closely with the business.

Then, many demand experience in the specific business domain such as financial, insurance... The experience might help speed the process, but unfortunately they may eliminate the real Architects.

Anyway, as in the previous case, this is not really a requirement for an Enterprise Architect which should work with and mobilize the business to design the specific architecture. An Enterprise Architect would apply method and frameworks to your EA rather than attempting to substitute software designers and business people and their expertise; he would model any business, on any IT platform, following the same process, no matter what industry, beginning with products and stakeholders' interaction specification, continuing with the functional decomposition and process design and engineering and, not really ending with the architecture of the resources executing it, IT and people.

How to select an Enterprise Architect (iii)

Jul 11, 2008

http://it.toolbox.com/blogs/ea-matters/how-to-select-an-enterprise-architect-iii-25649

Until now, I neglected the architecture skill, the most important in fact in the selection process. What is an Architect? It is someone with a structured mind, who likes to discover and use patterns and is willing to do this tenuous job. The Architect digs to discover the essence, like a true IT intellectual, and feels the inner need to understand how parts fit into the whole. A craftsman and artist, since Enterprise Architecture is far from being a science right now. Usually, is experienced in more structured disciplines such as hardware and software design. The architect also struggled at some point with OO UML and distributed components technology, hopefully not too much CORBA.

So ask what architecture is, what are the artefacts for an EA, how are they linked, what is a metamodel, how would the candidate design, implement and maintain an

EA, what would be the work breakdown, what are the architecture principles or styles...

Finally, you've got yourself an Enterprise Architect. But will you get an Enterprise Architecture? Probably not. This is a problem: all companies have Enterprise Architects but no Enterprise Architecture. Life goes on; the company survived without an EA for many years already.

Anyhow once you have the Enterprise Architect in situ, the problem seems to disappear: the EA box is ticked and the peace of mind descends upon everyone, including management. No Enterprise Architecture though. But since few know what that is, a few diagrams of interconnected applications will quench the thirst for it.

But remember what the Enterprise Architecture is: the documented structure and operation of your company. Hence EA is a necessary evil in this era of fast change, growing complexity and amount of information. The Enterprise Architect must be a dedicated and well rounded man that has to apply creatively the existing body of knowledge since the current state does not support well your endeavour to create your Enterprise Architecture.

What an Enterprise Architect does!

Jul 27, 2008

http://it.toolbox.com/blogs/ea-matters/what-an-enterprise-architect-does-25133

In the previous posts I tried to describe what Enterprise Architects actually do. It did not surprise me to discover that Enterprise Architects don't do much Enterprise or business architecture work for that matter. What is business architecture anyway, a few business process diagrams? It is true nevertheless that Enterprise Architects tend to be experienced people who may engage and solve most IT situations, in a flexible and clever manner.

What an Enterprise Architect should do though?

The job starts with putting together an EA business case to justify the EA development once for all, then sell the EA to business and management to get sponsorship and resources. Afterwards, the EA framework selection, customization or creative design since most frameworks are not going further than general patterns like matrices, layered pyramids, cubes, process and best practices etc. This is a critical success factor for the rest of the EA development!

The architect establishes the design principles, the process, breaks down the EA work into workstreams and organizes the teams to discover and document the current Enterprise state and blueprint. The Enterprise Architect validates other Enterprise developments from an EA point of view: all solutions architecture design have to comply to EA principles and conventions reuse the same components and link to other artefacts. Also, the ERP, SCM, CRM, MDM, Portal and business specific applications, suites and activities have to be properly documented at the process and technology layers.

As the EA becomes the knowledge DB of the Enterprise, the content has to be organized early in an EA taxonomy and exposed on the Intranet. The EA architect leads this effort.

Then the architect looks at the Business and IT Strategies aligns them to the Enterprise Map, determines the future state of the EA and establishes technology standards, guidelines and roadmaps. Then the EA architect specifies the EA compliance criteria and process controls, evaluates EA maturity and not least, coordinates the entire EA development work. Most Enterprise Architects don't do that. (They do though, validate most IT developments against their own professional experience which is good but leads to variable and debatable outcomes.)

Well, there is an explanation for that. The "body of EA knowledge" is scarce, fragmented, contributed by practitioners from experience rather than academia. There is a reason for that too. EA crosses the boundaries between the theory and practice of business (existing since the dawn of time) and IT (still young and playful, celebrating about half a century of existence)... disciplines that until now have been treated in utter separation. The Business side concocts a system specification, the business analyst translates it and the IT implements it. But business and IT have different cultures, objectives, vocabularies and require very different skills. Hence, the division between Business and IT does well without an Enterprise Architecture to align governance, goals, processes, communication language...

EA consultants, what are they?

Aug 15, 2008

http://it.toolbox.com/blogs/ea-matters/ea-consultants-what-are-they-24636

Consultancies, do they have EA frameworks? Most of them yes, some variations of the "legacy" ones. They count a lot on the collective consultants' experience with plenty of former projects to serve as examples. Aggregation or consolidation of all work in a single framework is seldom performed though, to the best of my knowledge.

Consultancies worry less with the selection of an EA consultant. There must be a hard working chap with a mortal desire to travel a lot, camp in hotels, hostels, managed apartments, dine in planes and trains, be mobile connected till late, live with an allowance of about 30-40$ a day but be able to impress customers with a no nonsense EA talk leaving few questions unanswered or providing the legacy answer "there is no silver bullet". More often than not, customers don't expect wonders anyway. In fact, in most cases consultants are more like "contractors", in that they do what the customer tells them rather than tell the customer what to do.

For a consultancy, a typical framework - that changes and varies quite often - is based on the few known layers (business, information, applications, technology etc) conveniently surrounded by a few great Zachman style questions, such as Why, Who, When, Where.... Orthogonally one will always find a security slice. Some have Strategy on top to show how important it is. These frameworks look like triangles, two dimensional boxes, tables, cubes, pyramids that really give you the impression of Architectonic monuments and with it, the good warm feeling that we talk about architecture.

When the EA exercise ends, the customer remains, with a diagram occupying a boardroom wall displaying and impressive myriad of connections and actors. At the top there always are the customer channels since the customer is king - that's marketing speak. There is a little bit for everyone but not enough to keep the interest long. Not quite touching the business issues or views. A bit hard to read, standing there and who's going' to maintain it? The consultant. One cannot print it since equipment like this is a rarity.

Consultancies usually have other Enterprise wide assignments, not only Enterprise Architecture design. That saves the day. The consultant must be flexible and inventive. Must be self-reliant, confident, bendable, ductile, non-vertebrate, cool and an "accomplished communicator" so that he can inspire confidence and sales even to his own boss. Communications to level Cs if not higher is a must.

The EA consultant is often compared to a body in a body shopping process, i.e. engaged in whatever work the customer desires over a while. The body may have a soul but that is not part of the contract. There is a striking similarity with the oldest trade in the world.

But a consultant, like Faust, would sell his soul for a viable framework.

The EA Architect's key traits from a recruitment perspective

Feb 21, 2012

http://www.ebizq.net/blogs/ea_matters/2012/02/the-enterprise-architect-and-specialist-knowledge.php

The core requirement (the "Must") for an EA architect is a candidate that knows how to uncover the structure of systems, use the proper methods to document the enterprise operation, link parts into the whole, and understands architecture roadmapping and strategy.

An EA architect will see the whole (forest) without neglecting the parts (trees). This comes only with experience in "various business and technology fields" and training.

But more important is the mindset, or better a personality trait, for analysis and synthesis. Not everybody enjoys or can do that, that is, dealing in abstraction, discovering patterns, designing etc. This is what you should be looking for.

Would the employers rather have another specialist in a business field (of which there should be enough already in their business), or would they rather have someone who has the capacity to analyse and strategise and approach problems of all sorts encountered at the confluence between business and technology, someone who fits the parts together?

In plain terms, what a recruiter and employer should be asking for, "do I want another specialist or a generalist the architect is? The EA architect should be the universal man of the business. The Renaissance man. This is what you should be looking at.

Ask yourselves or your clients this question, because that determines your EA candidate selection. Your rarely can get both at the price of one that is, at the quality you demand for the price you pay. Employers have to balance the EA with the specialist demands. If you go on asking for both you would probably end up with a specialist with TOGAF or Zachman training. Beware.

In practice, such a practitioner with ready solutions to your problem domain is hard to find and dear to keep, for a few reasons, at least. One of them is the architect's slim job satisfaction in a narrow domain. Another one is that specialisation prevents progress in the EA career.

Most EA architects would employ elements of existing EA frameworks. But none of them is good enough. Without a framework, you will not get the integrated whole of parts EA, that is, the business, technology components and describing artefacts all interconnected.

Very few EA architects would be able to create their own framework able to link the disparate parts of your business in a big picture. This is what you ideally want. But it's hard to find. You'll discover a lot of show off, ranting and hype.

You'll have to make sure that the architect understand how business parts and designs fit together in a blueprint or set of them. Ask them to show you a sample integrated blueprint.

The architect may document and design for you the many parts of an enterprise. But if you put them together would your enterprise fly same as an airplane does when you fix the parts together?

Having placed your designs in a Zachman matrix, have you gotten an EA blueprint? Certainly not. Having followed all the TOGAF steps and prescribed outcomes have you obtained an EA? Indeed not. But that's what you will usually get. Populated frameworks not EA. People often populate one framework or another (for example Zachman or TOGAF) but that does not mean that they do EA. In fact that contributes to the downfall of EA.

Ask them the EA definition and purpose. If they talk about many but a blueprint then you should look elsewhere. EA, once designed, can be employed by any stakeholder (rather than EA architect) for own purpose: fix parts and operation, to do strategy, manage complexity, control change etc.

But because EA is often associated with transformation, your EA architect should be able to do strategy and in particular roadmapping. Ask them how they did and do it.

Is programming knowledge necessary for an EA architect?

March 9, 2012

http://www.ebizq.net/blogs/ea_matters/2012/03/is-there-programming-language-necessary-for-an-ea-architect.php

Currently, many EA architects come from and work in IT. That does not necessarily have to be so. As it happens, some have some knowledge of programming. But that does not mean that such knowledge is required for an EA.

IT, from a systems and software design practice (OO...), often comes with an understanding of the Architecture side of Enterprise Architecture.

Business though comes with the knowledge of the Enterprise part of EA but with little ability to architecture it.

An EA architect has to understand both how a business works and how to structure and describe it rather than comprehend programming languages in any depth.

Many EAs come though from software development where they learned the ropes of software architecture - client-server, OO, UML, web services and SOA. Because applications architecture is part of EA, this is welcome even if it is in the domain of a software architect rather than that of an EA architect. But importantly, the object methods, may be used to model any system and as such transcend the software domain.

But even a software architect deals with object repositories, libraries, modules, frameworks and APIs (take for instance JavaEE) rather than pure programming.

Moreover, in other lands, the system analysts/designers are not the same as the programmers. They just hand over the design to the programmers.

It is true though that sometimes job descriptions confound software with EA architecture and eventually require programming experience.

The EA should know software architecture to a degree but should know much more: technology in general, business applications, infrastructure and products, networks, business frameworks and tools, planning and the whole science or art of managing an enterprise and its strategy.

As such, the architect is a generalist rather than a specialist in any of the above domains. They are simply too many to master in-depth.

Hence, there is a long way to go from a programmer background to an EA architect.

So, when recruiting, a programming language could come, at best, on a wish list rather than a must have list, and only when your EA architect has to specialise in the applications tier. In fact it is not the language itself required but the ecosystem of frameworks, libraries and objects you need.

Taking the view of MIT's Jeanne Ross, the architect would have to have the skills of a clinical psychologist in order to defeat the resistance of the top management who stubbornly just don't get it. This is one notch up from the soft skills we usually blubber about. Looking through this glass, programming sounds OK though.

It becomes easier to say what an EA must not know than what he has to.

12 Questions to help you recruit an Enterprise Architect

May 3, 2012

http://www.ebizq.net/blogs/ea_matters/2012/05/questions-to-help-you-recruit-an-ea.php

How do you make sure that you chose the right candidate for an EA job? Here are a few questions that, if answered to your satisfaction, may clear the way to the appointment.

Indeed, there may be other questions that you may ask that would be more related to the specifics of the job.

Publications clear the way as well since you can evaluate first hand some of the opinions held and the communications skills of the candidate.

Not least, you have to assess that the chemistry works between you and the candidate.

But here are the questions:

- 1. What is architecture and what is EA and its scope?
- 2. What is BA? How does it look like? How do EA and BA relate?
   Do you use a BA framework?
- 3. What are the EA/BA deliveries one can expect? And how would they look like.
   What would be the key artefacts?
- 4. How do you design an EA, what the key few process steps?
- 5. How would the EA governance look like?
- 6. How would you organise the team?
- 7. What is an EA framework and what framework(s) would you use?
- 8. What is the relationship to other enterprise functions such as

Strategy and Programs?

- 9. How would EA support business alignment?

- 10. How would EA enable complexity and change management?

- 11. What would you have on an EA 6 months delivery plan?

- 12. How do you justify EA and how to assess progress and value delivered?

Past experience with examples would reinforce the answers.

The CV is a key document that may answer your preliminary queries about business and IT knowledge, experience in managing stakeholders, soft skills...

An important step is to make sure of the veracity of the deliveries in the related positions held, by questioning the nature of deliveries (was it a diagram, a document...?).

The right candidate will vary though since different interviewers can expect different answers.

Is industry experience a must for an Enterprise Architect?

Feb 22 , 2012

http://it.toolbox.com/blogs/ea-matters/is-industry-experience-a-must-for-an-enterprise-architect-50492

Here is a LinkedIn debate on the issue.

The core requirement (the "Must") for an EA architect is a candidate that knows how to discover and structure a system (the enterprise), use the proper methods to document the enterprise operation and link the parts into the whole, and understands roadmapping and strategy based on EA.

This comes only with experience in "various business fields" (not specialisation), training, and not least mindset. Not everybody enjoys or can do that: dealing with abstraction, discovering patterns, designing etc.

Would the employers have another specialist in their business field (of which there should be enough already in the business), or would they rather have that architect that has the capacity to analyse and synthesise and approach problems of all sorts?

In plain terms, what an employer should be asking is, do I want a specialist or a generalist (the EA architect is)?

The answer to this determines the candidate selection.

You rarely can get both at the quality and for the price you pay. The employers have to balance the EA with the specialist demands. If they go on asking for both you would probably end up with a specialist with TOGAF training.

In practice, such a practitioner with ready solutions to your problem domain is hard to find and dear to keep, for a few reasons, at least. One of them is that specialisation prevents them from progressing in their EA career.

I discovered that many job descriptions for EA architects are so overloaded and under paid for the tasks, that they only address the market of the pauper CEOs.

EA TRAINING, CERTIFICATION AND HIGHER EDUCATION

EA training and certification, does it help?

Sep 3, 2008

http://it.toolbox.com/blogs/ea-matters/ea-training-and-certification-does-it-help-24310

 The EA (and SOA) training and certification courses will surely help, won't they?

A few companies offer training and certification courses, but did they really help you with the EA job? The test would obviously be to ask a certified architect to design, plan and coordinate the implementation of an Enterprise Architecture. I guess you know the results.

These courses could be also quite extensive (more than ten days) and expensive (more than $10,000).

EA certification attempting to fill the gap to an experienced IT professional, quite frequently does not provide a clear EA framework to guide the development work. And it does not provide guidelines or templates for business, information... architectures.

An Enterprise Architect needs to understand at least the EA IT layers not to mention the business architecture concepts and strategy.

As such all these IT layers (applications, information, technology) are typically presented extensively in a training course. You will see long chapters about network, DB, server technologies, type of applications etc.

Is that what you expected? It depends where you stand. If you don't have experience in IT that may be your need. But as a chartered IT professional aspiring towards an EA role, you would not need this, but the knowledge that differentiates and IT from an EA architect: an EA framework, metamodel, method and business concepts as Value Chains, Business Models, Business Process Maps...

I would say that a true Enterprise Architect needs to understand a business operation and the framework connecting the layers and its navigation, rather than the layers in detail.

Does training and certification provide the Enterprise Architect with a practical framework to design or lead the implementation of an Enterprise Architecture? Most probably not since it is not an objective of certification to design an EA framework but to teach and explain the existing ones.

If such an EA framework is not provided, training and certification courses do not really guarantee the ability of the EA architect to deliver an EA.

Enterprise Architecture training and certification

Mar 26, 2010

http://it.toolbox.com/blogs/ea-matters/enterprise-architecture-training-and-certification-37154

I found that people graduating from certification courses were unable to define what Enterprise Architecture (EA) is. Well that is the root problem, isn't it? How do you certify someone for something you can't properly define? Let's not accuse the newly certified alone. Asked an EA architect then. You shouldn't be surprised to discover that some don't have a clue.

I make a distinction between EA training and certification. While any sort of EA training may be all right for a starter, one would only be certified for a particular method anyway. And there are many. In fact most true EA architects build their own because the existing "frameworks" are rather incomplete. For instance:

- Zachman is only a mere taxonomy or ontology, if you listen to a self assessment. That is, it is not really a framework. It doesn't give a structure for the Enterprise or a method to transform it.

- TOGAF is an (IT) development process framework if you really insist to call it a framework. It addresses a program management rather than architecture audience. As a process without a structure, it does not really guarantee a result.

It might be worth getting trained in abbreviated courses but the certification what is it worth? If all you are after is a job solely, then do it because some jobs descriptions require it. But they won't help you do the job. As in most cases your manager does not know what to expect then that may be OK. You should deliver large and great documents full of side knowledge. Everybody does that. Nobody uses the documents afterwards because they are just a collections of observations, facts, methods, disclaimers, quotes...

Assuming that one is trained, the new EA architect has to browse now EA books (each and everyone is different, do we really write about the same thing?) and articles, stay put in the EA community, publish own view, and do work, eventually as a consultant to learn that each assignment is different.

And after all, anyone who pays becomes a certified EA architect. That shows in our EA groups discussions. This is why we have so many EA architects and so few Enterprise Architectures with so much secrecy surrounding them.

How do you distinguish the real EA architect? First you know what you want, and compare to what EA can do. EA is a set of integrated blueprints. That is what your architect should generate. Stakeholders then would use them for their own purposes. Just ask the question: what are you going to deliver? If the answer is long and circuitous then you surely found a certified EA architect.

But convince me otherwise.

EA means more Business Architecture nowadays but certifications are still IT based.

Nevertheless, if you work for the US government, for instance, there is sense in being certified in their method, FEA.

Open CA and Ea certification, take it or leave it?

Jul 19, 2012

http://it.toolbox.com/blogs/ea-matters/open-ca-and-enterprise-architecture-certification-take-it-or-leave-it-51885

In the following, I would like to debate certifications in general and in particular, the Open CA of the Open Group. This post comes as a result of a LinkedIn discussion on this topic.

The number of EA methods and certifications is increasing but the supplying parties continue to ignore each other, as if they don't exist. Currently, many do take EA training and certifications in the hope they'd improve their career prospects. But do they improve or guarantee the practitioners' prowess to do the job? How useful is an EA certification?

See a few posts on certification Tom Graves', here, and then my experience with TOGAF.

We have, obviously, the problem of regulating the EA profession. Too many claim they are EA architects, saturating the market. The title is used too loosely by practitioners, recruiters, companies and certifications bodies. Recruiters and customer firms have little support in their endeavour to select an EA professional. Their most specific demand is TOGAF, unfortunately, for now.

 That encouraged many parties to come out with certification schemes claiming that they fill a necessary gap in the market.

But, the EA problem stems, in the first place, from the fact that the current EA frameworks are improperly focused, incomplete and fail to deliver the integrated outcome.

In any case, the application of the EA methods does not produce to expectations. Unfortunately, there is no standard to assess the propriety and completeness of an EA method.

Then, how could EA certifications deliver quality guarantees when the EA methods themselves cannot? Certifications typically test the knowledge and experience for a specific method.

To avoid the issue, the Open CA certification body claims that an architect is evaluated based on the success achieved in practicing EA, independent of method.

What is the Open CA certification and what is the value it delivers to customers, practitioners and companies alike? Is the Open CA worth the cost and the effort, taking into account that we have been practicing architecture for many years today? Who needs it and who benefits?

First, here is the Open Group's (OG) CA link. Also check

 Mike's post overviewing the Open CA, and follow the links. Yet again, you'll find out that there is too much information. No different from TOGAF.

Open CA certification is Open Group's IT certification. It was formerly known as ITAC (IT Architect Certification).

Mind you, the EA architect is just a step in a stream of IT certifications, starting from the lowly IT architect and ending with the Chief Architect, of which the last few are ranked "distinguished".

To start with, since EA covers much more than IT, such as business, organisational and other technology views, Open CA can hardly certify you as an EA architect. How could it do that in a sequence of IT certifications? It should be fair to say that the EA certification is around IT alone.

"The Open CA program requires applicants to demonstrate skills and experience against a set of conformance requirements through written applications and peer interviews. There are no training courses to attend and no written exams to complete".

So, Open CA has and tests no EA theory, methods or body of knowledge, not even TOGAF. Open seems to mean exactly that that, that it is independent of TOGAF!

That leaves us with the dilemma of what do we make of two entirely different EA certifications from the same body? More on that later.

But based on what criteria, would the written evidence be evaluated as an EA practice? We, in the EA community of practitioners, have not even agreed so far what EA or its scope is.

Please do say your opinion here, because the proliferation of these dear certifications will affect us all. They may become de facto standards for architect selection in the near future. You may be soon asked by employers to get certified in order to occupy even the most obscure EA architect position. These things have a way of creeping in. When we finally take time to notice it, it's too late to act.

Open CA and EA certification, take it or leave it? (II)

Jul 27, 2012

http://it.toolbox.com/blogs/ea-matters/open-ca-and-enterprise-architecture-certification-take-it-or-leave-it-ii-52548

"The Open CA program requires applicants to demonstrate skills and experience against a set of conformance requirements through written applications and peer interviews. There are no training courses to attend and no written exams to complete".

Since an EA practice is successful if and only if it delivers the EA first, how would one define the certification criteria to validate the EA outcome if it is unclear what the EA delivers?

What does the certification body tick as successful if the EA is not only defined differently but produces differently in each and every case?

For instance, an EA architect delivers strategy, as outlined by some analyst and consultancy firms. For others, EA implements operating models. I, myself, aim to deliver the Enterprise integrated blueprints, on top of the above, using my own "successful" framework, FFLV-GODS.

But how would the Open CA certification be able to assess all these strands of EA practices, considering also the fact that there is no own reference EA model?

Nevertheless, playing the devil's advocate, we could argue that an engineer (similar to an architect), for instance, could similarly be assessed as Chartered after a similar test of professional experience.

True, but the engineering degree has been already independently assessed by numerous exams and papers during the university course. That is, the engineer has already been certified for the engineering knowledge theory accumulated during the formal study.

But there is there such prerequisite (university...) study for the Open CA? There is no one agreed EA method to be studied, not even own Open Group's TOGAF.

What kind of experience is then Open CA assessing in the absence of certified EA knowledge?

Perhaps the answer to the above issue is that Open CA certifies your experience in IT (architecture) alone, as it was initially meant to. Remember ITAC, the precursor of Open CA.

Had the Open CA certification be truly about EA, it would be prone to many challenges since, given our EA debates today, most EA practitioners would have different opinions about the deliveries of an EA practice and its criteria to assess success.

As a sideline, one may ask the legitimate question, which EA certification to sit, TOGAF or Open CA?

To sum up, TOGAF trains and certifies you in a "method" while Open CA aims to certify your architecture practice success, your work experience.

Problem is both come from IT and are about IT. Moreover, Open CA is not based on TOGAF and as such there is no path between one and the other.

On top, TOGAF has not been proved fruitful. Open Group may have a suggestion on that, which is welcome!

I further dare say that few EA efforts were proved "successful" today even if some claim so according to their own criteria. But even these efforts may not be successful judged by the certification criteria. So, if Open CA certifies the successful practice, what is there to certify?

Cui bono then this certification? And, more importantly, who loses?

I think that the enterprises at large, practitioners and the EA profession as a whole would not gain anything from it since the certification looks like re-badging the chartered IT professional.

Well, you can take it or leave it, that is the Open CA (EA) certification. Isn't that what they all say at the end of an argument?

If the certification takes off for whatever reason, even top EA professionals could be sidelined if "choosing" not to take this costly IT certification. Most EA job ads today require TOGAF. But TOGAF is easy to fake because nobody dares ask even what that is. What would you do though if the job demands Open CA?

Enterprise Architecture in higher education

Nov 21, 2011

http://www.ebizq.net/blogs/ea_matters/2011/11/enterprise-architecture-and-higher-education.php

The EA concept should be taught in any business study. Unfortunately the body of knowledge is too fragmented and incomplete right now to arm the student with a method that delivers results.

What one can teach today is the EA state of art, that is various approaches, questions still unanswered). The course would teach the state of art, raise awareness of the issue and enable further research. For this reason all approaches to EA should be investigated rather than only a selected few or a single one.

The idea whether to include EA in an MBA program appears to be agreed upon by most though (see LinkedIn discussion here). But what specifically should be in? Unfortunately, business academia has done little about it.

In practice, EA takes place in IT. Most frameworks originated in IT and most EA architects do their day to day job in solution architecture, architecture review boards and IT strategy. I dare say that this is not what an MBA should cover. The IT EA component might be taught in more detail in technology courses though.

An MBA teaches enterprise operation, strategy development, planning, organization design etc. The question is what value would the EA add to the MBA?

EA is the architecture of the Enterprise describing what the enterprise delivers and how it does that. Then how can the Enterprise be transformed implementing the strategy. It is about documenting the Enterprise operation in order to improve it, adapt it to market changes and roadmap it to achieve your strategic goals. As such it is essentially a business management discipline.

What EA could bring to the MBA:

1. EA may offer generic models or typical architectures for the enterprise. EA comes with the Capability map concept which unfortunately is not standardised or mature enough to be employed yet.

2. May provide the framework that links and integrates all the tiers of the Enterprise together: business process, technology and organization. That is a "true" EA framework. Currently there are a few meta-models that are an expression of the framework rather than the framework itself.

3. Last but not least, EA would provide the method of

implementing the target enterprise state in alignment to strategy.

Existing EA methods propose various processes to do exactly that.

As such, the EA contribution to the MBA (i.e. the Enterprise model, EA integration framework, the Enterprise alignment to strategy) would enable the MBA to create a model of an Enterprise, analyse it, transform it and assist the transition of the Enterprise to the desired state. EA it would also enable the MBA to understand how to implement various business and operating models proposed by the executive management.

Vote here in the Computer Weekly "IT industry blogger of the year" where this blog was short listed.

Enterprise IT outsourcing

Nov 30, 2011

http://www.ebizq.net/blogs/ea_matters/2011/11/enterprise-it-outsourcing.php

I just want to expose in one picture the various types of IT outsourcing a Enterprise can employ today. Here is a self-explanatory picture:

You can notice a mixture of good old traditional outsourcing such as Data Centre and Managed Services that will take place at the same time with Business Process Outsourcing (such as Call Centre, Recruitment, Payroll...) and Cloud Computing (IaaS, PaaS, SaaS).

The secret of success is too rationalise the number of outsourcing suppliers and harmoniously integrate their services. To achieve this you need this picture.

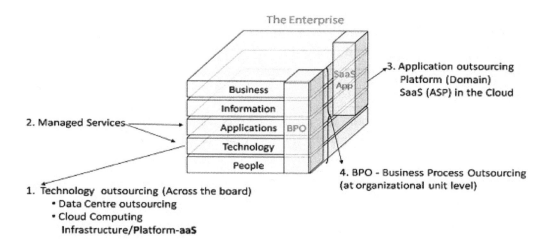

Enterprise outsourcing options

EA, should it be part of an MBA syllabus?

Nov 21, 2011

http://it.toolbox.com/blogs/ea-matters/enterprise-architecture-should-it-be-part-of-an-mba-syllabus-49436

The EA concept should be taught in any business study. Unfortunately the body of knowledge is too fragmented and incomplete right now to arm the student with a method that delivers results.

What one can teach today is the EA state of art (various approaches, the questions still unanswered). The course would raise awareness of the issue though and would enable further research. For this reason all approached to EA should be investigated not only a selected few or one.

The idea whether to include EA in an MBA program appears to be agreed upon by most though (see LinkedIn discussion here). But what specifically should be in?

In practice, EA takes place in IT. Most frameworks originated in IT and most EA architects do their day to day job in solution architecture, architecture review boards and IT strategy. I dare say that this is not what an MBA should cover. The IT EA component might be taught in more detail in technology courses though.

Unfortunately, business academia has done little about it.

An MBA teaches enterprise operation, strategy development, planning, organization design etc. The question is what value would the EA add to the MBA?

EA is the architecture of the Enterprise describing what the enterprise delivers and how it does that. Then how can the Enterprise be transformed implementing the strategy. It is about documenting the Enterprise operation in order to improve it, adapt it to market changes and roadmap it to achieve your strategic goals. As such it is essentially a business management discipline.

What EA could bring to the MBA:

1. Offer generic models or typical architectures for the enterprise. EA comes with the Capability map concept which unfortunately is not standardised or mature enough to be employed yet.

2. Provide the framework that links and integrates all the tiers of the Enterprise together: business process, technology and organization. That is a "true" EA framework. Currently there are a few meta-models that are an expression of the framework rather than the framework itself.

3. Last but not least, EA would have the provide the method of implementing the desired enterprise state according to strategy. Various existing EA methods propose bits and pieces of that.

As such, the EA contribution to the MBA (i.e. the Enterprise business blueprint, the EA integration framework, the Enterprise development alignment to strategy) would enable an MBA to create a model of an Enterprise, analyse it, transform it according to strategy and assist the transition to the desired Enterprise state.

The MBA will be able to map various business and operating models to the EA.

EA POLITICS

Politics of Enterprise Architecture

Apr 3, 2007

http://it.toolbox.com/blogs/ea-matters/politics-of-enterprise-architecture-15491

Is Enterprise Architecture a breeding ground for politics? As with any human activities and relationships, there is politics, but to what degree?

Some time ago, someone, reviewing my book, pointed out that there is no section on the politics of Enterprise Architecture (EA). I was not convinced then that there is politics, or at least, no more than in any other complex human undertaking. Nevertheless, EA spans business and technology knowledge domains and crosses many internal organization boundaries and, as a result, it is prone to politics. Now, that I am closer to publish an updated version of the book, I started looking at politics in relation to EA. To find out, I searched the web, looking for a definition:

"Social relations involving authority or power".

"Politics is the process and method of making decisions for groups... While politics operates, all decisions are provisional!"

"Although it generally applies to governments, politics is also observed in all human group interactions including corporate, academic, and religious".

And about office politics: *"social alliances often formed between colleagues of similar interests who may team up against other perceived competitors"*.

However, while formally correct, is this really what the suggestion was about? What about the day to day usage of the word. Since, this time, I could not find anything much on the web (?), I dared define it myself (with all the possible drawbacks) as consisting of:

- Promises, frequently made by politicians before elections, seldom enacted
- The impossibility to get straight answers from politicians when asking even the simplest of questions

- High ground moral stances driven, in reality, by self interest.

On a positive note, politicians must be energetic, skilful negotiators and decision makers to balance legitimate and conflicting interests of many parties. But what has all this to do with an Enterprise Architecture development and the Enterprise Architect? Enterprise Architecture and its promoters, myself included, promise a lot, but does it, or do we deliver?

Don't we sometimes assume the same moral high but safe ground when over selling the concept for the higher good of the Enterprise? The reality is that the typical EA development outcomes, more often than not, do not significantly change the structure of the organization or convey the much-touted agility to the firm. In other words, EA may not deliver to the promise. The truth is that the EA development can easily end up in various forms and shapes in the absence of an agreed definition or framework, since there is too much variability in terms of scope and deliveries. That is why US government mandated reference models to set expectations and be able to assemble the resulting artefacts in a coherent framework. A proper EA framework, reference model and process will fix this.

I heard rumours that IT fears the business reaction when confronting them with EA/SOA programs. Therefore, IT avoids naming it, substituting it instead with a discourse on benefits. This sounds a bit like the politician, avoiding a sensitive topic, with a convoluted response. But isn't this happening because EA and SOA have been grossly over hyped and over sold even before they were properly defined and scoped? Or, is it the "nervousness" of business, created by so many recent prophecies of "do EA/SOA or die"?

In reacting to this technology push, business does not contest the potential benefits but requires a business case and careful planning to justify and roadmap the move from the current, not badly yielding "status quo", to the revolutionary services based business (e.g. SOA) since the costs of the business disruption, might brake rather than make the business.

The divide between business and IT is a major source of debate in the Enterprise world and I would dare say, a breeding ground for politics. Business and IT speak different languages. They might look like two political parties engaged in a quest for the same holy grail, the budget. However, is it not the organization of the company and its governance, failing to align business and IT functions to a common strategy and objectives?

And is it not the Enterprise Architecture now charged with aligning the IT to business, that is, in effect, cross the political divide with the Enterprise Architect is in the lead?

The conclusions I can draw so far: an Enterprise Architect has to be politically astute to justify EA/SOA, argue the business case, rally support from stakeholders, keep management informed and optimistic, do the work and survive the process!

The politics of EA (ii)

Apr 13, 2007

http://it.toolbox.com/blogs/ea-matters/the-politics-of-ea-ii-15673

The EA is commended because of the state of high entropy of the Enterprise: high complexity, poor availability and understanding

induced by years of patching, point solutions, silo operation, organic growth, mergers and a growing divide between business and IT. Business needs to change and compete faster and faster while IT can no longer cope with mending the legacy of the past, unwiring the architecture "hair ball" and integrating technology generations from various eras, including the mainframes, the dinosaurs of IT.

Business got tired of the exotic IT acronyms like WS, SOAP, REST, UDDI, WSDL, mashups, AJAX, ESB, BPM, BPEL, XML, UML, TOGAF... some badged 2.0 now (and technology is changing at an exponential rate these days - Ray Kurtzweil's law-, so it is getting worse). IT is not talking either about Value Chain, business models, process improvement, Six Sigma, regulation, customer satisfaction, Balanced Scorecard, SWOT, KPIs, NPV, payback, the terms the business understands.

But, on the other hand, is business providing, in the first place, the process architecture, business information and vocabulary necessary for IT to comprehend and align the technology?

The net result of all this is the great divide and an increasingly high charged atmosphere progressing towards a blame culture

And the solution is the EA which ought to mend all the evils of the Enterprise, to cure the silo culture and patch the divide between IT and business In a nutshell, EA becomes the ground of the already existing political battle but, at the same time, the tool to mediate the political divide.

While the EA encompasses alignment of business, strategy, technology and people, the IT takes the driving role without business and top management support. How is this supposed to happen? After all, more than half of the EA is not IT, i.e. business processes (how), strategy (why), data (what), organization (who)... In fact without a strong business leadership and participation, EA would lack political support and fail to deliver on its promise since IT alone cannot specify SOA business services, improve processes, determine usefulness of data... Over-hype has already placed EA and SOA at the top of the curve where the credibility is not sustained yet by realisations. The IT history lessons would not concur to support the EA far-reaching claims; the result is that the business doubts it!

In this phase, the best you can do is be convincing i.e. gain support for the EA business case which you should be expressed in financial terms. Spend energy to rally critical stakeholders' support in business and top management. Involve them by planning adequate EA artefacts, in response to their requests, explaining what is in it for them.

Without critical business input, the resulting IT only Enterprise Architecture would provide mainly the Applications, Infrastructure and may be Data architecture, which is frequently the case, but not sufficient for releasing of all goods of the EA: process improvement, agility, strategic planning etc. The business people will have little reason to consult it, the word spreads, and, progressively, the EA losses its momentum everywhere. The loop is closed now. The business was right to doubt it, after all.

The politics of EA (iii)

Apr 20, 2007

http://it.toolbox.com/blogs/ea-matters/the-politics-of-ea-iii-15767

Thinking in many Enterprises is tactical, at best, fire fighting would better express the facts. The EA is strategic, a long term transformation accepted because of its strategy promise but its acceptance may become a lip service only, with its execution ever postponed to cope with tactical crisis. In truth, EA will compete for resources with many other activities which have not been included in the EA scope, in the 1st place.

Supposing the EA development moves slow and is delayed, it will be generating a lot more tactical-strategic conflicts: business people need solutions yesterday, the market cannot wait and the EA will provide the feature who knows when! Tactical projects are approved then and have to co-exist and compete for resources with the EA program. The chance to accomplish the implementation of EA slips away.

There is no easy solution to this except delivery on time and fit for purpose. To reassure everybody have a clear, simple plan in place that you are confident you can deliver to. You probably have one single try. Deliver often, iteratively, emphasize value returned. Prioritise business needs, deal with the EA trigger cause first and deliver what the stakeholders requested. This is a program, so business process discovery projects will have probably to be executed in parallel to Applications, Infrastructure, Data architectures and other streams. Then add views as DW/BI, Content Management, procurement processes, network architecture etc stakeholders typically need. With a delivery plan in front, people can wait, if they trust you. Otherwise, tactical projects win.

There are EA execution mistakes: ignoring important stakeholders, not communicating properly or enough in simple clear definitions and messages, not consulting relevant people, not referencing and recognizing contributions, to name a few, provoking the syndrome of "not invented here" i.e. you have not consulted us, where did this come from"?

From your side, lack of EA development experience and poor definition of scope and deliveries not fit for purpose, i.e. (typically large documents with poor focus) can increasingly deteriorate credibility as the development process is stalled by unusable outputs and by disputes about if and how the artefacts are to be used.

Define an EA vocabulary, for both business and IT to use, and Frequent Asked Questions to avoid confusion and display the progress dashboard on the Web for transparency.

The politics of Enterprise Architecture (iv)

May 3, 2007

http://it.toolbox.com/blogs/ea-matters/the-politics-of-enterprise-architecture-iv-16078

Enterprise knowledge is locked in people's minds. To release this collective wisdom you need negotiation skills, "selling not telling", to move to a culture of recognition and reward. Otherwise the information you may get for the EA may be of little value.

The EA team must have a vast knowledge spanning business, IT and people issues and be socially and politically astute. Selection of the proper EA team constitutes the major risk in this development. This team will not only have to develop the EA properly, but will have to explain it in simple terms everybody can understand, and then gracefully deploy EA compliance controls in all major business processes without meeting resistance.

EA is perceived as a threat since, in reducing duplication in process, platforms and projects it creates redundancies, it brings change. Change Management (CM) becomes essential in the Enterprise transformation execution process since people can and will resist, will do partisan fighting since, after all, their job is at stake for no grander purpose. CM has to work along to provide a path forward for all affected by the migration process to expose the greater good, to motivate. Early preparation is essential to avoid problems.

Agile processes with frequent deliveries and wide consultations will help make the process transparent and as such, accountable. Bottlenecks have to be quickly discovered and eliminated. Observe EA inhibitors since they could stop your EA development early, and find ways to conquer them from the beginning.

The governance team has to be properly chosen to reflect all interests and has to have enough authority to make it happen. Roles and responsibilities have to be well designed to avoid overlaps generating confusion and conflicts and, in the end, politics. Work as a team is crucial as the domain and span of activities is much too large.

Accountability and empowerment, recognition and award as company values will pave the way to progressive success in eliminating a culture of politics.

After the first few deliveries, it is important to police all other development work, install EA compliance controls (checkpoints) in all relevant business processes, provide training and easy access. Otherwise your EA may be ignored, forgotten.

The art of Enterprise Architecture politics

June 13, 2012

http://www.ebizq.net/blogs/ea_matters/2012/06/enterprise-architecture-politics.php

Is Enterprise Architecture a breeding ground for politics? As with any human activities and relationships, there is politics, but to what degree?

EA spans business and technology knowledge domains and crosses many internal organization boundaries with often conflicting silo interests. As a result, it is prone to politics.

What is politics? Various answers from the web:

- "Although it generally applies to governments, politics is also observed in all human group interactions including corporate, academic, and religious"

- "Social relations involving authority or power"

- "Politics is the process and method of making decisions for groups".

- And office politics is about "social alliances often formed between colleagues of similar interests who may team up against other perceived competitors"

Simply put, politics is about how to govern, and in particular for our context, how to get to govern. That applies to individuals as well.

However, while all definitions are right, what about the day to day usage of the word in the office? I dare define the term myself, with all the possible drawbacks. Politics is the technique of

- promises seldom acted upon later (for example those frequently made by politicians before elections),

- evasion of straight answers for the simplest of questions

- assuming high ground moral stances driven by hidden interests

- discourses with deliberate multiple, too general or no meaning at all to cloud the outcomes and avoid responsibility

- bogus smiles that hide antagonist behaviour

- elbowing and back stabbing, against the background of team work and against merit

- "means that justify the ends"

- ...

In other words politics is the art of spin for getting ahead. The art of serving oneself while seemingly serving others.

The problem with politics is that it impedes every day honest efforts,

shrouds work in an ineffective governance and duplicitous

communications... that end inevitably in failure. Politics leads to an

irreparable atmosphere of distrust and cynicism. Colleagues start avoiding real work and making decisions for fear of mistakes that are heavily penalized e who wishes to take political advantage at any cost.

And EA, as a discipline in search of its place in the chain of authority, in order to be able to accomplish its mission, is prone to politics.

In particular, politics is harmful for the EA, as a new discipline, making it look like the saviour of the enterprise that seldom saves it. EA has been grossly over hyped for selfish interests and over sold even before it was properly defined and scoped.

Enterprise Architecture and its promoters promise a lot, but do we

deliver?

Don't we sometimes assume the same moral high but safe ground when over selling the concept for the higher good of the Enterprise?

The reality is that typical EA outcomes, more often than not, do not really support strategy execution, organization transformation or convey the much-touted agility to the firm. In other words, EA may not deliver to the promise. The reason is that we may not have a proper body of knowledge and as such we have to spin it.

The divide between business and IT is already a major source of debate in the Enterprise world and I would dare say, a breeding ground for politics. Business and IT speak different languages. They might look like two political parties engaged in a quest for the same holy grail, the budget. But is it not the Enterprise Architecture now, with the EA architect in the lead, charged with aligning the IT to business, that is, in effect, to cross the political divide?

 On the positive side, politicians must be energetic, skilful negotiators and decision makers to be able to balance the legitimate and conflicting interests of many concerned parties.

 The Enterprise Architect has to be politically astute to justify EA, argue the business case, rally support from stakeholders, keep management informed and optimistic, do the work and survive the political process.

Enterprise Architecture politics and their roots

July 2, 2012

http://www.ebizq.net/blogs/ea_matters/2012/07/enterprise-architecture-politics-and-their-roots.php

Thinking in many Enterprises is tactical at best. Fire fighting would better express the fact. This is a main source of politics in the enterprise, since stakeholders would often question the resources allocation to the EA effort.

The EA thinking is strategic in nature, a long term transformation accepted because of its strategy promise. But it may become a lip service alone, with its execution ever postponed so that the enterprise could cope with the never ending tactical crises. In truth, EA will compete for resources in the enterprise with many other tactical and operational activities which have not been included in the enterprise transformation program in the 1st place.

Supposing the EA development moves slow and is delayed, it will be generating a lot more tactical-strategic conflicts: business people need solutions yesterday, the market cannot wait and the EA will provide the feature who knows when! Tactical projects are approved then and have to co-exist and compete for resources with the EA program. The chance to implement EA slips away while the EA goalposts are forever moving away.

There is no easy solution to this except plan integrally. To reassure everybody have a clear, holistic plan in place that you are confident you can deliver to. You probably have one single try at the EA. If you don't achieve it, EA would be incriminated. Most of all, EA may end up as a policing function without a reference code law, the EA itself, to guide its operation.

To mitigate these risk, try to deliver often, iteratively, on time and fit for purpose.

Emphasize, communicate the value returned.

Prioritise business needs, deal with the EA trigger cause first and deliver what the stakeholders requested. Otherwise they would not support the EA. Success is in the eye of your stakeholders.

With a delivery plan in front, people can agree and wait, if they trust your delivery. Otherwise, tactical projects win and the role of EA diminishes.

There are a few political EA execution mistakes:

- ignoring important stakeholders,

- not communicating properly or enough in simple clear definitions and messages,

- not consulting the relevant people may provoke the political syndrome of "not invented here" i.e. you have not consulted us, where did this come from?

- not recognizing or referring to valuable inputs (in truth assuming their work)

And, in addition

- the lack of EA development experience

- poor definition of scope

- deliveries not fit for purpose, i.e. (typically large documents with poor focus) can increasingly deteriorate credibility as the development process is stalled by unusable outputs and by disputes about if and how the artefacts are to be used. The debate about whether the EA delivered value or not becomes political.

As such, define an EA vocabulary, for both business and IT to use, and publish answers to Frequent Asked Questions to avoid confusion that may raise questions about the EA credibility.

Display the progress dashboard on the Web for transparency so that no one can say they were not informed or aware.

Publish EA realisations so that people can use asap all EA results.

The politics of Enterprise Architecture

July 9, 2012

http://www.ebizq.net/blogs/ea_matters/2012/07/politics-of-enterprise-architecture.php

Why should there be EA politics in the first place? Because EA is a complex, long term human activity, demanding cooperation of many parties and expensive skilled resources. And politics is all about human interaction and competition. Because EA is challenging the status quo of the Enterprise by altering its normal course for the sake of the future: EA is about strategic planning which inherently collides with the tactical thinking and action of Today - perhaps because the change is coming today at tactical speeds.

What are the drivers for EA? From a business perspective, it is the inflexibility, slow change and high costs of IT. From and IT perspective it is the lack of business process and requirements clarity, inherited obsolete technologies and the tangled IT spaghetti architecture.

Pre-existing conditions for EA politics

 - Businesses are already organized in silos which means politics already exist inside and between silos

 - The existing great divide between business and IT, makes any new IT initiative a political issue.

Politics escort EA along its life cycle.

A. At the concept phase, where the main debate is about the meaning and definition of EA. The scope agreement in this phase, if any, can determine if a true EA is going to be developed, an IT only architecture, an ITIL implementation or other. This dispute hits the balance between the tactical and strategic thinking and it is crucial as the benefits diminish at the same rate with the scope reduction. And hence the "nay" sayers.

B. At initiation, the argument is about To Do or not To Do Enterprise Architecture, argument most often not supported by compelling business cases. The EA benefits, like for many other architecture developments, are hard to quantify in a business case but it should be done on a best effort basis. There is also the hype or overhype which may animate the IT and annoy the business. Hence business prefers not to hear about it while the IT world is shouting.

How many times SOA was presented as a technology, while the reality is that it deeply affects the way your business works? The business under direct market pressure cannot afford to play with technology trials. This may explain the half-hearted buy in from business the reluctance to hear about EA or SOA.

Furthermore the EA is a threat to "status quo" we all like.

C. The discovery and design is a milestone for the EA since a poor design would leave its internal customers baffled not able to understand what to implement. The classical example is the "tome" delivery. A such another kind of politics of "passing the buck" to the next team.

There is no Business Architecture in the first place to guide the Technology architecture. The EA would be the common ground where business and IT meet and talk the same language. But the IT would have to drive the business architecture which is not perceived as necessary by business, hence reluctance and scepticism. Here is where, without communication and sanction from the top the EA will fail in politics.

True, the initial confusion starts with the world of EA design frameworks, which was compared to a jungle. The deliberation about frameworks can be bitter. A mixture of them is usually the answer but there are acerbic camps. Then the Enterprise knowledge is locked in people's minds. The ability to extract that information may be a political art. Not consulting the relevant groups breeds the "not invented here" syndrome.

D. The execution, if defective, trailing for too long or not solving the immediate business pains, will surely spawn heated arguments. There is little tolerance for long programs with uncertain results. Slow, delayed development, revive the tactics to deploy tactical. Lack of transparency in execution, rumours taint the atmosphere.

The EA governance will most certainly create political debate again if it does not involve all concerned parties.

E. At utilisation: Make sure EA is not ignored, forgotten or considered a dead weight because you have not implemented architecture controls, check points in business processes. And some good practices:

Preventive actions:

- Define clear EA and scope

- Ensure business and management support from the beginning

- Prioritise business needs, deal with the EA trigger cause first and deliver what was requested, listen to your stakeholders

- Observe potential EA roadblocks from the very start

- Define an EA vocabulary and Frequent Asked Questions to avoid confusion and display the progress dashboard on the Web for transparency

- Select a quality EA team quality since it is the major risk; the EA team must have a vast knowledge spanning business, IT and people issues and be socially and politically astute. Introduce EA accountability, recognition and rewards

- Employ agile processes with frequent deliveries and wide consultations which will help make the process transparent and as such, accountable. Bottlenecks have to be quickly discovered and eliminated

- Police development work, install EA compliance controls

(checkpoints) in all relevant business processes, provide training and easy access.

EA ROADBLOCKS AND MYTHS

EA inhibitors, politics and remedies

June 22, 2012

http://www.ebizq.net/blogs/ea_matters/2012/06/-the-ea-is-commended.php

The EA is commended because of the state of high entropy of the Enterprise: high complexity, poor availability and understanding induced by years of patching, point solutions, silo operation, organic growth, mergers and a growing divide between business and IT.

Business needs to change and compete faster and faster while IT can no longer cope with mending the legacy of the past, unwiring the architecture "hair ball" and integrating technology generations from various eras, including the mainframes, the dinosaurs of IT.

Business got tired of the exotic IT talk like WS, SOAP, REST, UDDI, WSDL, mashups, AJAX, ESB, BPM, BPEL, XML, UML, TOGAF... some badged 2.0 now (and technology is changing at an exponential rate these days - Ray Kurtzweil's law-, so it is getting worse). Business has no need to understand this language.

IT is not talking either about Value Chain, business models, process improvement, Six Sigma, regulation, customer satisfaction, Balanced Scorecard, SWOT, KPIs, NPV, payback, the terms the business understands.

But, on the other hand, is business providing, in the first place, the process architecture, business information and vocabulary necessary for IT to comprehend and align the technology to the business operation? No.

In brief, neither IT nor the business pay their due for the alignment of the enterprise and a proper collaboration. The net outcome is the great chasm between the business and IT and an increasingly high charged atmosphere progressing towards a blame culture. And as such politics.

And the solution is the EA which ought to mend all the evils of the Enterprise, to cure the silo culture and patch the divide between IT and business.

In a nutshell, EA becomes the ground of the already existing political battle but, at the same time, the tool to mediate the political divide. While the EA encompasses alignment of business, strategy, technology and people, the IT takes the driving role without the business and top management support. How is this transformation supposed to happen then?

After all, more than half of the EA is not IT, i.e. business processes (how), strategy (why), information (what), organization (who)... In fact without a strong business leadership and participation, EA would lack political support and fail to deliver on its promise since IT alone cannot specify (SOA) business services, describe or improve processes, determine usefulness of data...

Over-hype has already placed EA and SOA at the top of the curve where the credibility is not sustained yet by realisations. The result is that the business doubts it!

So IT proceeds with the EA under a cloud of hype with no business support.

In this phase, the best you can do, is try to remedy the relationship with the business. That needs trust.

As such put forward a business case for EA expressed in financial terms that may gain business approval.

Sell the EA benefits specific to each key business stakeholder. Spend energy to rally critical stakeholders' support in business and top management. Involve them by planning adequate EA artefacts, in response to their requests, explaining what is in it for them.

Without critical business input, the resulting IT only EA would provide mainly the Applications, Infrastructure and may be the Data architecture, which is not sufficient to deliver to business expectations (such as process improvement, agility, strategic planning etc). The business people will have little reason to consult it, the word spreads, and, progressively, the EA losses its momentum everywhere. The loop is closed now. The business was right to doubt it, after all.

 Thinking in many Enterprises is tactical, at best. Fire fighting would be a better expression. The EA is strategic, a long term transformation accepted because of its strategy promise but its acceptance may become a lip service only, with its execution ever postponed to cope with tactical crisis. In truth, EA will compete for resources with many other activities which have not been included in the EA scope, in the 1st place.

Supposing the EA development moves slow and is delayed, it will be generating a lot tactical-strategic conflicts: business people need solutions yesterday, the market cannot wait and the EA will provide the feature who knows when! Tactical projects are approved then and have to co-exist and compete for resources with the EA program. The chance to accomplish the implementation of EA slips away. There is no easy solution to this except delivery on time and fit for purpose. To reassure everybody have a clear, simple plan in place that you are confident you can deliver to. You probably have one single try. And plan tactics and strategy at the same time to alleviate resources conflicts.

Then deliver often, iteratively, emphasize value returned. Prioritise business needs, deal with the EA trigger cause first and deliver what the stakeholders requested. With a delivery plan in front, people can wait, if they trust you. Otherwise, tactical projects win.

There are EA execution mistakes: ignoring important stakeholders, not communicating properly or enough in simple clear definitions and messages, not consulting relevant people, not referencing and recognizing contributions, to name a few, provoking the syndrome of "not invented here" i.e. you have not consulted us, where did this come from"?

Poor definition of scope and deliveries not fit for purpose, i.e. (typically large documents with weak focus) can increasingly deteriorate credibility as the development process is stalled by unusable outputs and by disputes about if and how the artefacts are to be used.

Always have a plan to prove the current status and deliveries to come.

Define, Terms of Reference and an EA vocabulary, for both business and IT to use, and Frequent Asked Questions to avoid confusion and display the progress dashboard on the Web for transparency.

Enterprise Architecture is overly simplified

Jan 4, 2007

http://it.toolbox.com/blogs/ea-matters/enterprise-architecture-is-overly-simplified-13695

In the previous post I discussed two Enterprise Architecture (EA) development inhibitors; EA is typically reduced to an IT Architecture and it does not cover any other type of technology except Information Technology. As a result it's difficult to get traction from firm's management, business or manufacturing people or, for that matter, from any other stakeholders outside IT.

Yet there are a few other factors which may add to the problem of preventing a wider EA adoption. More often than not EA does not mandate architectural views - reflecting the interests of many stakeholders - or a functional architecture thus preventing adoption by a wider range of users.

.1. Enterprise Architecture is overly simplified

EA frameworks typically consist of four architectural layers: business, information, application and technology. The EA development is often considered finished soon after an inventory of technology is compiled, the application architecture is drawn, the process documentation is initiated by business analysts and data architecture is sketched.

This leaves out other aspects or "views" of the Enterprise such as real estate, parking, accounting or, in IT, email or printing architectures though they probably exist, are documented elsewhere in some form and are of real interest to you and quite a few enterprise stakeholders.

The lack of points of view reduces even more the interest and usage of EA to just a few stakeholders. Due to this simplification, EA architect positions are sometimes advertised directly for Information, Infrastructure or Applications roles in the IT space, already confining the activities to this narrow scope before the development has even started.

By default the only stakeholder considered is the customer, leaving out though owners, partners, employees... views, thus limiting the scope yet again. A good practice would be to listen to stakeholders and capture their views as part of the EA architectural layers. The Enterprise discovery should be initiated by Stakeholders' interaction and needs expressed as Use Cases.

.2. Frequently there is no EA functional or logical architecture view

The lack of a functional architecture inhibits understanding of the Enterprise operation and of the Enterprise Architecture itself. The functional architecture outlines the key units of the firm interconnected to support your enterprise value chain and business model. Enterprise functions as Sales and Marketing, Distribution, Manufacturing, Supply Chain, Product Development, HR, Payroll ... are rather standard nowadays.

The logical architecture may also help linking the process, applications and technology in a function and enable the partitioning of the EA development work. For a technical system design, the logical architecture specification is one of the first steps an architect has to perform to describe the system operation and its components.

A functional architecture, added to the business, information, application and technology layers, will improve comprehension and enable organization optimisation and EA specification. It will also make possible a SOA design approach where services are built around functions.

People and organization are outside the scope of EA

Jan 11, 2007

http://it.toolbox.com/blogs/ea-matters/people-and-organization-are-outside-the-scope-of-ea-13839

Not long ago I felt that Enterprise Architecture (EA) had not been growing at the pace I, at least, thought it should. I asked myself why and came up with a couple of issues. I never thought though the list would expand. I realised it does and I am not sure yet if I should quit numbering the inhibitors. This being the case, no wonder that people are reluctant about an EA development then: it may be costly, takes time and resources, its business case is not proved and the outcome may not live to expectations.

What I found until now: EA is seen as an IT architecture only. All technologies besides IT seem to be ignored. EA is overly simplified to four architectural layers with no other "views" to respond to non-IT stakeholders' concerns. The functional architecture, a good practice in systems design, is not really adopted and Use Cases, coming from the world of software design, are not really used. There is seldom a link to the enterprise Value Chain or business model. And if that is not enough, there are a few more:

3. People and organization are not included in the EA scope

Typically business processes or parts of them are still performed by people rather than applications. These processes, in fact more accurately workflows, are still relying on human interventions for data input, validation, phase approval... In other words they are not automated. Processes lag too because people taking decisions are away or technology fails at the hands of poorly trained personnel. More often than not the human intervention is not described in business workflows for the simple reason that people are not part of the framework. If human performance is not accounted for the overall workflow will perform as well as its weakest link, the people. But EA looks like an unfinished business without people manning processes and technology.

Organization (people) design is often the object of an entirely separate and non-correlated initiative. I witnessed in a company a process and best practices optimisation effort, an organization re-design process and an Enterprise Architecture program performed by three different groups, in parallel. That is process, people and the EA activities were executed in isolation, without correlation.

The organization chart should be aligned to your Enterprise Architecture so that people take ownership of EA functions, processes and technology. Culture and people communications also affect your Enterprise performance, but this is quite a topic in itself.

After all, "the Company is the People" who govern, plan and operate the Enterprise.

No commonly accepted Enterprise Architecture framework

Jan 22, 2007

http://it.toolbox.com/blogs/ea-matters/no-commonly-accepted-enterprise-architecture-framework-13968

I have been gathering for a while now grounds for the Enterprise Architecture's lack of adoption at the pace foreseen years ago. I trust that by exploring "inhibitors", EA development obstructions would be better understood and eventually neutralised. I would also try to elucidate the scope of the EA if not for all, at least for particular developments. Every so often EA suffers from and is restricted by narrow scoping. This should be extended to reach the whole Enterprise audience with views reflecting the work of various stakeholders in business, organization, IT and non-IT technology.

4. There is no commonly accepted EA framework, the diversity of approach hindering adoption

After examining the core body of EA frameworks literature I decided to count on what's left in my mind once I close the books. It is definitely a confusing scenery. Some of the existing EA frameworks are, by and large, cognitive aids asking key questions as why, what and how. A few others mainly handle implementation program management and best practices aspects. Some are mere reference models describing outcomes and implementation guidelines to serve as models for other EA developments. A few approaches are confined to BPM or Enterprise Integration only. Some specialise on domains as government, defence, manufacturing or telecoms. Most frameworks leave out people and organization ("who") or are narrowed down to business process architecture (the "how") ignoring technology. Some have been applied for a while with less than convincing results or are obsolete and used no more. Some are not taking the EA development very far. In other words there is no consensus on approach or scope.

The four layers framework (business, information, application and technology) appears to be the largest common denominator for many developments. It is not clear though how or to what level of granularity the four architectures are described and how are they linked. At a minimum, the deliveries would consist of at least four diagrams, one for each layer. This may not meet normal expectations though.

Now and then, a few mapping matrixes are used to link elements in or outside layers but they hardly support navigation between components or consistency in artefacts design. The four layer framework, while useful, is an over simplified approach revealing few aspects of the real Enterprise and reducing the number of EA stakeholders to a few, in IT.

How do we choose a framework? Are there any recommendations for framework selection? Do you have to create your own framework? There are more than you would hope for though. Are frameworks enabling drawing of a complete picture of the Enterprise? A first check for this would be a map on Zachman's; are there all questions ("why", "when", "who"...) answered? Is the chosen EA framework fit for purpose or I would add, scope of your endeavour? All legitimate questions.

To address real business concerns and to improve business and management support and participation, an EA framework should cover, besides the four layers architecture (business, information, applications and technology), people and organization, the functional structure of the Enterprise and other stakeholders' views describing aspects of work and type of information such as the real estate blueprint, financial and HR support views and document management architecture.

Why does not (Federal) EA work?

Feb 2, 2011

http://it.toolbox.com/blogs/ea-matters/why-does-not-federal-ea-work-44076

Here is a report on "Why Doesn't The Federal Enterprise Architecture Work" by Stanley Gover:

Mostly quotes in this post, to leave you read the doc but comments will follow.

"*This research culminated in a completely unexpected and unsettling conclusion: Enterprise Architecture within the federal government hasn't been working, and far more often than not hasn't delivered useful results. Moreover, significant parts of the federal EA program have been complete and utter failures.*"

"*each analysis brought a new discovery that yet another part of the federal EA program was misunderstood or poorly implemented or just plain broken.*"

"*This paper is now more than four years in the making. It's not that the material has actually required four years to research, process, and write about. Rather, many times I doubted where my findings and conclusions were taking me. More than once I abandoned the project, thinking that I must have been missing something or that my understanding of Enterprise Architecture must have been wrong. After all, how could Enterprise Architecture not be working?*

How could so much work be performed, for so long, by so many, and yet too often produce nothing of value?"

"*But with the passage of time, extensive research and, finally, by the act of writing this paper, I now know how this can be the case. I'm now confident that my findings and conclusions are correct. And any lingering doubts that I may have had (and there were some) have been erased by recent developments within the federal Enterprise Architecture program.*"

"*In early October 2010, the Federal CIO Council hosted a meeting attended by approximately 80 senior architects, CIOs, and CTOs from throughout the federal government to discuss the concerns of federal EA practitioners and stakeholders and plan for the future of the federal EA program. The concerns raised at this meeting echo many of the findings of this paper:*

The case that the Federal Enterprise Architecture isn't working is presented on the following pages as seven exhibits... that will collectively prove the case that the Federal Enterprise Architecture is, in fact, not working.

1: A Growing Realization Across the Industry

EA often doesn't work well anywhere because the problems with Enterprise Architecture are fundamental in nature.

2: The FEA Reference "Models":

Tragically Misnamed Calling these "models" has caused massive confusion and misunderstanding, and is the biggest single factor causing the federal EA not to work.

3: Problems with EA at the Agency Level Many or even most agencies experienced many of the same problems and failures while attempting to implement their EA's. These shared experiences are examined and explained.

4: Problems with the Federal EA Program

Many of the initiatives of FEA program failed or produced very little value.

5: GAO Reports on Federal EA Show a Long History of Problems Many GAO reports on EA in the federal government reveal both fundamental and long-running problems

6: A Confused Understanding

Confusion and misunderstanding about Enterprise Architecture has been widespread from the start and exists to this day.

7: Confusing / Misleading / Incorrect FEA Diagrams Some of the diagrams in FEA documents are both evidence of the confusion within the FEA and are also propagators of some of this confusion.

...

"This research quickly led to an understanding that the Reference Models were completely misnamed. They weren't actually "models", but rather taxonomies, and calling them models was causing significant and widespread confusion.

We still cal TOGAF or Zachman frameworks. Do we still claim EA is a success? My comments come later. But before that

"The problems with Enterprise Architecture aren't unique to the federal government; many of these same problems are also found in commercial EA, so much of what is covered in this report is also applicable to the entire practice of Enterprise Architecture. But the focus of this report is on Enterprise Architecture as practiced in the federal government, what's wrong with it, what has caused it to fail, and what steps can be taken to fix what's wrong."

Enterprise Architecture myths

Oct 9, 2011

http://it.toolbox.com/blogs/ea-matters/enterprise-architecture-myths-48814

True, most if not all myths contain a bit of truth, but the key word is "bit".

Myths you heard about:

.1) That you need to "sell" Enterprise Architecture.

Do you? For one, the concept is straightforward. Anyone understands a plan or a city map and everyone wants a "schematics" of the Enterprise. EA is self selling.

But are those loose IT diagrams you are going to provide to your business really delivering the sold benefits? Selling promises you may not keep will not help your effort or the EA. Can you deliver on your promises?

.2) That EA is about strategy.

What about documenting the day to day operation of the Enterprise to reduce duplication and unnecessary complexity, to improve and optimise the Enterprise, what about describing the key processes and technology to enable tactical change. Strategy existed long before and will survive without EA. The EA is the Enterprise blueprint for managing complexity and change. It enables strategy specification and execution but it is more than strategy. EA is related to many other Enterprise disciplines but it does not replace them, it just works along them.

. 3) That you have to do the To-Be first.

How would the target Enterprise state look should it be not anchored in the reality of the current state? Do you suggest discarding your present systems and processes? Are you committed to a revolution, i.e. starting from tabula rasa and abandoning current investments, rather than to an evolutionary path departing from the existing state? At least, you get rid of the gap analysis phase. And soon after, when the To-Be becomes the As-Is, would you be ignoring it as well, in the strategy development cycle?

.4) That you need an Architecture Review Board.

You definitely need a decision forum to sanction process, architecture and technology change. But the EA strategy will be the Law book for their judgments. Without the EA the forum cannot properly function. Care should be taken though not to duplicate the tasks of the existing governance boards.

.5) That architecture principles are key to EA.

In my mind, there are just a handful of useful architecture principles. And those are already known to whom it matters. Any more than that and we would have a problem employing them. Architecture Principles are there to guide our architectural choices and design. Usually they come mingled with principles that have little to do with architecture.

How are you going to use the principle, for what decision or purpose? This is a question that you should answer before producing "the principles". Otherwise they would be quickly buried in the graveyard of EA artefacts that no one ever uses.

.6) That we do not need an EA framework.

How do we make sure we deliver an EA, the same EA? How can our effort be predictable and replicable? Does every EA architect need to concoct an own framework? An EA framework consists of a frame/chassis on which the EA artefacts mount on to construct the whole. The whole can be broken into parts as such, that can be documented or designed independently. It helps us manage complexity. But if you don't have a proper or a single one then you may have to go on your own. An extended framework would consist of the development process and governance best practices.

.7) That we have EA frameworks

We have a process framework like TOGAF (found useful by IT folks unaware of project management good practices), a cognitive EA approach such as Zachman's and its clones, and other frameworks often consisting mainly of acronyms such as POLDAT. Also there are specialized frameworks for the public sector (FEA), not generic enough to be used the business sector and design methodologies like D/MoDAF... for the defence industries and so on. But it is still a matter of debate if they returned results or are suitable to your purpose.

Imagine a manufacturer having to produce a car using a process like TOGAF or a framework like Zachman! They don't even describe the parts of an Enterprise.

.8) That EA is about business rather than IT.

That's true, in theory, but, in practice, most if not all EA groups are part of IT and are tasked to deliver a technology EA. Nevertheless, without the business view, the IT architecture explains little and has a very diminished audience. Which is what happens.

.9) That the Cloud has an impact on EA

It does but no more than anything else. The business blueprint is about the same except that you don't care about the insides or the How functions are implemented. The infrastructure is abstracted in terms of servers, storage and networking. The applications becomes a business service. Indeed, you have to integrate the business service into your landscape.

Reference Enterprise Architecture

Feb 11, 2011

http://it.toolbox.com/blogs/ea-matters/reference-enterprise-architecture-44262

Reference models provide guidance, repeatability and predictability to your work, whatever that is. They save cost and effort since they embed past experience that streamlines your development, avoiding mistakes. They provide confidence to your stakeholders because their expectations are set from the beginning.

They also ensure that organizations have a common approach in developing EAs. That is they get similar outcomes that can be compared.

There are generic architecture models that describe a system, domain, industry or any industry. TOGAF speaks about the EA architecture continuum.

Generic models may become reference if they pass the test of time and are adopted.

A reference business architecture, for instance, should reflect both the business structure and operation. Be simple enough (a page would suffice) to address the enterprise wide audience.

A reference IT architecture would show a generic IT blueprint of a generic enterprise.

I put together a few generic models for business and technology infrastructure, applications, information architecture... described in my book and site.

On the other hand, in the EA space, one still needs to employ a reference framework that describes how different Functions, Flows, Layers, Views and reference models of an Enterprise fit together.

But a reference EA framework is not the same as a reference model

Zachman and TOGAF do not really provide reference models or even EA frameworks so that enterprise components could be attached to.

They would not be of much help in this sense.

Zachman, and most similar matrix like frameworks (such Cap Gemini's...), return a taxonomy of basic EA artefacts rather than enterprise components in interconnection, as in the 1471 architecture standard.

TOGAF itself is a reference development process rather than an EA framework or reference architecture.

You do not have to show any reference models to customers though. Models should be included in the architect EA toolkit.

THE EA FRAMEWORK DEFINITION, CATEGORISATION AND PATTERNS

The importance of the EA framework

Sep 9, 2009

http://it.toolbox.com/blogs/ea-matters/the-importance-of-the-ea-framework-34026

The framework importance is de-emphasized deliberately sometimes.

Without a framework though, it is impossible to have foreseeable and repeatable outcomes. Every EA development would have a different path and different outcomes. Each and every EA development might link the same parts in different ways. Two EA teams would come at very different results for the same Enterprise. Without a framework there can be no true metamodel to describe the Enterprise entities.

Stakeholders' views must all feed and fit back into the framework where they belong, once completed. Otherwise one ends up with a simple folder of unrelated, unnavigable artefacts whose sum does not reveal the whole. Impacts of change cannot be analysed. The IT alignment to business, a chief aim of EA, would not be achieved then.

A process framework like TOGAF would specify EA deliveries but not how to mount them in the whole and how to navigate from one to another to analyse dependencies.

Zachman does not specify how to relate the Who to What, Why to What ... although there are composite views. It only tells you to document them. And so on.

POLDAT and its variants look more like a list of views.

A framework describes the architecture of the architecture, that is the meta-architecture of the Enterprise, that is an EA structure with hooks where components fit back in, like the car parts mount on the chassis.

An extend framework has to cover not only the structure, operation, and layered resources but the development process, governance, value measurement, ... all aspects of the EA. You do not have to do this framework work again and again. Such a framework would enable navigation.

Let me explain. You need a framework to have at least:

 - a high level philosophy (Why, How...) to scope, explain and sale EA (like Zachman)

 - the business and process map for any Enterprise (like SCOR, VRM...) for business architecture

 - the key layers/domains we need to describe (business, technology...)(like FEA(F))

 - a method of modelling the architecture(like structured design, OO/UML) and metamodel DODAF is good at that.

 - a process with deliveries at milestones (like TOGAF)

and principles, standards eventually maturity models etc. That is why I put together a framework called GODS, describing the key artefacts and their components, linked by a metamodel.

As an architecture is a blueprint not a thousand pages, a Single Page Architecture concept is also useful, together with architecture templates for business, applications and technology architectures.

The importance of frameworks

Feb 15, 2010

http://www.tmforum.org/community/groups/frameworx/blog/archive/2010/02/15/the-importance-of-frameworks.aspx

The framework importance is de-emphasized deliberately sometimes. But without a framework though, it is impossible to have foreseeable, repeatable and integrated outcomes. Same development would have a different path and different outcomes at different times. Every development might link the same parts in different ways. Two teams may come at very different results for the same development.

A framework describes the architecture of the architecture, that is the meta-architecture of a system or an Enterprise.

Stakeholders' views must all relate back to the framework. Otherwise, one ends up with a simple folder of unrelated, unnavigable artefacts whose sum does not reveal the whole. Impacts of change cannot be analysed.

An extend framework has to cover not only the structure, operation, and layered resources but the development process, governance, value measurement, ... all aspects of a development. You do not have to do this framework work again and again. Such a framework would enable navigation.

A framework should have at least:

- a business process map (like eTOM) to describe structure

- an Information map (like SID) to establish key entities and vocabulary

- a business flows map to describe the behaviour

- the key layers/domains (process, information, applications, technology, people...)

- a development method/process with steps, deliverables...

An Enterprise Architecture frameworks classification

Nov 10, 2010

http://it.toolbox.com/blogs/ea-matters/an-enterprise-architecture-frameworks-classification-41824

 It is important to distinguish between different types of frameworks since they serve different purposes.

Some frameworks help you structure the EA thinking by asking investigative questions (what, how, who...) from various development perspectives. The matrix "question-perspective" is then filled in. This is, essentially, Zachman's framework. I call it a "cognitive" tool as it structures the process of discovery of the Enterprise or of any other system for that matter. Another example is the IFEAD's E2AF framework. Both frameworks look like matrixes.

The problem with this type of frameworks is that when you assemble your artefacts back in the matrix they still do not constitute an EA but an artefacts taxonomy.

They are not ontologies either since they describe neither the elements of an Enterprise Architecture, nor of an Enterprise but a number of potential artefacts.

Many frameworks consist of four basic layers: business, information, applications and technology (the common denominator framework). Some frameworks add on top a business strategy and objectives layer. These frameworks look like cubes or pyramids. They are simplistic in nature and the outcoming EAs consisting of a few diagrams have a limited audience.

Some add a deliveries checklist, known as reference models (e.g. FEA) to align the products of all development parties. These look like lists of diagrams, standards, technologies and matrixes of information exchange and components interconnections. These framework come from practice. Suitable to keep up an IT inventory of assets and interconnections. Fail to render the big picture for either business or IT.

Some are specifying a business process map (SCOR, VCG VRM, APQC...) consisting of a process hierarchy. They are typically found in the BPM domain rather than IT. They fail to distinguish between functions and flows most of the time. As such they convey neither the business structure nor its end to end flows, for improvement or benchmarking. People struggle to use them.

Some EA frameworks offer development and implementation best practices and program management guidelines such as Spewak's EAP. They are mostly described in text documents and business like planning. Good stories but little structure. Good for books. They may be better addressing the planning assistant rather than the architect.

TOGAF is mostly about a process(ADM). It is IT oriented, no matter the claims. It is also hard to study or use since it is a tome more than 800 pages long. The knowledge is not structured in layers of increasing detail. you have to read it all. It is hard to criticise since there will always be a paragraph somewhere that may be claimed that deals with the critique.

Frameworks of the defence type are based on a metamodel and artefacts that seem to come from the OO era. Even if that is not too bad, the metamodels are overly complex and themselves and they do not constitute a framework that humans (except SW designers) can understand. The terminology is too specific to be used elsewhere.

Some frameworks are combinations of the above.

Certification, typically based on a framework, helps candidates find a job but solely guarantee that candidates have graduated a course rather than they are able to do the EA job.

Many frameworks limit the scope of the technology to IT, although, until 50 years ago, there were few Enterprises served by IT, if at all.

Few frameworks are pointing at organization and people issues which appear to be in different knowledge domains Only a few are offering views or viewpoints, e.g. aspects of interest for various stakeholders, and a very limited set of them at that.

Navigation and linkage between EA entities in artefacts remain a point of debate for most EA frameworks. Typically, applications, technology and information architectures have little in a common: separate diagrams with different entities, drawn by different architects without a common picture.

In truth, the existing EA frameworks recommend you do the usual business, information, applications and technology layers and leave you at that. Is this a problem? No analysis transcends from one view to another, changes are not propagated, impacts are not resolved and IT is not aligned to business or strategy. Hence it is a problem.

In summary, the existing EA framework types can be loosely categorized as:

   A. *Matrixes (Zachman, E2AF...) for artefacts classification, Thinking/Cognitive aids*

for scoping and discovering the Enterprise and providing answers to What, How, Where and Why the Enterprise delivers from various development perspectives

   B. *Business Process Maps (APQC) for generic business process hierarchies*

C. *Layered structures: Cubes and Pyramids (FEAF, TEAF, PBGC, BPTrends …)*

describing a few typical Enterprise layers: Process, Information, Applications and Technology, from strategy to resources layers

D. *Process /Method (TOGAF)*

E. *Planning and Best Practices (EAP)*

F. *Reference checklist of deliveries (FEA)*

G. *Metamodel such as DoDAF*

Most of them help in limited ways. In the end, if you really are tasked to produce an EA, do your own EA framework. But most of the EA work relates to solution architecture guidance and reviews and IT roadmapping. This is usually done without an EA. That is why there are so many architects and so few EAs.

Check this frameworks critique here.

EA method made of Framework, Process, Models and Design

Apr 6, 2012

http://it.toolbox.com/blogs/ea-matters/an-extended-ea-method-made-of-the-framework-process-models-and-the-design-view-50986

What would you need to develop an Enterprise Architecture?

I would propose an extended EA framework (or methodology if you like) consisting of four distinct classes, described in four posters illustrated in the link included:

1. *The Framework*

Describing the structure of the Enterprise Architecture enabling the EA decomposition based on various criteria such as processes, layers... and facilitating the navigation across the structure.

A metamodel that describes the key EA components and relationships.

Architecture Patterns must be described here.

Vocabulary and definitions should be provided with the framework.

2. *The Process*

Starting with the EA Setup, then on-going iterations from the enterprise Discovery, Planning, to Implementation and Exploitation phases.

The Process may also include good practices for EA business case, strategy mapping and roadmapping, EA governance, maturity and value measurement frameworks, team and site organisation structures, communications and cultural issues, roadblocks, recruiting...

3. *The Models*

To ease the EA documentation and design, reference models should be provided for the EA context, business partitioning, business capabilities and process maps, one page architecture, Information map, IT applications map, Infrastructure blueprint template, organisation design...

Also best practices for SOA, Security... architectures.

4. The Design

A synoptic view of the design process and diagrams describing the layers of the EA, the artefacts in layers and their relationships and the potential sequence of design production.

The Models should be customised and filled in the Design.

The design diagram shows the metamodel and the populated **Models** artefacts and their relationships mapped on the **Framework.**

Additional artefacts may appear here such as the data model, IT inventory of systems and interconnections, technology standards...

The Design supports embedding the EA in a tool.

Here are the four posters: **The Framework, The Process, The Models, The Design** for the FFLV-GODS extended methodology (click to enlarge).

An Enterprise Architecture framework definition

Oct 14, 2010

http://www.ebizq.net/blogs/ea_matters/2010/10/an-enterprise-architecture-framework-definition.php

Continuing one of my own recent posts: "the question is for us if we do need an EA framework... We do because the framework embodies, in a structured manner, the long experience of the many of us and our companies... The framework saves a lot of effort and costs since it leaves the architect focus on own Enterprise issues. It makes the EA development predictable and repeatable. And ensures that professionals are certified against a single standard."

But can we talk about Enterprise Architecture frameworks without defining them? Apparently we can, quite garrulously, in some fora, with little closure nevertheless.

If we do not agree on what EA is, it consists of and what its scope is, how can we say what EA can achieve; can EA aligns IT to business or facilitate strategy specification and execution? And if we don't agree on an EA definition how can we agree on an EA framework, which should be the EA backbone? How can we make sure that we achieve similar outcomes using different frameworks?

A popular opinion is that we don't even need an EA framework. It is typically uttered by professionals superior in the knowledge that they alone know how to do it, but you don't, that they know how to answer, let's say, the W questions while you don't.

They really guard their experience for competitive advantage but that favours them in the relation with the customer, who often live in expectation and doubt till, at the end, they see the results, whatever they are. And then it is too late for the customer to say "no way". In fact these professionals sell their reputation, assuming they have one, in a way consultancies do. But it is also true that some attempt to guard their IP coming from a hard won experience. But how can we progress in the field if nobody shares successful case studies and methods? How do we know whether EA pundits talk about the same EA? The probability is that they don't having not even the definition in common.

I begin with the critique of existing "frameworks" to explain why we need to move on. In the first place they are too many and few of them deal with the same aspects of EA. There is also an ever stronger current of opinion that they became obsolete, that we may need a new generation framework. Nothing great have been achieved in using them and nothing significant has been added for a long time now.

Zachman's is called a framework but some say it is an ontology; in truth it is mainly a method of analytic thinking used more for scoping and selling EA than anything else.

TOGAF is a process (ADM), buried under plenty of additional and often disjoint information, hard to read and use.

FEA is a US federal program, a process (FSAM) and a set of a few common EA views that should bind together the EAs developments in each government agency. Is there enough commonality though to achieve that? I don't think FEA is called a framework any longer. FEAF was, but it might be also obsolete.

DODAF starts with a solid metamodel, which is public, but then most of the work is obscured from public view.

But what is a framework or what should it be?

"The most common method of creating an Architecture is to use a framework to break down and categorize the various parts of the architecture; this approach allows focus on design while retaining the overall context within which the object is being designed." That was Zachman's. According to this, Zachman's matrix is not a framework since we assemble the parts in a matrix (the same, no matter what Enterprise) rather in our own EA.

In my view, an EA framework is the architecture of the Enterprise Architecture, that is, the meta EA. And it would consist of the common elements and their links that could describe any EA. But a framework should be complemented by development process, reference models (for a typical Enterprise structure for instance, IT infrastructure etc) and design method (design artefacts in interconnection). Let me elaborate. An EA method should consist of

1. EA Process: the EA development process and Best Practices for

- EA team organization

- EA governance, team and program organization

- Tools to measure maturity, value created and assess EA business case

2. EA Framework, the meta EA consisting of the specification of

- Key EA framework elements/patterns

- Metamodel showing the EA entities and relationships

- Key Views like Location, Information, Security, Financial, Performance etc

3. EA (Reference) Models

- Generic Business Architecture, reference functions/capabilities map

- Typical IT Applications Map

- Generic Infrastructure architecture

- Typical organization design charts...

4. EA Design method consisting of

The key EA artefacts and design sequence using metamodel & framework elements

Discussion on the EA framework definition and ISO/IEC42010

Oct15, 2010

http://www.ebizq.net/blogs/ea_matters/2010/10/discussion-on-the-enterprise-architecture-framework-definition-and-isoiec42010.php

Since the post on the EA framework definition has raised discussions (please read comments to previous blog) I'll post this article separately to respond to concerns expressed, since it is worth clarifying the points of view with wider participation. Please chip in.

Rich wrote "the Standard does not define functions, flows, resources, or any other constructs. The intent is that these are defined in viewpoints or by frameworks".

True, ISO/IEC42010 does not attempt to be an architecture framework.

A framework helps you build and decompose a system; the framework represents the meta architecture, that is the architecture of the architecture. Bu what does a framework consists of? As an (meta-)architecture, a framework should consist, according to the ISO42010, of the common elements of a system (that is architecture), in interconnection.

I found these elements to be the Functions, Flows, Layers & Views. Any system could and should be described by these elements.The Functions describe the structure, the Flows the behaviour of the system, the Layers, the physical resources (implementing Functions and Flows) and the Views, the many angles the stakeholders see the Enterprise from which, put together and properly aligned, form the EA.

Rich also wrote "You are incorrect that the Standard is limited to "technical" dimensions and lacks the human dimension. The Standard, and its predecessor IEEE Std 1471:2000, have taken a "wide-spectrum" stance on Architecture since the beginning. In 42010, an architecture description must address the stakeholder concerns relevant to the system of interest. By definition, these include those system concerns that "pertain to any influence on a system in its environment including: developmental, technological, business, operational, organizational, political, regulatory, or social influences."

Well, nothing to disagree with, except that the 42010 standard, being more general, does not have to take into account the fact that people are part of an Enterprise system, not only part of the environment since humans are not only stakeholders but resources of an Enterprise.

People form a separate Layer of the FFLV framework three layers: Business (logical), Technology and People (Implementation). And the People architecture is part of EA. Ana as an observation, a system, in my view, should be described by both a logical and an implementation (physical realization) architecture.

Does the ISO/IEC42010 standard differentiate between the logical and implementation architectures?

Rich added: "The goal of the Standard is NOT to define an architecture development method, but provide a foundation on which users and enterprises can define such methods in a coherent manner."

In the EA space, Spewak's, TOGAF... are mainly about the EA development process. Because of that most professionals would expect such a development process to be The framework. And the process is useful indeed. I'll just say that such a process should come with an extended EA framework. Agree, that should not be the case for the ISO/IEC42010 standard.

I found 42010 useful in defining what architecture is since many associate EA with a strategy process alone. Still, EA is architecture in the 42010 sense. I also found the views concept to be useful even though rather ignored in the EA developments; my initial concept in FFLV was "planes" since I represented the framework as a cube (three dimensions: Functions, Flows, Layers+Views) where planes looked like CT scan cross-sections in the body of the Enterprise. If you need to see the BI architecture, just select a cross-section in the technology layer.

I felt the need to develop an overall EA approach that contains

 - definitions and EA framework

 - EA architecture reference models (to ease up the modelling of the Enterprise)

 - the EA design that shows the key design artefacts that map on framework and use the metamodel elements.

 - the EA development process

Should there be one, none or more EA frameworks?

Nov 16, 2012

http://www.ebizq.net/blogs/ea_matters/2012/11/should-there-be-one-none-or-more-enterprise-architecture-frameworks.php

In EA, we came to the rather original situation where everybody has his own EA approach and there are more frameworks than we can count.

How many frameworks does one need though to design, document develop the same system and achieve same results? Ideally one. In practice, two or three perhaps, at least until the domain matures.

If more than that, we cannot call them any longer frameworks for that specific purpose, that is EA frameworks. In fact, neither Zachman nor TOGAF are specific to EA.

Currently, most professionals don't use any specific framework; that is, we use bits and pieces of knowledge from everywhere and anywhere: Zachman, TOGAF... Value Chains, business models, operating models, balanced score cards, process frameworks, all kind of business methods, ITIL, COBIT...

Hence, some may even say that they don't need no frameworks. True. As long as the academia and the big firms cannot come with anything good, what can the practitioners do when there is such a demand for EA?

The one good framework should incorporate all the knowledge and experience in a discipline with consistency and without conflicts, overlaps...

 Without this framework, our volume of work would significantly increase and the results won't be similar, predictable or to expectations.

Each project is different. Yet we have the same project management method or framework. One has to use indeed own experience as well, on top of that.

Each enterprise has a product make and delivery function, a product development one, an HR, Finance and pretty much the same processes for accounting, payroll, marketing, sales, services... Plenty of commonality as such between enterprises. That would be described by a business architecture framework like GODS. And that is why SAP is in business.

Besides an EA framework like FFLV describes how (work)Flows, Functions, Layers (technology and people) and stakeholders' View entities relate to each other in various artefacts and fit the EA whole. They can only link in one way. Hence, the EA metamodel is the same for all enterprises.

Yet, any framework would do, even TOGAF, if the only criteria is to satisfy the requirements of the job.

The fact of the matter is that the EA is the blueprint of the enterprise, nothing else. How it is used by strategists, operations etc is a distinct matter. As such, to my mind, the requirements are the same for all EAs and EA frameworks but different for various stakeholders that use the EA, depending on the problem they solve and the domain.

Nevertheless, in practice, due to lack of definition, scope and the wide variability of EA job descriptions and expectations (such as architecting a Java application for instance!) many other questions can be asked that can be relevant to the job at hand but not relevant to the EA production.

The problem with EA is that not only it is inconsistently defined but there is a real distinction between what we think of it and what is demanded or performed in reality.

Enterprise Architecture framework patterns

Jul 30, 2010

http://it.toolbox.com/blogs/ea-matters/the-enterprise-architecture-framework-patterns-40264

What are the key elements of any Enterprise Architecture framework? Well, currently, there is no definition for an EA framework. In fact EA development processes. matrices, pyramids, cubes are all called alternatively frameworks.

The EA framework is the architecture of the Enterprise Architecture, that is the meta EA. The patterns or structure of the EA framework is in fact the meta-meta-EA. Too many metas.

But what are these patterns of the EA framework?

How can we describe the business structure?

By using functions/capabilities. Or let's differentiate: functions are abstract while capabilities consist in addition of the people and technology that execute them. But we'll elaborate on that in another post.

Functions are the key element of business structure.

How can we describe business operation? Processes or flows is what we use to do that. Or value streams... I'll call them Flows.

Information is what the customer needs or has to provide or, in the end, the enterprise teems with. Information exists in Functions and is transmitted in Flows. And in truth, it exists everywhere.

Note: I'll avoid making things more complex than necessary by describing business goals, strategies, projects or even information at a later time.

Still Functions and Flows solely describe the Business operation of the enterprise. The real enterprise consists of People and Technology (including facilities).

Let's call Business, People and Technology "Layers", a name as good as any. At extremes, an enterprise may have no technology or no people. Usually we have both technology and people manning the Functions and executing the Flows, in interaction. But that is all we have with exception of finance which I would prefer to mention later for simplicity.

So we have the Functions and Flows in what we will call the Business Layer. And we have the Business, People and Technology Layers. What else?

Still many stakeholders would not be able to use our description of the Enterprise. Where is my view they would ask? Where is my (Business Intelligence) function?

The way a system is perceived is through views. The Enterprise, seen through the eyes of a stakeholder, consists in a View or set of them, reflecting mainly his own work and concerns. Of course the stakeholder would like to understand the whole in order to improve his own operation in context.

Views are like filters or cross-sections in our Enterprise body.

An Enterprise consists of many views showing activities such as strategy, IT, culture, finance...

The task of the EA architect is to come with a framework that can integrate all these aspects in current and future EA development iterations in order to assemble all these stakeholders' Views consistently in the EA whole. The more open this framework the better.

The Functions, Flows, Layers and Views patterns is what I assembled in the FFLV , a true EA framework.

The silent competition between the EA frameworks

Aug 6, 2011

http://it.toolbox.com/blogs/ea-matters/the-silent-competition-between-the-enterprise-architecture-frameworks-47776#

The silent competition. And it is silent because the proponents of a framework are tacitly saying that the other frameworks are no fit for purpose; that's why they came with a new one.

Let's recap. TOGAF ignores the existence of Zachman, Spewak's,... Zachman may claim to be the first but it never considered the merits of later frameworks.

Archimate is accepted in TOGAF even though it is not integrated. In fact Archimate and TOGAF appear to have different metamodels. Archimate also unnecessarily invents an own new architecture language, unlike any other framework. FEA(F) acts like there is no other framework out there. DoDAF is an industry in itself. Gartner talked about emergent EA, what is that though? And others, like Cap's IAF, E2AF and so on and so forth do pretty much the same even though they ask questions like Zachman does. Few, if any EA framework acknowledges the others.

True, usually in a tacit pact, framework supporters do no not denigrate each other. Business is business. But they do not recognize each other either.

What TOGAF says, in a minor admission, is that it can be used with any other framework. But isn't TOGAF a complete framework then? What would the other framework add to TOGAF? What would a complete framework look like? How could the frameworks be so different? That also means that the training courses and certifications they come with are also very different. Does an architect trained in one framework deliver the same outcomes as an architect certified in another? How do we select then an EA architect after all? It may well be that the framework does not matter, as some says. But, in my mind, the framework represents the streamlined body of EA knowledge.

So why the competition amongst frameworks is so silent though? Maybe because there is profit to be had in this diversity.

Still, a few practitioners, in search of the holy grail of EA, struggled to position the EA frameworks by comparison. The results are poor though, not because the studies have not put in best efforts but because the frameworks are not alike at all. TOGAF is a process mostly for solution architectures. Zachman, a structured way of thinking about constructing a system, any system for that matter. Why do we call them Enterprise Frameworks? Same reason we call Java, Enterprise Java? FEA is more like a program that chiefly describes the government services, the need to assess their performance and depict the technology implementing them. DoDAF extracts inspiration from the good old times of OO design, more than anything.

Why is that? After all, these frameworks aim to describe, improve, roadmap... the same old enterprise operation. And we would eventually all profit from comparing them and taking the valuable bits of each approach. But how many frameworks does one need? What is each framework good for? How much effort is there left for us to build an aggregated framework?

The question also is why no organisation takes leadership, in studying the existing frameworks, noting down what they essentially deliver, how can we combine them or select the best bits of most for one quintessential framework. But there is no authority to regulate the EA domain.

Or why not coming with a definition and components of a true EA framework starting from scratch, with a basic definition like Wikipedia gives: a framework is like "scaffolding, a structure used as a guide to build something"; or it is like a "chassis, a vehicle's framework". and then see what existing framework bits fit in.

And last but not least. An architect could be trusted to construct a building, bridge or a town. But could we trust an enterprise architect to deliver an EA given this profusion of methods for building it? Would the architect deliver what we expect? Probably not. Most of the time EA architects deliver and review solution architectures, but having been doing that for a few systems, they are called architects with Enterprise wide reach, that is Enterprise Architects. Same as with

Enterprise Java.

Perhaps because of this state of affairs, there is no reluctance anymore to loudly express opinions on EA, even when one's knowledge and experience in the matter is inappropriate, to say the least.

That being said you may find here a "critique" of a few better known frameworks and here a comparison of business process frameworks, both by this author.

About EA frameworks, how useful they are

Dec 24, 2009

http://it.toolbox.com/blogs/ea-matters/about-ea-frameworks-how-useful-they-are-35338

The existing EA "frameworks" help, but not much. In fact, are they really frameworks? According to whatis.com, a framework is "a real or conceptual structure intended to serve as a support or guide for the building of something that expands the structure". Current frameworks simply don't do that.

Zachman's matrix tells us what the cells are not how to model them. It helps us think about EA (or any system for that matter) but not how to built the EA which is the job of the architect. The matrix stands for a taxonomy to store artefacts rather than for an Enterprise structure to glue the parts together, which is what we need from a framework.

TOGAF serves us with a simple process (we use it every day to plan the move from point A to B) with delivery checklists for the known layers. In fact, it may be called a process "framework". Views are considered, but in isolation. No navigation, impact analysis or integrated view of the Enterprise is possible. Also, for TOGAF, the business architecture is an afterthought, a late addition to IT. TOGAF was created by the Open Group, an IT forum, with no obvious interest or expertise in business matters. It is too large to manage comfortably.

Neither TOGAF nor Zachman provide a generic Enterprise structure, as a framework should do, where components and artefacts fit back into the EA frame. As such, even if widely adopted, the existing "frameworks" cannot ensure consistent, predictable or repeatable results, fact confirmed by practical results. An EA development process or taxonomy support your effort but without a structure you are effectively left to design a black box.

People, aware of the dire situation, are bold enough to come with their own EA definitions and easily claim the rank of Enterprise Architect in business or IT.

More, EA is currently driven by IT for IT. Infrastructure architecture is predominant because it can be done separately. But no matter who drives or sponsors the EA, it would hardly deliver, except in cases where the architect builds an own approach and framework claiming compatibility though with de facto standards.

The original EA vision covered the entire Enterprise. Nevertheless Zachman was an IBM-er, looking at how to build IT systems with the rigor of the airplane industry. So the vision was directed to IT which embraced it gladly, liberally using terminology like Enterprise for its technologies: EAI, ESB, EJB...

The EA, as a concept and asset, is still valuable. It should start though from modelling the business. Then continue with the alignment of the technology and organization resources.

Enterprise Architecture Frameworks

May 16, 2010

http://www.ebizq.net/blogs/ea_matters/2010/05/enterprise-architecture-frameworks.php

From time to time it is worth assessing the progress of Enterprise Architecture body of knowledge. Not much has happened in the past few years.

It was said SOA is dead or at least the hype. With the EA the problem is no better. It is barely moving, that is its body of knowledge. No remarkable results have been published. Most use own frameworks because the EA frameworks are what they are. But EA has yet a lot to deliver since the concept is very promising.

Zachman covers a high level philosophy, Socratic in that it asks various questions to define an entity. It is called sometimes an ontology or taxonomy. It is not practical, it does not take us too far. After asking the first few questions, the road ahead is too open to interpretation. There is no more guidance. It is appealing in its simplicity to top management as it enables an executive's analytical approach. But, at the next level of depth, another framework is required.

TOGAF covers extensively the process and its deliveries, ADM. Its technology standards chapter is said to be obsolete. TOGAF 9 adds a few hundred pages, some structure and Archimate, an architecture language which looks more like describing a metamodel. People are looking hard for examples because it is not clear how to use it. It introduces services and interfaces although most Enterprises, having evolved organically, cannot be described using the SOA service concept. And that does not help TOGAF.

Neither of these frameworks is specific to the Enterprise, i.e. they can be applied to most technical systems. For instance Zachman thinking can be applied when you intend to have a house built. You asked the obvious questions including "how much" which is absent in Zachman, from different perspectives: the owner, architect, builder...

Zachman covers a high level taxonomy while TOGAF a process. In a sense they are complementary. None of them provides guidance for the structure of an Enterprise which is essential for an EA framework.

As a result no two EAs outcomes are similar. Everybody pretends to know Zachman and TOGAF. It's easy to pretend to be an EA architect as Zachman's matrix is a straightforward one pager while few can verify that an answer is compliant or not with 800 pages of TOGAF.

FEA and DODAF are more prescriptive but specific. And even so no two departments EA look or feel quite the same.

EA frameworks should enforce repeatable or predictable results so that even if you build your EA in two different Enterprises in the same industry, they should still have the same fundamental structure and components. So you can compare apples with apples.

Some have delivery checklists but architecture is about diagrams not lists. No framework offers reference designs (templates), not even for IT, except, maybe, for the old model-view-controller paradigm for software.

As with SOA, the first step is to design the EA Business Architecture. It is not the business of IT, in the first place, but IT understands "architecture". The business schools, academia, management consultancies have not quite put together a business reference map to guide the architecture. What are the typical parts of an Enterprise? You would wonder why they don't need an EA in their work.

There are a few tries though at process architectures. (APQC, VCG, SCOR, eTOM...). They do not help too much though. They are virtually unknown in the IT domain. They are used by business people for benchmarking and quality improvement. The Value Chain concept, the closest attempt to an architecture in the business world, looks foreign to the IT world.

How can you build an Enterprise Architecture (essentially the Enterprise structure, operation and strategic planning) starting from technology, IT for that matter?

Imagine an electricity utility company that has other technologies. How can the EA IT architecture describe what the Enterprise does? It can catalogue the IT landscape and document front-ends, back-ends etc. But there are networks of transformers, transmission lines, couplers, switches, meters, SCADA systems not part of IT. Not to mention the people operations.

The natural expectations of business and management from the current EA i.e. to deliver the Enterprise blueprint, roadmap, transformation are far from being fulfilled then. The solution would be to limit the expectations to technology standardisation, reduced platform duplication and complexity and integration of the islands of IT.

To succeed, in its full meaning of structure and operation of the Enterprise, the EA has to be started top down from the business architecture in scope (for instance for the Operation or Shared Services) and then the supporting technology architecture. But the division between business and IT does not help.

ENTERPRISE ARCHITECTURE TOOLS

The success of EA depends on EA tools (part i)

Feb 11,2007

http://it.toolbox.com/blogs/ea-matters/the-success-of-enterprise-architecture-depends-on-ea-tools-part-i-14156

Enterprise Architecture "inhibitors" are, in my definition, approaches to the EA design, implementation and exploitation which do not promote further usage and limit the number of stakeholders. Amongst other, usual candidates are a lack of business and management support (because EA does not address their concerns), limited interest inside the IT function itself (since the EA scope is too narrow even for IT) and a lack of clarity with regard to other Enterprise approaches (such as BPM, SOA, ITIL...) and existing technologies (ERP). I'll touch these topics in the near future.

The success of Enterprise Architecture depends on EA tools

EA would eradicate issues like multiple EA vocabularies, inconsistent terminology, notations, conventions or input/outputs and the proliferation of Visio, Power Point drawings or even word processing documents which generate similar issues, in documentation at least, to the ones EA aimed to eliminate in the first place, such as duplications.

Usually teams design EA artefacts, reflecting own concerns, with a tool of choice. While this is not a bad practice in itself the fact is that the artefacts have no common component repository, are poorly linked, if at all, and are inconsistent with most other stakeholders' diagrams. Entities in different diagrams may not be linked to each other and may have different properties even if they represent the same component.

A simple change performed by a team has to be endorsed by all other groups and propagated to their diagrams, stored in various places. That demands a considerable effort and fosters architectural data integrity issues easily avoided with a tool. Since, without a tool, maintenance of the EA is hard work, the artefacts are rapidly becoming obsolete and after that, seldom reused.

With time, the EA development may change course a few times, with the outcome that EA artefacts will not implement any longer all requirements or even cover the initial scope. As such, requirements management is necessary to control the requirements churn and render the EA artefacts fit for purpose.

With a potential large participation and even wider audience, web presentation is mandatory and access to the EA artefacts needs to be controlled; each team should manage own entities and produce own artefacts but aligned to and within the constraints of the EA framework.

An EA tool would support consistency in definitions, inputs/outputs and look and feel by employing a single vocabulary, metadata, repository and set of architectural patterns, principles and conventions for all designs and all people; an EA entity would be represented only once for all to share and reuse. The tool would enable configuration, change management, collaboration, requirements tracing, access control and web presentation.

The success of EA depends on EA tools (part ii)

Feb 19, 2007

http://it.toolbox.com/blogs/ea-matters/the-success-of-enterprise-architecture-depends-on-ea-tools-part-ii-14412

Enterprise Architecture is about documenting, communicating and utilizing the knowledge about the Enterprise to enhance its operation. Artefacts, relevant to each and every stakeholder, have to be structured around the same EA framework; components, designed according to same principles, notations and conventions and have to be available to everybody concerned, according to established access rules. The EA collaborative development has to be supervised, the artefacts versioned, the on-going program portfolio managed and the EA knowledge base controlled and updated on an on-going basis. An EA tool is invaluable for such a process.

"Presentation" only diagrams do not allow drill down to components at various levels of detail in "zoom in/out" like actions. As a result, large diagrams, aiming to provide all things to all people, proliferate. The sheer size and detail of such diagrams become a deterrent, discouraging their consultation. Take for instance, ISO A0 formats (1189/841mm or 46.81/33.11") I discovered on a few occasions; not everyone has equipment to print them (in fact few), wall space to display them or is patient enough to extract solely the aspect of concern or even less to update them. The diagrams become too large and they look and are too complex. Few are interested in the whole Enterprise at such level of detail.

An EA tool would reduce the size of architecture drawings by enabling "zooming" in and out of diagrams for navigation of the Enterprise decomposition tree; it would also allow "openness" to the addition of more architectural views.

From a management perspective, a tool capable of process simulation, would enable business process improvement through the modelling of process performance and implementation of correcting actions. Management also needs to understand the impact of a business strategy or process change on the supporting applications and infrastructure.

An EA tool would enable business process improvement and change through simulation and by returning, "on-demand", the dependencies between specific processes, applications, infrastructure, organization and other views.

More often than not, EA tools will not cover the whole repertoire of EA artefacts (roadmaps, spreadsheets, Word documents ...) which have to be inspected, linked and stored. Some tools have a business process orientation, some are IT oriented (such as network design) and some are looking at portfolio management or organization design. EA artefacts could be also imported/exported between tools and eventually converted and presented as web pages for universal access.

An EA tool enables process simulation, dependency reports, navigation of the EA decomposition tree, "zooming in and out" and would support integration and import/export to other tools to handle a wide range of EA artefacts and notation standards.

The EA tool would pull together the wide spread EA development efforts and artefacts in a single control process and repository enforcing the reuse of same components and design rules and offering a common look and feel.

THE CRITIQUE OF TOGAF, ZACHMAN, DODAF, BIZBOK, TM FORUM

TOGAF, is it an EA framework?

Nov 9, 2009

http://it.toolbox.com/blogs/ea-matters/togaf-is-it-an-ea-framework-35232

An EA framework counts because most EA efforts build, again and again, their "own" frameworks at great costs, with poor results and in most cases to the detriment of the profession.

A framework, according to whatis.com, is "a real or conceptual structure intended to serve as a support or guide for the building of something that expands the structure", like the chassis of a car or the frame of a bike where the parts mount on.

An EA framework should similarly describe a structure to which the components and artefacts fit back.

TOGAF though, is an EA development process (ADM), mostly. As such, I would call TOGAF a process framework.

But a process is not enough of a framework to guarantee predictable and repeatable outcomes. A process stays the same for a bike or a car or no matter what. That is why probably most (TOGAF based) EA developments have little in common and look so different leaving the stakeholders disoriented.

An EA framework should be based on a business architecture framework that shapes the overall EA. TOGAF though, does not propose a business architecture or any structure for what it matters.

The Open Group is an IT forum, not overly concerned with business architecture. TOGAF's organization, and in fact, all non IT activities are lumped in the "business" layer as the context for IT. TOGAF does not cover non-IT technology either. For these reasons, TOGAF looks to me like an IT EA process framework.

Can TOGAF be updated to deliver EA?

Oct 30, 2012

http://www.ebizq.net/blogs/ea_matters/2012/10/can-togaf-be-extended-to-deliver-ea.php

Here is a LinkedIn discussion on "What would make TOGAF more usable?" that prompted my post here.

A framework, according to whatis.com, is "a real or conceptual structure intended to serve as a support or guide for the building of something that expands the structure". TOGAF is not a framework in this sense.

TOGAF is not a framework, in the sense that artefacts or building blocks plug into, to give an EA.

Essentially TOGAF is about ADM (Architecture Development Method) an IT project management guide + lots of additional advice from other domains such a requirements and risk management which should not be part of, in my opinion, but referenced by TOGAF. In fact, ADM seems to cover more than the architecture development effort itself.

ADM also extends to such phases that an architect hardly ever controls such as implementation and change management.

Besides the process of transition from one state to another is hardly news. It is common sense. We all do that in our everyday work and life.

 TOGAF specifies or I'd rather say "mentions" in the ADM Business Architecture (BA) phase, concepts like capabilities, functions, processes, Value Chains and even People... . It does not provide though any guidelines on how to build or relate these constructs or how to build a business architecture in the end, which is an integral part of an EA.

TOGAF hardly mentions strategy or roadmapping that are often expected from an EA.

Hence, TOGAF can barely serve the development of an EA. That explains the lack of results.

There is little point in extending TOGAF since it would be too much to prune and too little left afterwards.

Unfortunately, TOGAF has become a production band for unproductive EAs.

The TOGAF training

Jun 17, 2011

http://it.toolbox.com/blogs/ea-matters/togaf-training-46799

I studied TOGAF at my own pace, along the years. The lush 800+ page were always a challenge. I also listened to and participated in many discussions. Still, last week I decided to go onto a formal training course.

The trainer proved to be experienced in many matters and in the training process itself. When matters were foggy, he often came with answers springing from own experience. And that saved the course in many ways.

The best definition of TOGAF, I came out with at the end of it, is that it is a process (ADM) coming with a plethora of guidelines and techniques. Most of them were almost unnecessary in the context, in that they could be referenced rather than described as part of TOGAF.

Guidelines and techniques about Risks, Security, Governance, Contracts... do not really belong to the architectural discipline alone. Architectural contract ...., have you ever used that?

TOGAF is not a framework, in the sense that artefacts or building blocks plug into, to give an EA. Can one arrive at an EA by following a process and a set of guidelines, if the object the process develops, is not specified either as structure or behaviour? I'll let you answer this.

The ADM circle specifies phases. But Business, Information Systems and Technology are domains/tiers of an EA, rather than EA development phases.

In the first place, there is no clarity around the As-Is and To-Be EA states. They don't really exist in fact. It looks like their analysis and design happens inside each of the Business, IS and Technology architectural "phases". So be it.

Following, there is an Opportunity and Solutions phase after the architectural phases, that seems to consolidate facts discovered in the gaps analysis hidden in the architectural analysis.

The ADM moves then to the Migration Planning where the notion of roadmap, so often associated with technology and architecture, is missing. Planning is also not an activity associated with EA team, normally. But in the general training rush from one section to another the audience doesn't even notice.

Where is the Design phase of the ADM though?

There is the Implementation (Governance) phase which is about executing the migration in which yet again the EA architect is engaged to observe conformity to EA rather than perform it, that is implement or govern it. That should be clearly stated to avoid confusion.

The Change Request phase, that I would call, business as usual enterprise operation, is involving the EA architect solely in assessing and resolving the impacts of change in conformity with the EA. Maybe the ADM circle describes only the involvement of the architect in a delivery process. The process should equally then apply to Planners, Implementors etc. But do they use it?

The ADM goes around in circles.

The strategy which execution, many claim is enabled by EA, is rarely mentioned, if at all!

While the Preliminary is an One Off phase, it appears though in the iteration cycles described later on in the ADM!

In exchange, the ADM circle shows requirements in a middle disk, affecting all phases. But architecture requirements are few; anyway they should probably look more like architecture principles. And requirements are typically specified in relation to solution and their delivery process rather than in conjunction with the EA. That leads me to believe that the TOGAF ADM attempts to describe a solution rather than an EA development process.

Technology is solely IT. Non-IT technology is ignored!

Business architecture is not really approached except in lumping people and process together in the non-IT part of the enterprise, which is not good. People organisation is really a separate discipline as it is BPM but both are equally important parts of EA and the enterprise and as such they deserve more from TOGAF.

As an input, there is an Architecture Request document which has to be signed off by stakeholders; but who ever had seen or signed such a doc?

As a delivery from a phase, there is also an Architecture Description Document. But what is the audience of such a document? It looks like a big tome consisting of all architectural artefacts. How would one use that? Where is the linked set of architecture artefacts, navigable at that, where each stakeholder can readily discover the blueprint and component of interest?

Architecture views are in general innumerable. As a matter of fact any stakeholder has or should have an own view (printing, file sharing....). TOGAF limits them to a few, described in a table. Does the resulting EA, if any, cover the whole enterprise then? No.

TOGAF describes deliveries only as lists, matrices, diagrams but then later on it introduces the Architecture Description Document. This is one of the many inconsistencies of TOGAF.

The Architecture repository (the organisation of EA artefacts and information related to team and process), is incomplete and little related to the Content Metamodel or the ADM process.

The metamodel mentions capabilities which are just hanging there in a corner, not connected to anything.

Also the presence of service oriented business services in the metamodel, characterised by a defined interface..., gives you the impression that SOA or service orientation is already the norm in the enterprise. It is not.

The Technical Reference Model and the Standards Information Base are obsolete apparently, for many years now. Why aren't they removed or updated?

Pictures/Diagrams seem to be inconsistent all along the course. It is also hard to understand the relationships between main TOGAF constructs and diagrams.

Also, TOGAF makes no clear distinction between capabilities, building blocks, business functions, components and so on. Every section seems to come with a different interpretation reusing little from the ones before. In fact, every section seems to be designed more or less in isolation with weak efforts of integration taking probably place as an afterthought.

Was there a capability map? Not that I can remember. But a Capability Framework is part of TOGAF to define the team capabilities necessary to develop an EA.

Both TOGAF designers and audience come, perhaps, from the IT world. That may explain the ardour they put in describing some well known business techniques and discover the "complexities" of TOGAF which abounds in loose detail.

There are many things to be said. It is not a light training since everybody tries to make sense and think how to glue concepts together. But things were not integrated in the first place.

I am trying to remember what was good about it. Can you tell me the TOGAF follower? Of course, the certification is the best good thing for many.

But how can you use TOGAF to built an EA? What TOGAF parts do you use? Do you use TOGAF at all? Or you just pay lip service.

What is TOGAF offering in terms of Business Architecture?

Jun 25, 2011

http://it.toolbox.com/blogs/ea-matters/what-is-togaf-offering-in-terms-of-business-architecture-46819

TOGAF specifies or I'd rather say "mentions" in the ADM Business Architecture (BA) phase, concepts like capabilities, functions, processes, Value Chains and even People... . It does not provide though any guidelines on how to build or relate these constructs. That is left to the newly TOGAF stamped EA practitioner.

In TOGAF, "people" are added to the BA lot, most likely because the time will come, when increased attention can be paid to the issue. This is much better than ignoring it. At least we rest secure that that time will come.

In a way, it looks like the BA in TOGAF is the entire outside world, seen from the perspective of IT.

This post is questioning what is the role, if any, of business methods like Value Chains, business and operating models... in the realm of TOGAF but also in the larger worlds of Enterprise and Business Architecture.

TOGAF does mention Value Chains. One has to do it, it says. But it does not specify how or what is the place of Value Chains in relation to the rest of the Business or Enterprise Architecture. If you decide to use value chains you are on your own.

Should you use them? What for? These are questions you would find to answer in the process.

The Business Model concept is not included in TOGAF, to my mere knowledge. Nevertheless, numberless EA practitioners would be willing and trying to employ or deploy a business model to shape their enterprise architecture.

The Business Model (BM) addresses the specific way in which an Enterprise returns value to stakeholders by configuring the enterprise resources and processes to deliver a product to a market segment, through particular channels. Osterwalder et al, and many others, have analysed it, at length.

The Operating Model (OM), chiefly popularised by the "EA as Strategy" book describes the organisation of an Enterprise with regard to the integration and replication of its operations. At one end is the McDonald's replication of its operations around the globe, while at the other, could be, for example, recently merged telecom companies where each operates differently. An OM could be part of your enterprise strategic intent. Your enterprise operation can be migrated to a target OM. TOGAF does not use or elaborate on it. What other frameworks do that though?

TOGAF does not really refer to most existing frameworks either. Why is that, can one ask?

Many of us would have felt more comfortable if TOGAF would have tried not to describe the difference or similarity to Zachman's, the archetype EA framework, but to integrate it in the ADM process. After all, they are pretty similar in that they describe the same layers (business, IS... and the well known rows of Zachman). They do not compete either: Zachman's is a structured method of thinking about the design of a system while TOGAF represents the development process and the associated guidelines, mostly.

That would enable Zachman supporters the use of TOGAF process and vice versa. I hope someone will see that soon.

Similarly, while TOGAF claims to have roots in the Defence framework, it exhibits little resemblance to it. DODAF though has probably a better design approach in that it specifies artefacts in its formalised views that show how to describe the structure, behaviour and relationships of a system; this approach could be easily employed by TOGAF. I can only hope that TOGAF will approach this constructively.

I would also mention FEA framework which, while not referenced by TOGAF, could easily provide a few useful paradigms such as the performance view, for instance.

Spewak also published a book on Enterprise Architecture Planning which precedes TOGAF by long and would have been worth looking at since, in many respects is similar in intention to TOGAF. It describes the planning of an EA. It is a good source of inspiration, if not already done so.

Last but not least, TOGAF describes the Enterprise as an organisation... But what is an organisation in its own? This looks to me like an unfinished definition job.

I would define the enterprise as a group of people organised to deliver a product, employing technology.

That would give technology its right emphasis in the EA definition. After all, that is what TOGAF is about. And that would define "organisation" too as a group of people organised to deliver....

Is TOGAF incomplete, complex and sucks?

12 Feb 2013

http://it.toolbox.com/blogs/ea-matters/is-togaf-incomplete-complex-and-sucks-54935

In his "TOGAF Demystification Series", Mike The Architect claims that TOGAF is not incomplete, complex or sucks. Here is my take.

Mike, does not prove that TOGAF sucks not. He only raises the question "If TOGAF sucks, aren't we to blame?"

That we are to blame for accepting something that sucks is a different matter all together. There are explanations for that. And unfortunately, we have to accept everyday things that suck. Because we have little choice.

People adopt methods coming from reputed firms or open fora exactly because they believe that there are less chances to suck. Some of them still suck though. But not everybody wants to make own EA definition and framework, starting from scratch. Professionals need to deliver EA not to re-invent it.

People (claim to) do TOGAF because employers demand so or because it is pushed by the many who make today a profit out of it.

For someone like you and me, to make a contribution one has to become a member of Open Group, pay fees, eventually represent a company and then engage in meetings with the same TOGAF veterans that know it all, in order to convince them that the proposal is worth. Indeed some egos are at stake here, since these veterans produced this TOGAF in the first place. I had this experience first hand.

I, for one, tried. I sent a contribution to TOGAF that was ignored.

TOGAF is not even open enough to acknowledge or integrate other frameworks like Zachman or concepts like business and operating models... So much for its openness to change.

I think that TOGAF has a lot of problems but I would not use the term "suck".

"TOGAF is incomplete"

TOGAF ADM is a solution rather than EA development process. That was stated in TOGAF 8.x but conveniently obliterated later. ADM just tells us the phases of a process that those with experience know better. Half of those phases are about implementation having little to do with architecture. While ADM talks endlessly about requirements it mentions little the strategy and roadmaps... which determine in fact the target EA.

TOGAF is not a modelling framework either, because it does not tell us how to put the parts together in the whole.

On top, TOGAF is IT. And is not even integrated with Archimate.

I would say that "incomplete" is not strong enough.

"TOGAF is not complex".

Its content is not, in fact it is rather bland, the form is though. It's simply too large, consisting of sections that are not specific to architecture but overlap, unnecessarily, with other methodologies.

TOGAF is an unstructured, not integrated collection of views coming from various work groups, each with its own approach and definitions. The only thing complex is to understand what to use, how and where is it in that tome. And the fact that each and everyone of us has to reconcile all those conflicting and overlapping concepts and definitions that TOGAF did not even bother to align. There are surely, good bits but how do you find them in that lot?

The reality is that most of us do the training and certification but don't use TOGAF in practice, if you watch what they say in discussion groups. Except bits and pieces.

To me you either do TOGAF or EA.

At the end of the day, the losers are the customers, the enterprises.

Is TOGAF incomplete, complex and sucks? Second instalment

15 Feb 2013

http://it.toolbox.com/blogs/ea-matters/is-togaf-incomplete-complex-and-sucks-second-installment-54969

Mike The Architect and Dave Hornford responded to my comments to the demystification series. Thanks. Here is my view, expressed at large, in my own blog.

Let me begin by telling you how, in my experience, a TOGAF debate goes on. This discussion was no different.

You raise an issue. In response, the TOGAFer refers you to the near 1000 pages tome. Now you feel little and like giving up. You tried to study the lot but it was too much, too large and too disjoint. But how can you talk about TOGAF if you hadn't read that lot, the TOGAF-er implies? You feel a degree of guilt. You are sure the term is mentioned somewhere since everything is in there, but who knows where, in what context, and whether it would answer your question. Probably not. You give up. You are not going back to the tome.

Had the TOGAFer provided a reply? Well, he rather referred you. guess what, back to the volume. End of discussion.

In any case, has anyone here read the weighty tome? Raise your hand. I tried for months even though most prefer to pay for the training, no matter what, rather than having to have a go at it.

Even if an issue you raise is not mentioned in TOGAF at all, no problem, it's still in there, somewhere. Mike, for instance, says that business and operating models are not missing, really, you can just "plug them in" on demand, in phases B to D. "It's that simple". Why bother?

An industrious TOGAFer may even recommend you to study Chapter x, Verse y. Well, TOGAF does feel a bit like the bible. You have to use your memory rather than logic and trust it without asking.

In any case, to pass the certification exam one has to memorise the TOGAF answers like verses, rather than come own adequate answers. Otherwise you go back to the queue and are left again short of a hundred bucks.

And TOGAF looks like the bible indeed, in that it is a collection of texts created at various times by different authors, with different points of view. TOGAF does not tell us the EA story end to end. There is no end to end logic. And there is so much room for interpretation.

Then TOGAFers claim to have employed TOGAF successfully, how could you not do it? This is supposed to silence you. Well, my experience is different. Many claim to use bits and pieces but few claim to use TOGAF in its entirety. In actually practice, even fewer do employ it, if at all. But it's coming down to your experience against theirs.

And if TOGAF "sucks" whose fault is it? Ours, to make it better we should have asked to join the forum, pay the fees, sat in conference calls, convince the esteemed audience and travel at our cost, to the community chats taking place, true, in various sunny resorts. All that, in order to offer the forum our ideas for improving TOGAF, for free. Perhaps I should say that again.

Well, I know how things go in these fora since I worked as the Chief Architect of TM Forum's Frameworx, the EA framework, standard for the digital media and telco industries. - At least the framework exhibited Business Process, Applications, Information maps and a services (SOA like) framework.

The TOGAF team, if true to their mission, should research the field, invite and adopt EA developments from the outer world rather than work in isolation or wait for the world outside to plead with them in oder to donate contributions.

In any case, EA does not equal TOGAF and vice-versa. There are alternatives to TOGAF even if some are equally inefficient and distracting us from the EA job. While we keep talking about TOGAF, some people have to do EA though.

And the question for many is why TOGAF and not another method? Many have given up to the degree they use no framework at all or a loose, variable mix of them depending on the enterprise.

I am an independent consultant. And my duty is to deliver EA, independent of method, rather than adopt or improve TOGAF. In my view, the TOGAF team has to be proactive inviting valuable contributions and making it simple for everybody to engage rather than conferencing in closed circles and looking from above at the rest. It's for the good of TOGAF.

I, for one, had my hard time with TOGAF. Only when I found that there is little to achieve, I proceeded to do my own framework, at great effort. Nothing personal as such.

Nevertheless, some specific issues were raised in the posts. The concept of requirements applies to a solution (architecture). You don't document the current EA based on requirements. What requirements? You just devise the current EA using a modelling EA framework which TOGAF is not. (DODAF is, beside other things.)

And you draw the target EA based on vision, goals, strategy and tactical solutions developments rather than requirements. The tactical and strategic programs that are all aligned by EA, have to gather and document the specific program requirements, not the EA.

And in the centre of the ADM circle, should be the Strategy rather than the Requirements, were we to use ADM at all.

Anyway, have you seen an EA team gather all the development requirements lot for an enterprise, as TOGAF recommends?

To my knowledge, TOGAF was defined as a solution architecture process. I've read that time ago in TOGAF 8.x, but TOGAFers should know better.

Mapping of other EA approaches, - TOGAF says it does that - is not the solution. It makes it look like TOGAF does the same thing in a different way. It doesn't. It does not cover what other frameworks do, for instance modelling, business models, strategy... TOGAF is not a modelling framework indeed, that is, it does not point you to what models, how to design and how to integrate them in a single navigable EA. That is what we all miss most in EA, contrary to superior opinions.

Besides "mappings" often consist of only a few paragraphs that look like they were done just to quell the demand for that rather than support interworking.

And what should the architect do, go through the ADM and afterwards check the mappings? The approaches, if good, have to be incorporated in the method, with credits indeed.

Not even Archimate has been incorporated today. Neither the metamodels, nor the basic definitions coincide.

But let's recap some: TOGAF

- does not propose a business architecture,

- it is not a modelling framework (DODAF does that and more) that integrates the

EA out of the business, information, technology architecture... from phases

- it does not integrate the business or operating models paradigms, value chains

- it does not align to other frameworks like Zachman, FEA, DODAF... but only maps them as an afterthought for those who may complain,

- the requirements rather than strategy drive the EA development, rendering, ADM, as such a solution rather than an EA development process

- it does not have process, information, applications maps/templates..., it does not even have an updated technology set of standards

- it is complex in form to the degree of being unusable for training or references; chapters have little continuity, coming with new pictures, definitions and concepts that relate little to the ones before or introduce alternatives

- TOGAF is about IT, even if that is denied, because contains little about business, people organisation or other technologies; it was designed by IT and is used by IT for IT alone

- ...

To paraphrase Mike, in my opinion, TOGAF competes with other frameworks, rather than working with them, creating as such "fragmentation" in the EA space rather than alignment. The Open Group's CA creates an alternative path to TOGAF for the enterprise architect certification.

TOGAF drives the EA discipline on the wrong path, while delaying the EA delivery to the enterprise. It evolves so slow that it may grow obsolete before long.

Should TOGAF be open to critique and outside developments, rather than pout offended, it could make faster progress. For starters, it would be enough to honestly survey if, how and what parts are in use, if any. After all, were TOGAF good, why would everyone come with own framework?

Mike stated about my comments: "I find a great deal of the feedback to be extremely high-level, abstract, uninformed and conjecture".

I found Mike's assertions and responses superficial, lacking objectivity, foundation and understanding of EA.

My answer to Mike's "If TOGAF sucks, aren't we to blame?" is No. But I don't join the blame game.

And enterprises lose today because TOGAFers deliver TOGAF rather than EA, that is they check the ADM deliverable lists rather than coming with what the business and IT need or with the integrated EA architecture set that depicts the whole enterprise.

TOGAF misconceptions

April 1, 2013

http://www.ebizq.net/blogs/ea_matters/2013/04/togaf-misconception.php

This post comes as a response to TOGAF Misconceptions blog by Mike Walker citing Dave Hornford which responds to some misgivings I have about the method.

How does TOGAF serves your effort to develop an Enterprise Architecture? Let's have a look at the ADM.

ADM Phases B, C and D are part of an Architecture Development Method (ADM) indeed. But the rest of the phases such as F,G and H are rather part of a different sort of process, an enterprise Transformation process which is not the responsibility of an Enterprise Architect, except perhaps in an advisory role, because the focus of the whole process is not to design or even implement the architecture itself but to transform the enterprise, eventually employing an architecture.

ADM should perhaps clearly state that for these phases there is latitude to employ alternative and proper business methods.

The name ADM (Architecture Development Method) is a misnomer as such, not suitable for these phases.

Nevertheless, businesses don't use ADM as the enterprise transformation process and probably they never will.

It is debatable whether B, C and D, layers of a standard EA stack (Business and Information Technology tiers), should be made separate phases. If their activities and deliverables are similar, and they are, they shouldn't be separate. Moreover, would you include as phases of an entity development process, all the elements of its decomposition tree?

About TOGAF's focus on requirements. Neither an EA nor an enterprise transformation process need requirements.

The current architecture development process in phases B, C and D does not use requirements. I think we could all agree that because the task in these phases is to discover and document the EA, the requirements have no role to play.

Moreover, the Architecture Vision in phase A should be essentially based on the enterprise vision, enterprise strategy and goals rather than requirements, because these constitute, if you like, the requirements for the target enterprise and its architecture.

Even in practice, the EA team has been never known or asked to collect all requirements for the transformation of an enterprise. That is a matter for individual solution projects. The transformation roadmap, strategy, planning and target architecture would consider the outcomes of these projects rather than their requirements.

In any case, there cannot be an Architecture Vision in phase A Before one discovers and documents the current architecture in the phases B, C and D, because the vision has to be rooted in the current reality. One has to follow an evolutionary approach (rather than revolutionary) that starts with the current state and continues to build on it. The business though would be thrilled to hear that the EA team wishes to start from "tabula rasa", to re-design their enterprise from scratch.

On top, this architecture vision should have the same components as the architecture layers (mentioned in phases B, C...). Otherwise how can one later assess and fill in the gaps?

One can clearly see that the architecture phases C and D cover only the Information technology. If TOGAF claims to cover the whole enterprise, then IT should not be the only technology included. But that would obviously would increase the ADM phases (B,C D...) to the whole alphabet.

ADM is indeed more of a solution development process, as it was also stated in one of the early TOGAF releases, because

 * any solution starts with the requirements collection and analysis and takes into account their changes at each iteration

 * a solution development process includes indeed implementation phases like F, G and H

Besides, as above, there is nothing in the ADM that makes it applicable at the enterprise level. On the contrary, phases F,G and H do not apply as explained above.

I can only assume that a solution development process was applied to EA without considering the implications.

One does TOGAF and not EA because the TOGAFer attempts to deliver according to TOGAF's phases lists of deliverables (which are in fact small and prescriptive subsets out of an unlimited number of potential EA artefacts), rather than to deliver the integrated EA, the linked set of blueprints of the enterprise, made possible by a modelling framework. TOGAF doesn't cover modelling, as it was proudly stated. The outcome of TOGAF, is not an integrated EA but a number of independent and disjoint enterprise artefacts listed in a table. These artefacts, disjoint as they are, used to exist in the enterprise long before the advent of TOGAF or the EA for that matter.

On top, the ADM demands such a thing as a "Request for Architecture work". Once the work has been approved, no EA requires such a formality. It is usually the architect that has to sell the work product to the business rather than compelling the business to make formal requests for ADM phases. And, who would consent to issue the EA team with formal "Request for Architecture Work" at each architecture phase?

Archimate and TOGAF. To my knowledge, they still have, after a long time, different if not conflicting metamodels. One reason is that TOGAF has different and even variable definitions for concepts such as for Functions, never mind a plethora of alternative concepts such as building blocks, capabilities, services which are not sufficiently differentiated to be properly modelled.

Even the training for TOGAF or Archimate is done independently. It may be even the case that the two compete. It looks to me like a marriage of convenience rather than an integrated method.

TOGAF was said to be a set of tools too. Can TOGAF specify then what these tools are? Then that you may add any tool you like. For what purpose though? What are we trying to achieve? And yet again, what tools, for what and when to use them? What is missing in TOGAF that we have to come up with? How much does TOGAF cover out of this plethora of methods? What other frameworks does TOGAF recommend? Do we need TOGAF at all if we have all these tools?

In any case shouldn't TOGAF have included value chains, business and operating models and, at the very least, a modelling method? But TOGAF does not even offer the models that TM Forum's Frameworx does: Process, Applications and Information maps. TOGAF does not offer a business architecture model or modelling guidelines at all.

Now, if anyone wishes to join the Open Group to attempt to derail TOGAF from its path, please do that. There is just the small matter of cost, time spent and nice travel, just to render TOGAF usable to the community. But you are not paid to do theoretical framework work but rather the EA of your company. You might be interested to use your good methods for your own development rather than surrendering it to TOGAF and even pay for that good deed. Then, in my experience, it's easier to move a mountain than an organization with such a legacy cash cow or the people of the many and various member companies who have their own vested interests, which sometimes aim to preserve the status quo.

Zachman is neither a framework nor an ontology, but a process

Dec 15, 2012

http://it.toolbox.com/blogs/ea-matters/zachmans-is-neither-a-framework-nor-an-ontology-it-is-a-development-process-54236

This is a challenge with regard to Zachman's table: it is neither an ontology nor a framework, as it was often said, but a good old system development process.

Whatis.com states that "an ontology is the working model of entities and interactions in some particular domain of knowledge or practices."

In which case, an ontology sounds more like a metamodel, which Zachman is not.

In Zachman's table the interactions between the elements/cells that would define an ontology are missing.

The cells are not entities in the EA domain of practice since the matrix is neither enterprise nor architecture specific. It can apply to any system. And solely one row is in fact, about architecture. In fact, cells are artefacts themselves rather than elements of an ontology.

As such, Zachman's is not an ontology because it describes neither the entities of the knowledge domain nor their relationships.

Zachman's is not a framework either. Here is what Whatis.com (and it is not the only source) writes about frameworks:

"A framework is a real or conceptual structure intended to serve as a support or guide for the building of something that expands the structure into something useful"

Hence, Zachman's is not a framework because it does not represent the structure of the enterprise or its architecture. Creating the artefacts in cells, and putting them back in the Zachman's "framework", does not constitute an integrated EA but still a table of disjoint enterprise representations. In fact, we already have these isolated enterprise representations. The How describes enterprise processes, the What the information map, the Who the organisation charts...

Zachman's is a simple but veiled process though. The vertical dimension describes the system development process beginning with objectives establishment and concept design and ending with Implementation.

The process is described by either deliverables (the business model, the logical, physical...) and/or by phase owners (planner, business owner, architect, designer...) rather than by process phases.

Were we to describe the process, the following phases would be evidenced:

1. objectives specification (row 1),

2. concept definition (row 2),

3. logical design (row 3),

4. technology design (row 4),

5. implementation (row 5)

6. (and eventually functioning view (row 6) or I would say deployment)

Row 6, added later by some, demonstrates that Zachman's was indeed perceived as describing a process since the system functioning view comes naturally at the end of a system development cycle. Every row follows logically in this system development process.

It is uncommon too that each phase is executed by a different participant or firm. The process would be often executed end-to-end by the same entity. In this case repeating questions like why, who... etc for each phase of the development makes little sense. Why should one ask the why question again and again, once the business case for the development has been already established in a previous phase?

Nevertheless, the same "w" paradigm can be applied to other processes such as TOGAF's ADM. Just ask the "w" from questions at each phase of the process, if you think it useful.

To sum up, Zachman's looks to me like a straightforward system development process specified on the vertical dimension of the matrix by its deliverables and/or owners rather than by phases.

If the owner of the phase does not change, the "w" questions make sense only once for the whole development process, rather than repeated for each phase.

If each phase has a different owner, then again the "w" questions make sense only to each owner in part.

It is obvious that the EA architect is not responsible or accountable for all the activities in rows/phases. Take for instance he is not in charge of the planer's, the contractors' rows... In a RACI scheme the architect may be listed as interested, at best. But the architect should be clearly in charge of the architecture, logical/system phase (=row).

You cannot document or design an architecture using Zachman. It does not tell you how to design the artefacts in cells or how can they be navigated. It does not give you a metamodel to describe the EA elements in relationships. It does not offer integration between the what, the how, the where... The questions are rather interpretable, do "what" refer to information...?

You cannot track an end-to-end process in Zachman's table. You cannot analyse impact of change by navigating to the resources that implement it.

Zachman's is valuable though as a historic development in that it brought to light the role of EA in the enterprise. Given this, I use Zachman's to market EA to top management. They like to and even need to ask questions like why, who... at the relevant phase of a major development. That is because top management has responsibility for the whole outcome, not only architecture, to ensure that it is fit for purpose and delivered in time by the participants (in rows).

Zachman's is a process rather than a framework or an ontology

Dec 3, 2012

http://www.ebizq.net/blogs/ea_matters/2012/12/a-view-on-zachmans.php

I would like to launch a challenge with regard to Zachman's table by saying that it is neither an ontology nor a framework, as it was often said, but a good old system development process.

Whatis.com states that "an ontology is the working model of entities and interactions in some particular domain of knowledge or practices."

In which case, an ontology sounds more like a metamodel, which Zachman is not.

In Zachman's table the interactions between the elements/cells that would define an ontology are missing.

Furthermore, the cells are not entities in the EA domain of practice since the matrix is neither enterprise nor architecture specific. It can apply to any system. And solely one row is in fact, about architecture. The cells are artefacts themselves, composites of such entities.

As such, Zachman's is not an ontology because it describes neither the entities of the knowledge domain nor their relationships.

Zachman's is not a framework either.

Here is what Whatis.com writes about frameworks:

"A framework is a real or conceptual structure intended to serve as a support or guide for the building of something that expands the structure into something useful"

Hence, Zachman's is not a framework because it does not represent the structure of the enterprise or its architecture. Putting the artefacts in cells, back in the "framework", does not constitute an integrated EA but still a table of disjoint set of enterprise representations.

Zachman's is a simple veiled process though. The vertical dimension describes the system development process beginning with objectives establishment and concept design and ending with Implementation.

The process is described by either deliverables (the business model, the logical, physical...) and/or by phase owners (planner, business owner, architect, designer...) rather than by process phases.

Were we to describe the process the following phases would be evidenced: objectives specification (row 1), concept definition (row 2), logical design (row 3), technology design (row 4), implementation (row 5) (and eventually utilisation (row 6) or I would say deployment).

It is uncommon too that each phase is executed by a different participant or firm. The process would be often executed end-to-end by the same entity. In this case repeating questions like why, who... etc for each phase of the development makes little sense. Why should one ask the why question again and again, once the business case for the development has been already established in a previous phase?

To sum up, Zachman's looks to me like a straightforward system development process specified on the vertical dimension of the matrix by its deliverables and/or owners of the phase.

The "w" questions that help justify and qualify the activities in each phase, make sense once only for the whole development process, rather than repeated for each phase, at least because the owner of the phase does not change.

In any case, the EA architect is not responsible or accountable for all the activities in phases. Take for instance the planer's, the contractors' rows... But the architect should be clearly in charge of the architecture, logical/system phase (=row).

You cannot track an end-to-end process in Zachman's table. You cannot navigate to the resources that implement it.

I solely use Zachman's to market EA to top management who needs to ask questions like why, who... at each phase of a major development. That is because they have responsibility for the whole outcome to ensure that it is fit for purpose, delivered in time by participants and resourced accordingly.

Zachman framework, how does it help you?

Oct 14, 2009

http://it.toolbox.com/blogs/ea-matters/zachman-framework-how-does-it-help-you-34758

I recently read a post of Mike Walker in response to Robin Meehan's, on a Zachman presentation. I heard Zachman's speech once, time ago. From Robin Meehan's post, the speech looks unchanged over the years, pretty much standard now. But to be fair, how much can one speculate on this approach? Zachman is a forceful, passionate advocate for EA. He is good at selling EA to the world. That pretty much sums it up.

If you think about a house, you would have to ask yourself the same questions: Why do I need it? Who's going to live there? What should it look like? Where should it be, in case I buy or build a new one...

And then you need an architect, designer, parts supplier etc. All good thinking. The matrix just tells you what the involved parts need to do; it does not tell you how to draw the architecture, how to build it...

Zachman in fact leaves you exactly where the EA work begins. It might help an executive make his mind about EA but it does not help you build the EA. It asks the initial questions but gives no answers.

So it is not about EA execution or method.

IT Enterprise Architecture and DODAF (1)

Feb 29, 2008

http://it.toolbox.com/blogs/ea-matters/it-enterprise-architecture-and-dodaf-1-22591

DODAF, one of the most elaborate and mature EA frameworks, has been making steady progress and rallied customers along the way. But what does it mean to us in the business world?

I am attempting here to summarily compare DODAF and variants to the "standard" four layer IT EA (Business, Information, Applications and Infrastructure) approach, accepted in the business world, TOGAF is proposing for instance. I do this because DODAF appears to be so different, so unapproachable from the business world, while I started believing that this should not be necessarily so. But it is true, in my belief, that the metamodel is complex and the vocabulary is different.

Even before we start I have to admit that I am not a DODAF specialist. But without much ado, here it is:

DODAF has four major viewpoints:

AV- Views for Summary and dictionary

OV- Operational describing the operational nodes, activities, information exchanged and organizational units and roles

SV- Systems depicting the systems, data and interfaces implementing the operational views

TV- Technical Standards View present and future standards and conventions the systems are subject to

Key DODAF Views:

Operational Viewpoint

OV-2 Nodes Model

OV-5 Activity Model

OV-3 Operational Info Exchanges, result of OV-2, OV-5

OV-4 Roles and Org Units

OV-6a,b,c Operational Business Rules, State Transitions, Sequence Diagrams
OV-7 Information Model

System Viewpoint

SV-1 Systems Interconnectivity Model

SV-4 System Functions Model

SV-6 System Data Exchanges, result of SV-1, SV-4

SV-10a,b,c System Business Rules, State Transitions, Sequence Diagrams
SV-11 Data Model (as opposed to the Information Model)

There are also performance, standards views and, in some DODAF variants, Strategic and Project Views. Also a few levels of detail and mapping/matrixes between the different Views, called also Views.

IT Enterprise Architecture and DODAF (2)

Mar 8, 2008

In the previous post, the take away was that DODAF while looking complex, is nevertheless a thorough EA framework. DODAF covers organization which is not common ground for other EA frameworks. In MODAF, a configuration of organization units and systems constitutes a resource. It also covers Systems not solely IT technology, that being the nature of DODAF business. IT, the way it still managed, may still fail to win the war.

The DODAF Viewpoints are Layers in the parlance of standard EA frameworks, since they appear to play the same function: grouping, categorizing Views - in the IEEE1471-2000 (now ANSI and ISO as well) spirit.

The Operational Viewpoint does not stand for military operation views, you would have said so - but no, it is a logical architecture. It is similar to the Business Layer, in my view (I have a few views as well). It includes organization.

The System Viewpoint is represented in the business world by the IT applications and technology layers. Information architecture exists in both the operational and system (called data) viewpoints. In MODAF there are "St" views which tie the strategy to capabilities and consequently to Operational and System Views. So far, so good, really.

Interestingly, DODAF mandates similar Operational and Systems views in terms of Nodes and Activities (OV-2, OV-5 and SV-1, SV-4), behaviour (OV-6, SV-10) or Information (OV-7, SV-11). This creates though a complex metamodel with many relationships. The System view SV-4 is similar, at the system level, to the Operational Activities view OV-5 which describe, in essence, the same processes. They are mapped to each other. SV-4 appears to represent the real processes, those embedded in the technical systems. But is it possible to document the real "as-is"? Even if possible, is it practical? An OV-5, on the other hand, at a higher level of granularity, can come close to the SV-4, it might even replace SV-4.

The idea is that other SV artefacts have similar OV counterparts that may substitute the SVs given sufficient level of detail. This way, the number of entities, artefacts and especially their mappings are significantly reduced. In truth, DoDAF v1.0 itself, proposed a minimum a set of artefacts (info from Wikipedia): AV-1, AV-2, OV-1, OV-2, OV-5, OV-3, SV-1, TV-1.

 No SV views appear except SV-1, the system nodes view. Leaving out, for clarity, the concept (OV-1), the summary (AV-1/2) and the

standards (TV-1) artefacts we remain with

OV-2, OV-5 similar to Business Functions- and Process Architecture

SV-1 similar to Systems /Applications Architecture to which we may add the information architecture.

* Functions here are not in the sense of DODAF System SV functions though. DODAF scores good although it speaks a foreign language for most of us.

In the next post I will briefly compare DODAF to the FFLV framework described in the Enterprise Architecture book, freshly reviewed by BPTrends' Paul Harmon here.

About Business Architecture (BA), BizBOK...

Aug 28, 2012

http://www.ebizq.net/blogs/ea_matters/2012/08/business-vs-enterprise-architecture.php

Nick Malik, in this post discusses the business architecture definition of the BizBOK 2.1. For completion, the BizBOK 2.1 definition cited is:

"A blueprint of the enterprise that provides a common understanding of the organization and is used to align strategic objectives and tactical demands".

First of all, EA is conspicuously absent from the BizBOK BA definition. Yet, business architecture should be a part of EA, at least because EA includes the technology architecture, without which the business blueprint is abstract and cannot be acted upon for either "tactical or strategic" causes.

Still, even if they can be developed independently to a certain degree, the BA and the overall EA should be built on a common EA framework that would natively align the architectures since, taken in isolation, they would be of narrow use.

Nick says in "conclusion: the BizBOK 2.1 defines the concept of "business architecture" in terms of an artefact that business architects do not create!"

It's hard to say what business architects do, at least because they have not even been around till recently. And so far, I have not seen any methodology for the development of business architecture except for loose lists of existing independent approaches. To the extent of my knowledge, for now, BizBOK just lists a raft of disjoint and overlapping activities (such as value chains, value streams, capabilities, process frameworks...), coming from various domains of activity, without providing any integration paradigm.

Nick continues with

"Clearly the concerns of the business stakeholders include "aligning the strategic and tactical demands" of the enterprise. I would not LIMIT the scope of enterprise architecture to this one concern. This is the other problem I have with the BizBOK definition... it is limited to alignment only. Perhaps that was intentional. I have not asked. But it is clearly limiting."

This, I entirely agree with. I would remove the statement of EA intent from the BizBOK 2.1 definition or I would make it more comprehensive. But what would be left of the definition then?

In the end Nick defines Business Architecture as

"1. A specialization of the Enterprise Architecture business function that collects and manages functional, structural, and motivation-related information for decision support purposes including eliciting and improving the alignment of strategic and tactical demands.

2. One of the four traditional domains of Enterprise Architecture."

I would say though that the relationship between the two is that BA is "a part of" EA rather than a "specialisation" of EA.

The definition then continues with describing what the EA business function does - such as collecting information... - rather than what the BA is, i.e. a blueprint, changing as such the object of the definition from the BA itself to the BA function that implements it.

In any case, the activities (such as collection of information) mentioned in Nick's definition reminds us of a business analyst job description that "collects" the information for the EA architect to produce the blueprint.

This is surely the case today when the business architect is in fact a mere business analyst with many business analysts jobs newly advertised as business architects, unfortunately.

Hence I can understand the position that a business analyst (even if badged as architect) cannot and should not produce a business blueprint.

Moreover the business analysts or the new "business architects" cannot do the job without a proper business (and EA) framework or experience in "architecture" which is not currently part of the business vocabulary.

But as long as EA means still EITA to too many, I can understand why the BA guild would want to evolve separately and eventually supply those business architects that can produce blueprints.

In any case, EA is the integrated blueprint of the enterprise, that includes BA. It does not really matter who produces the business blueprint, as long as they know how to do it and the blueprint contributes to the greater EA.

TM Forum's frameworks and Enterprise Architecture

Feb 5, 2010

http://www.tmforum.org/community/groups/frameworx/blog/archive/2010/02/01/gartner-highlights-key-predictions-for-it-organizations-and-users-in-2010-and-beyond.aspx

What is EA? I promise a down to earth definition.

We have all these plans for the CRM, data warehouse, portal, printing and floor maps, networks, manufacturing bands, buildings, locations... EA is supposed to integrate all plans or blueprints in a whole, the parts of which can be related. Not that we don't have these designs, we do. But they are devised with different components, diagramming techniques, symbols, tools... A plan is typically useful only to a small community which has its own vocabulary, conventions and tools, or may be, more importantly, own objectives to achieve that relate little to the whole. EA is supposed to link all these architectures/blueprints in a whole where one can navigate from one item to another, in a logical manner. For instance, one may track the performance of a flow from one process to another, from the beginning to the end, inspecting, at the same time, the resources (e.g. applications) executing it.

EA becomes, as such, the integrated set of enterprise blueprints. Of course, to get to that unique integrated set of views, one needs a frame that holds the views together exposing placeholders when the components have not been represented yet. Well, this is called an EA framework.

Today's EA frameworks are taxonomies like Zachman, development process descriptions like TOGAF or design method and metamodel like DODAF. Most are entrenched in IT though. That is why some fail to deliver to business expectations. One cannot draw a comprehensive Enterprise Architecture without a representation of the business operation. TM Forum's frameworks do describe a reference business architecture.

EA is used for many and various purposes, in fact, as many as stakeholders. Enterprise Architecture, EA, was compared to city planning. One needs to plan roads, public and residential buildings, parks, shopping malls, entertainment venues, water and gas pipes, electricity cables, telephone wires etc. But, as you know, city stakeholders like gas, cable, water, sewage, phone... companies, they are all digging incessantly each others' pipes and our pavements, having, apparently, little regard for a common plan or blueprint. I think there is a human tendency to choose the organic growth versus the planned and the tactical against the strategic. Nonetheless, cities are the result of an organic evolution over centuries of building for immediate needs, trends and styles. American cities are planned to a degree few other cities are because the rectangular grid was planned early in a city lifecycle. But many cities are too old already for reconstruction. As such, urban architecture, like EA, is a lot about managing the change from as-is to to-be, the two end states of the EA, in iterations.

As a practice, EA needs to roadmap all change in the enterprise, facilitate the alignment of structure and projects to enterprise ends and strategic directions. Ultimately, the TM Forum's Integrated Business Architecture would support the enterprise transformation effort, not only for technical reasons, but to enable the alignment of the enterprise operation to business needs, changes, goals and strategy.

The TM Forum's integrated frameworks may be positioned, in fact, as an EA framework, i.e. a template to build an EA. We have a Business Process Framework (eTOM) describing a reference process architecture, an Information Framework (SID), the template for your Information Architecture, and a generic Application Architecture, all in all, the key layers of an EA. We evolve towards SOE, too.

But there is also some work to do before we get there. We have to better integrate the parts and add technology and organization views, business and operating models, Value Chains, an EA like transformation method and possibly, some more.

Transforming your Enterprise and Frameworx

Mar 5, 2010

http://www.tmforum.org/community/groups/frameworx/blog/archive/2010/03/05/transforming-your-enterprise-and-frameworx.aspx

I choose to chat again about Enterprise Architecture and EA frameworks. "If you have ever watched a house being built, or if you have ever had an addition put onto an existing house, you know that the standard method of communication is a big piece of paper called a blueprint. Blueprinting is the standard method used to copy large architectural and construction drawings. A blueprint used to consist of white lines on a blue background. A more recent process uses blue lines on a white background." (from here).

The blueprint is designed by the architect and used by the plumber, electrician, owner, potential buyer... It comes with guidance documentation, when necessary. A plan of transformation is the result of strategy executed as (a portfolio of) projects transforming the blueprint components.

The blueprint reflects the structure that changes in time with its purpose. The architecture could be classic or baroque, depending on the architectural style. The relationship between structure and its purpose is shaped by the architectural style.

Similarly, the EA blueprint is not static. It should be constantly updated to reflect the change in structure result of all on-going projects in an Enterprise. That may not always happen but this is the role of the EA architect.

The EA blueprint is the base of all conversations on changing the structure to fit the purpose or fitness for purpose, maintenance, renovation and transformation. It should be the basis of change in the Enterprise, be it operational, tactical or strategic. Without a blueprint, the transformation cannot be properly managed; the Enterprise would grow organically until a point when nothing works properly any longer and its decay starts.

The EA, as a blueprint, should be seen as the cornerstone of any Enterprise transformation, as a strategy, as in the title of a well known but less practical EA book.

But the core of any EA development is the framework, i.e. its meta-architecture. And

Frameworx represents a reference EA meta-architecture populating the 4-layered EA model with true Business Process, Information and Application reference architectures. It may be used either stand alone or along TOGAF ADM (Architecture Development Method) for instance.

ON OTHER ILLUMINATED EA APPROACHES, GARTNER...

Gartner's Emergent Architecture

Sep 7, 2009

http://it.toolbox.com/blogs/ea-matters/gartners-emergent-architecture-33972

There were quite a few reactions to Gartner's Emergent Architecture proposition.

"Architect the lines, not the boxes" is one new precept. Well, lines without boxes would be lines going nowhere. Anyway, lines/connections were part of it since the dawn of architecture.

Quote from properties(?) of Emergent Architecture:

"1. Non-deterministic - In the past, enterprise architects applied centralised decision-making to design outcomes. Using emergent architecture, they instead must decentralise decision-making to enable innovation.

2. Autonomous actors - Enterprise architects can no longer control all aspects of architecture as they once did. They must now recognise the broader business ecosystem and devolve control to constituents.

3. Rule-bound actors - Where in the past enterprise architects provided detailed design specifications for all aspects of the EA, they must now define a minimal set of rules and enable choice.

4. Goal-oriented actors - Previously, the only goals that mattered were the corporate goals but this has now shifted to each constituent acting in their own best interests.

5. Local Influences: Actors are influenced by local interactions and limited information. Feedback within their sphere of communication alters the behaviour of individuals. No individual actor has data about all of an emergent system. EA must increasingly coordinate.

6. Dynamic or Adaptive Systems: The system (the individual actors as well as the environment) changes over time. EA must design emergent systems sense and

respond to changes in their environment.

7. Resource-Constrained Environment: An environment of abundance does not enable emergence; rather, the scarcity of resources drives emergence."

Sounds a bit pretentious, to say the least. It looks a bit odd that Gartner had uncovered these best practices so late, after such a long time practicing and preaching EA.

I'll summarize my understanding (hope I get it right!) and comment.

1. De-centralize EA decision making

Good management precept, rather fashionable. Applicable to any organization.

2. Devolve EA control to business stakeholders;

This sounds a bit like the 1st point and looks like empowerment or delegation to those in the know in business. Good find.

3. Emergent Architecture to establish only a minimum set of rules.

With the frameworks we have there is no danger of that. Every EA seems to build its own rules which are not many. This also adds to the de-centralization concept, 1st point.

4. Stakeholders to realise own goals, rather than corporate ones

And return to the old silos EA was trying to break. Add to 1st point.

5. EA to coordinate rather than dictate

Is that not a good practice for any management? Same as de-centralization.

We might simplify and merge these five commands into one: de-centralization.

6. EA to design adaptive systems

That looks like the talk about agility. EA does not design systems; an architecture like SOA though would enable agility, adaptability.

7. Abundance inhibits Emergence or, I would say, motivation comes from scarcity; that surely is a deep reflection upon life and a good American principle for education. Fine one.

These surely are governance principles rather than properties. But is it anything specific to Enterprise Architecture? Hardly so.

Now, why does Gartner call it Emergent? New buzz word? Is that a new term "Emergent Architecture"? From search, I came up with this. Not sure if related. Make your own mind.

From InfoQ sources: Mike Rollings, Research Director for Burton Group's Enterprise Architecture, in response to Gartner, thinks this is the right opportunity to stipulate the traits of an EA architect: rule-breaking, entrepreneurial, self-educating, bonding, revolutionary and visionary. That's a role model for me. The crisis changed the way people thinks, definitely. Maybe we, the architects, should demand a raise, in statute.

And there were other opinions as well, I would not bother you with.

To recap, Gartner in translation: the EA governance has to be decentralized, business involved, stakeholders' needs taken care of etc.

That's good stuff. Not sure it helps.

Gartner's emergent Enterprise Architecture

Jun 25, 2010

http://it.toolbox.com/blogs/ea-matters/gartners-emergent-enterprise-architecture-39320

Let me have another look at this issue.

"Gartner identified a new approach for Enterprise Architecture; it's called "Emergent Architecture" . There are seven properties that differentiate emergent architecture from the traditional approach to EA:

1. Non-deterministic - In the past, enterprise architects applied centralised decision-making to design outcomes. Using emergent architecture, they instead must decentralise decision-making to enable innovation.

2. Autonomous actors - Enterprise architects can no longer control all aspects of architecture as they once did. They must now recognise the broader business ecosystem and devolve control to constituents.

3. Rule-bound actors - Where in the past enterprise architects provided detailed design specifications for all aspects of the EA, they must now define a minimal set of rules and enable choice.

4. Goal-oriented actors - Previously, the only goals that mattered were the corporate goals but this has now shifted to each constituent acting in their own best interests.

5. Local Influences: Actors are influenced by local interactions and limited information. Feedback within their sphere of communication alters the behaviour of individuals. No individual actor has data about all of an emergent system. EA must increasingly coordinate.

6. Dynamic or Adaptive Systems: The system (the individual actors as well as the environment) changes over time. EA must design emergent systems sense and respond to changes in their environment.

7. Resource-Constrained Environment: An environment of abundance does not enable emergence; rather, the scarcity of resources drives emergence."

This appears to be part of the Gartner's series of EA messages, vague enough to generate various interpretations and lots of discussion. That's probably one of the goals. Trust, not judge seems to be the adopted critical attitude. Let's have a closer look at the seven commands:

1. Non-deterministic - does Gartner say in fact de-centralised? Another word, another meaning. In any case Enterprise decision making is not part of the EA governance; EA should be used by Enterprise stakeholders to do take their own decisions; is that what Gartner struggles to express?

2. Autonomous actors - This all sounds a bit esoteric; the constituents, are they the autonomous actors? Nevertheless, have you ever assumed that the EA architect would take all control, in particular for the business capabilities bits? The domain and solution architects take their own decisions in the EA environment where their parts have to fit back in the EA whole. Fine, if this is what they say. I wish they were more obvious here. The point looks similar if not identical to the first one.

3. Rule-bound actors - it looks like actors are all parties except the Enterprise Architects. What Rules though? Does Gartner mean that there should be an EA, EA framework, process, principles... that should bound all "actors"? I fear I put words in their mouth though.

4. Goal-oriented actors - the story seem to shape around actors that Gartner wishes to paint back into the picture. This though contradicts the known business strategy execution approach that recommends that strategy be cascaded to all functions; this tactics is also in opposition to one of the EA key goals: to align business and technology to strategy and may create dissent unless both local and corporate strategies are considered in the initial strategy specification.

5. Local Influences: getting back on track here; EA architect must "coordinate"; until this point Gartner recommended decentralization, autonomy...; there must be a difference between coordination and control larger than I thought. This point seems to complement the previous one though. The message seems to be that the EA must coordinate not dictate.

6. Dynamic or Adaptive Systems: always good to mention "panta rhea", the old Greek adage observing that everything is in motion, changes; probably, Gartner observes that EA should not take longer that it should since actors, goals, the enterprise itself can vanish in the meantime.

7. Resource-Constrained Environment: don't we know it all! We can't ever get enough of anything. I would not comment on that since this is obviously a truism, so much like the previous point. We already operate on that premise.

Overall I think Gartner discovered or assumed that a single EA function or architect does all the work and decision making and they say that this should not be the case. I don't think that the EA architects have ever had this authority though. They make a good point though: there are lots of EA architects wishing to wield influence without having devised an Enterprise Architecture establishing the solution design, investment and decision making context.

The question is what should we do about this set of EA governanance principles? It depends on your case. Can we call this "emergent" EA? I leave it to you. I am looking forward for the next batch of commands though. They have a tendency to appear around Gartner EA events timeframes, probably to provide a theme for discussion.

Gartner's 10 Enterprise Architecture pitfalls

Sep 7, 2009

http://it.toolbox.com/blogs/ea-matters/gartners-10-enterprise-architecture-pitfalls-33988

10 EA pitfalls. They include:

"1. The Wrong Lead Architect: Gartner identified the single biggest EA problem as a chief architect who is an ineffective leader...Gartner recommends that such a lead architect be replaced by someone with strong 'soft' skills.

2. Insufficient Stakeholder Understanding and Support:

3. Not Engaging the Business People:

4. Doing Only Technical Domain-Level Architecture:

5. Doing Current-State EA First:

6. The EA Group Does Most of the Architecting:

7. Not Measuring and Not Communicating the Impact:

8. Architecting the 'Boxes' Only: Integration and interoperability standards are high EA priorities

9. Not Establishing Effective EA Governance Early:

10. Not Spending Enough Time on Communications: "

The 10 pitfalls are the result of common sense, with exceptions, but who knows, they may be worth re-iterating.

Obviously the wrong people can wreck any undertaking. Soft skills are good as long as there are "hard" skills as well. Involving stakeholders, business is what architects usually do to extract, validate and insure participation etc.

Governance, communications, work in collaboration, team etc.

By removing the negation, we may call them common work principles applying to most endeavours.

Yes it was known that the EA team has tried to do it all. The quality of the outcome suffered because the EA architects are not domain specialists. It may also create resentment for lack of accreditation of people's input.

Logically the current state must be documented first. Otherwise how would you know what needs changing, what the gap is? Business strategy may dictate directions but the implementation program has to understand the current state in order to specify the change in systems and processes.

In each EA iteration of a spiral process both current and future states have to be specified, unless you choose a waterfall process, which seems improbable.

It all sounds a bit patronizing.

Gartner's EA hypecycle critique

Aug 10, 2010

http://www.ebizq.net/blogs/ea_matters/2010/08/gartners-ea-hypecycle-critique.php

Gartner's news on Enterprise Architecture leaves me a bit baffled as usual. This seems to become a quarterly forecast aimed to direct the community on the right EA track. Let's dissect a bit the news.

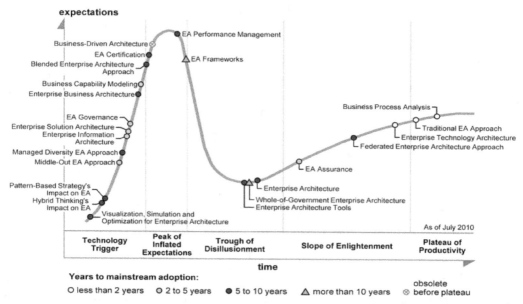

The message is centred around the EA hypecycle that Gartner wished to show us all. So many EA "technologies" were placed on it that the field looks teeming with activity. I wish it were so.

"Visualisation, Simulation..." is the first car climbing the curve, right at the beginning and rightly so because it was there and will stay there for a long time. Until we have an EA model.

"Hybrid thinking" is a way mixing design, marketing, accounting... and in general artistic, humanistic and technological thinking. Anyone here would have thought that this is the case for now; but it's not, just look at some ugly products out there. It looks like a popular buzzword with the business nowadays. It's still hard to envisage what this has to do with EA though. But let's trust them for now.

"Pattern based strategy" is next in line.

"There is a way to see things coming. It's a framework for proactively seeking and acting on the early and often-termed "weak" signals forming patterns in the marketplace. It's also about the ability to model the impact of patterns on your organization and identify the disciplines and technologies that help you consistently adapt. It's called Pattern-Based Strategy".

Looks like a Gartner concept that has more to do with strategy specification which is not really in the EA domain, unless you know EA architects who develop the strategy for their company.

An observation at this point: this really turns out to be a Gartner's hypecycle in that these "technologies" are really added because Gartner thinks so rather than being used out there. At least this is my feeling.

"Middle-out approach"-

"Middle-out architecture is an approach to EA whereby architects focus on managing the key dependencies among those parts of the organisation that have the biggest impact on the ability to change. A middle-out approach focuses on architecting interoperability by defining a small but rigidly enforced set of general, stable interface standards, while allowing complete autonomy of decision making for the specific technologies and products that are used within the solutions. This approach is highly suited for organisations and "business ecosystems," where the business units, partners, and suppliers are not under the direct control of a central EA team."

The middle out approach looks like a service based approach to architecture sometimes called SOA. Isn't this an old way to say good old things?

"Managed diversity":

"The standards process of the past no longer works to protect the management and security aspects of the enterprise. Gartner's enterprise architecture concept, "managed diversity," brings order to the chaos" and "project teams can decide which product best fits the project needs, rather than having a single standard imposed on them" says Gartner.

And "Gartner has identified four basic approaches to EA - traditional, federated, middle out and managed diversity. Analysts said that the majority of clients will, in reality, support a mixture of more than one of these approaches based on their business   needs."
It looks like whatever it is, the advice is to cover all bases in what you do.

It is coming well together in with "Hybrid Thinking", "Patterns based strategy", Middle Out" ... I am not sure they really happen out there where you and I live but they sound good. Good for management talk. Quote Gartner.

"Enterprise solution architecture" and " Enterprise information architecture" have been happening for a long time now with or without EA. They should be more or less past this cycle. Or the speed of crossing the cycle is very different from technology to technology. Any opinion? The only problem with these technologies is that they should be integrated in the EA.

"EA governance" should not be there. It is not really "emerging". After all, this hypecycle is used to analyse emerging technologies.

"Business capability modelling", "Enterprise business architecture" they are in their infancy, it is true since no one in the business has come with a business architecture framework. Does Gartner have one?

"EA certification" is old enough to be on the plateau. Only that there should be a single approach to be done against unlike now where one can choose to pass multiple orthogonal certifications. That does not guarantee that the candidate would be able to deliver EA, unfortunately.

"Business driven architecture" seems to have fallen in disgrace for some reason. After all that is what IT is doing in terms of EA now.

At the top of the curve is "EA performance Management"; that could be in terms of interest it raises rather than in terms of technology or deliveries. People don't know yet how to measure EA performance or value, for that matter. Should not be there.

On the downside, falling quickly is "EA frameworks". I agree entirely. We go through the "winter of discontent".

Then at the "trough of disillusionment" are the EA tools; those on the Gartner's Magic Quadrant as well? Very true. Well, the tool frameworks have no frameworks from the academia, no metamodels... They need help from us here.

Don't know about the "Whole-of-Government" EA. It outlived a few US presidencies though.

"Enterprise Architecture" itself appears surprisingly on the bottom of hypecycle where it may fall through.

How come? Later on the hype, doing quite well, is the "Traditional EA" approach though. What is the difference? After all EA consists of Information Architecture, Business Architecture placed on the climbing curve of the cycle. We need urgent explanations.

"EA assurance" whatever that means without a clear EA definition, scope and frameworks, is climbing though the plateau of productivity.

"Federated EA" seems to be doing well; "Enterprise technology Architecture" seems to be productive. I suppose this is IT, not just any technology.

Surprise, surprise at the end, being quite productive, is "Business Process Analysis". I asked quite a few times what is the role business process frameworks play in EA and never got an answer from architects. It looked like it does not belong here if you ask the EA architects. How is it integrated in the EA work? That is the question. How do we use business process frameworks?

How are we supposed to use this EA hypecycle? I think that the intention is that we ask Gartner.

Some questions linger though. Why "EA governance" "EA Information Architecture" are at the beginning of the cycle when "EA" itself is at the trough and "traditional EA" is nearly productive?

There are a few Gartner's EA proposals, as expected at the beginning of the cycle not really sanctioned by the community of EA. I also suppose that Gartner's "Emergent EA" was lost in translation somehow.

After all, the message is good:

"As IT roles shift away from technology management to enterprise management, EA is suited to bring clarity to these blurred boundaries, and, by 2015, increased adoption of EA processes and uses by business will further IT's alignment with the organization's culture, future-state vision and delivery of business value outcomes ...

We predict that by 2015, the marketplace of EA practitioners will find a landscape very different from today's environment," said Betsy Burton, research vice president and distinguished analyst at Gartner. "To prepare for 2015, EA practitioners need to ensure that EA practices are driven by a clear business vision and defined business context, and that their EA program has stabilized the practices and disciplines that are less than two years to mainstream adoption."

Stay put and positive. Things are happening.

Should Enterprise Architecture enter rehab as Gartner says?

Aug 19, 2010

http://it.toolbox.com/blogs/ea-matters/should-enterprise-architecture-enter-rehab-40718

Here is a Gartner post on EA entering the rehab. I am not sure what that means.

The EA problem consists in that we always preached about the ideal EA that promised to heal all ailments of the Enterprise while practising an EA that mainly covered solution architecture, its reviews and IT strategy, as a Forrester survey interpretation shows. I would not call this EA but let me not go there.

EA seldom provides, if at all, the Enterprise blueprint or operation as keenly expected by top management and business people. That is why it may be at the trough of disillusionment. That is, depending on viewpoint, since EA employs more people than ever, happy to use TOGAF, whatever that does for them ... And the IT management is not unhappy because the expectations are no different.

"EA" architects might be happy to take up a real integrated EA but they need a framework for that, that links business functions, flows, layers and technology components in a unitary navigable whole aligned to strategy. They don't have that and they are not expected to represent the Enterprise, each in their own way.

This won't come without innovation either no matter how assiduous we promise it, re-brand it, rehab it or add wondrous terms or approaches.

The EA landscape is unfortunately confused by the fact that the EA is too often associated to ITIL, software or IT technologies that have "Enterprise in the name" (ERP, EAI, ESB, JavaEE...) or even with the "glue" between strategy and..., business and....

As such lots of other practitioners claim to be EA architects.

In the end, EA just needs an honest definition of what we do and what we would like to do but cannot since we don't know how to build it. And that should be make public so that anyone can make distinction between what an EA role is or it isn't.

I would have expected that reputed for a would listen and arbitrate a solution if not coming with one. But that does not seem to happen.

Nothing as dramatic as rehab though.

The future of Enterprise Architecture according to Gartner
August 18, 2010

http://www.ebizq.net/blogs/ea_matters/2010/08/the-future-of-enterprise-architecture.php

I just thought that it is not a bad time to attempt to forecast myself the future of EA given the high interest still attracted by the topic. After all, Gartner does it with profusion of detail.

Is Enterprise Architecture going anywhere? This looks like a legitimate question. It is, albeit slowly in the absence of an agreed practical framework and clear proof of its business case. The reason is straightforward: EA is a necessary "evil". Any system needs a blueprint enabling proper operation, maintenance, planning... To fulfil the expectations, EA needs to satisfy its many stakeholders in top management, business, technology/IT and organization. Here are a few directions, I can see the Enterprise Architecture progressing, in no particular order, but happening in the next five years or so:

A.	EA will finally be recognized as a business discipline, having incorporated Value Chains, Business Models, Strategic Planning...

B.	The EA evolves to increasingly cover business architecture rather than IT alone; the Enterprise Architecture will be the result of the fusion of IT, Business and Organization/People architectures; what is the value of an applications architecture, without the process it implements or the people operating it?

C.	The governance for EA will be more & more business and top management heavy; this is because it would be used in mapping the strategy to components, to derive the enterprise transformation portfolio, make investments and take strategic and tactical decisions.

D.   The EA development will be increasingly triggered by Mergers & Acquisitions and outsourcing activities; IT BPO, SaaS(ASP) are riding a strong current right now.

E.   The Enterprise Architect would be more and more called in the business decision making process; because the EA architect deals with the business logic, technology operation and strategy, is able to understand both worlds and use both business and IT vocabularies.

F.   A combined EA framework emerges to take advantage of the strengths of various frameworks, such as Zachman, TOGAF, FEA and others.

G.   SOA is recognized as part of the EA program as the target EA style of architecture and technology, rather than executed in isolation as it often happens

H.   EA would be increasingly required by

shareholders/owners/investors to provide the blueprint of the business operation to describe assets, provide proof of regulatory compliance, map costs and profits on various operations and align strategy. The US government mandates EA to the public sector. EA would become a regulatory feature for public listed companies.

About Gartner's Philip Allega "Applying EA to your life"
Aug 22, 2010

http://www.ebizq.net/blogs/ea_matters/2010/08/about-gartners-philip-allega-applying-ea-to-your-life.php

It is often said that "life imitates art". According to Philip Allega of Gartner in "Applying EA to your life" we should apply Enterprise Architecture techniques to plan our acts of life or achievements. I sincerely hope we don't come to that, that is use TOGAF or a look alike to plot our lives.

Since the dawn of time people established goals, assessed where they were and what they have to do and then worked on it. The good news is that they could do without EA, especially given its failure rate today. Otherwise we would not have reached our venerable ages and current positions by chance alone.

Then Philip says that "If you have started your EA program and your first activity is to document the current state, STOP NOW. Refocus your team on analysis of the business strategy and development of the future state architecture."

I hope this piece of advice was not meant to be taken literally. Imagine going to your CIO or senior manager telling him that you have to stop the current state documentation work, now.

If you catch him on a good day, he will probably explain to you that you need to discover your IT landscape to reduce the undesirable diversity in platforms and applications and introduce standardisation, eliminate unnecessary duplication, and costs as such, enable integration of various applications, document processes for improvement, establish a common vocabulary, an inventory of assets... And he is right, of course. Not that it is a matter of your choice, that is, as an Enterprise Architect you don't do the decision to stop working.

Enterprise Architecture is not aimed at change alone and not all change is strategic in nature. EA is also about complexity management or aligning technology to business. And about many other things. But EA should be implemented in iterations where you analyse enough of as-is and to-be states to be able to deliver the goods in your scope. And there is no one final Enterprise state. What's target today is current tomorrow.

The target architecture cannot be established based on Vision alone. It is not practical or economically viable to start from tabula rasa each and every time you implement a new strategy. Competitors would be delighted though.

Questions arise, like how do I know how the future architecture looks like, without the current one, what do I do about the ERP system I just implemented and trained people in, what do we do about the projects transforming the Enterprise as we speak... how do you do roadmapping, if you don't care the current system is SAP? I am sure there are more questions like this.

This approach incites to continuous revolution, rather than evolution with the high price to pay for such sudden and mountainous changes. Anyway, once you go through a first target architecture development, you'll have a current EA, right? Or should we just ignore the works done and start from scratch again at the next cycle?

Philip's comparison of the exercise of current architecture design with "naval gazing" is worth quoting though.

He wrote, with regard to his friend conundrum to built a new career, for which I have sympathy, that the turnaround plan is "ambitious" and *the alternative scenarios we discussed were none too pleasant given where he's _starting from_*".

So Philip did consider the starting point.

I can also cite research that delayed gratification in children, that is first work and then achieve your goal, is a characteristic of later achievers. But then all these scientific observations, how reliable are they ? Wasn't it said that a nine years old is mature enough to function in society? Or that frustrated children increase criminality later? Criminality seems to be high anyhow, but children may be illiterate as well now.

On current and future Enterprise Architecture, (Gartner)

Aug 29, 2010

http://www.ebizq.net/blogs/ea_matters/2010/08/on-current-and-future-enterprise-architecture.php

Philip Allega of Gartner replied on my blog with "Future state first current state last" to the position stood last week on the debate on current and future EA. Thanks Philip, I'll take the challenge since this is an old debate for many.

The emphasis in his latest blog moved to the priority of the future state rather than doubting the current EA worthiness and stopping it as in the previous.

I'll summarise my position, upfront, for brevity, before going into explanations.

I'll say that a realistic Enterprise vision must be planned from the current state.

The vision remains a day dream, unachievable if the gap analysis necessary to plan the Enterprise transformation may be not performed because the current state is not documented. Mind you, a reasonable description is all right for there are many iterations.

The vision itself must be based on the current state.

The target Enterprise state must take into consideration not only vision but also the current problems which are documented by the current EA.

Tabula rasa (rather than rosa), i.e. discarding the current state, is not, in practice, an option for any business management in performing the Enterprise transformation to achieve Vision.

EA is more than vision implementation. It is about complexity management, alignment... To realise all these you need the current EA.

Now, to detail.

Enterprise Architecture enables much more than vision implementation alone. It enables change, be it operational, tactical or strategic.

EA is also about complexity management, or simplification of the organically grown Enterprise, about aligning technology to deliver the operation the business really needs, about increasing business agility, enhancing understanding in the Enterprise workings... All this is based on the current EA.

The target state is designed with the idea of fixing both the current state issues and achieving the vision. You need the current EA to fix the current problems not only to achieve Vision.

if you plan to improve your home, you first take stock of what you have (like size, location...). And then you build your "vision" on that because that tells you what is possible, what you can afford, what the land permits..., unless of course, you wish to demolish what you already have. You won't plan a shopping mall on a little cabin in the mountains.

Thus, the vision itself must be based on the current state.

About the failed EA example. It's rare when EA succeeds, given its IT orientation alone. Nevertheless, when transforming the Enterprise you have to consider all change, not duplication reduction... or vision in isolation.

I also cited <u>research</u> that states that delayed gratification in children is a characteristic of later achievers, to support a position of starting with the current state to achieve vision.

True, you can have brave visions if you don't know yourself or remember who you are.

Philip also liked this quote:

"Things are the way they are today because of the decisions we have made in the past. But just because they are that way today, does not dictate the future of how things will be tomorrow."

This really says, if you accept it as true, that one can change things, not that one may ignore the initial state. And that your past visions are now your current state, a truism. It is high time to document this state, once for all, rather than live in the future.

And not least EA is about Architecture. You use it, not only to achieve a target, but for instance to understand the Enterprise structure and operation.

To reply to a related comment, Deb's.

"My views are very strong on this Phil - current state is business-as-usual for every person in the organisation EXCEPT the architects. Their role is to collect the current state information that is a reflection of the future state being defined.

The minute any EA team starts the accept that they are responsible for documenting the current state then they are on a slippery slide down to oblivion.

Every business manager should understand, document and update their processes, information and solutions. Every IT manager should understand, document and update their technology. How can they manage if they have no idea what they are managing? What arrogance that they think they can delegate this accountability and responsibility to the architects?

My advice make them all accountable for the current state and get on with strategy and future state!"

It is common sense that the business is documented by stakeholders, the very people who own the work and know most about the business. And indeed, it would be unwise to do otherwise. But that work is mostly not suitable "as-is" for integration in EA, otherwise there would not be much need for an architecture.

It is the task of the EA architect to establish the framework in which all the stakeholders' parts fit in, to specify how the EA parts look like to fit the whole, what are the missing parts, what are the design constraints, architecture principles, what are the components of EA that have to be re-used by all stakeholders, how to navigate the EA whole.

The current EA (re-)work would be done by stakeholders so that they take into account all these and deliver to the same standards; the EA architect will integrate the these parts.

Current EA is about every stakeholder documenting own work consistently in order to be able to link it to the rest of Enterprise parts in a coherent whole, so that anyone else can navigate and analyse the Enterprise.

To paraphrase Deb, I would say that an EA architect would be indeed arrogant, not to accept the duty to integrate and model the current EA

After all, EA is Architecture, a blueprint that is used by stakeholders in different ways - operational, tactical, strategic- not only to realise Vision. For that you need the current EA before anything else.

Future or Current state EA, which one is first, Gartner cnt'd

August 31, 2010

http://www.ebizq.net/blogs/ea_matters/2010/08/future-or-current-state-ea-which-one-is-first-cntd.php

I am elevating this at the blog level since it is an important debate for many of us and well, the posts are too long for a reply. Philip replied to my latest opinion in this debate.

We agree to disagree; still, one of us is right and one is wrong, on the whole. Philip you have not answered many of my arguments though while I did try to reply to most of yours.

Philip's friend's challenge is in the current state (no job, money...). That is why he must come with a solution, a strategy that will solve the Current Situation problems. i.e. no job, no money. In this case we know well the current situation and more, the target state is only supposed to solve the current state problems, nothing else. I rather disagree with the gem that we never get to the future state. We do realise it. Buildings are architected, raised and delivered. Same with some Enterprises. The problem is that in some Enterprises, people play management and strategy "games". They come up with goals and strategies that are too vague to be implemented. But the Enterprise ignores them, for all the noise, and goes on living. In these cases, the visions are unachievable because they are not rooted in reality (current situation). They sound like "Increase the profit margins by 20%" in recession times. But how? Is it realistic? What is the situation?

I am saying that Enterprise Architecture is about the description of the Enterprise that one may use for many reasons like understanding, alignment, automation or change.

It often happens that EA is used for duplication reduction alone, as in Philip's example. It would have been much better, as Philip recommended, to include the business requirements and strategy so that EA included all factors from start because that is what makes it an Enterprise wide Architecture. But then, one should have also included the BPM automation, XSigma business improvement efforts, non-

IT technology plans...

Philip's writes about research study: "The scientific study I quoted also proved that, by considering where you are BEFORE considering where you want to be you will LIMIT your future target state. I'm not quite so certain I understand your reference as it's not explicitly focused upon making decisions based upon an unfettered future state versus creating a future based upon today's limitations."

I prefer not to rely on psychological research alone. That science is like EA. It has a long way to go. As I have mentioned, it was also discovered that nine years olds are ready to live in society. As a result of this, some people may behave like that the rest of their life.

In short I disagree with the research. Of course, one has to LIMIT the vision to one achievable from current situation. Otherwise the friend might have a vision of becoming the CEO of a hedge fund or win the Lotto, rather than getting a good job. He probably does that as I do. But do I count on it happening? More, the progress to that Vision should be measurable from the current situation so that we can see where we are.

I listened to a similar argument where people said that an EA framework would Limit their ability to the EA job. Well TOGAF does that, I agree. But in that case, any knowledge would limit your ability to perform in the future since it will train you to respond in specific ways. That does not mean you have to remain ignorant and start from scratch.

My research reference, in response to Philip's, concluded that a child that makes a deliberate decision to postpone achieving his desires (vision) in order to study and discover would achieve and reap the benefits later. That is the child is aware of the current situation, improves on it rather than jumping to vision. The child builds on his current capabilities. And that sounds true. But it may as relevant as that other research is.

If you create a vision of your Enterprise, that ignores the reality of your current Enterprise, you may end up with no Enterprise, most probably. And the business would never agree to this. You may have elements in the future state that are not in the current state. Starting from the current state is an evolutionary approach; beginning with the vision and stopping the current EA is a revolutionary approach that in fact may build an entirely new Enterprise.

This future state first approach is somewhat typical of IT that always wishes to jump to a new technology abandoning the last mess behind. But the business needs to keep the ball rolling no matter what technology.

The Enterprise Architecture entry in Wikipedia (i)

Feb 5, 2012

http://www.ebizq.net/blogs/ea_matters/2012/02/enterprise-architecture-entry-in-wikipedia.php

Here is a hearty LinkedIn debate about the Enterprise Architecture entry in Wikipedia. I'll comment only the outcome, the Wikipedia entry itself. It is informative indeed, but how useful is it in practice to you? Ultimately, I found it as good as the definitions quoted in the entry, which, in any case, have to be widely sanctioned materials.

The EA according to Gartner:

"Enterprise architecture (EA) is the process of translating business vision and strategy into effective enterprise change by creating, communicating and improving the key requirements, principles and models that describe the enterprise's future state and enable its evolution."

For a long time now, enterprises have had some kind of process in place to achieve vision and strategy, without employing EA. Not that the EA could not have a major contribution to this process.

 EA it's not about strategy and target enterprise alone, it is about documenting the current state. Can you ignore the technology, processes and organisation already in place in the specification of the target state and strategy? You need first to draw the picture of the current enterprise in order to specify an evolutionary path for your enterprise, rather than a revolutionary one that starts from scratch. This definition encourages practitioners to ignore the current enterprise state documentation.

According to MIT CISR:

 "Enterprise architecture is the organizing logic for business processes and IT infrastructure reflecting the integration and standardization requirements of the company's operating model."

This definition is partial again in that it defines EA as solely a "reflection" of the Operating Model. See my previous posts on the book "EA as Strategy",

What about implementing the strategy as mentioned in the Gartner definition? Or reflecting the enterprise Business Models? Or describing the business functions and systems in their interconnections (IEEE1410...)?

This definition also reduces technology to IT.

Both definitions narrow EA, if you ask me, to solely one of its many purposes and benefits, to either translate strategy into effective change or implement the Operating Model.

Nonetheless, a definition should not solely be based on purpose because there may be more ways to achieve the same purpose. Is it sufficient to define a car as a system that transports us from point A to B? An airplane or bicycle could do the same.

Both definitions assume that you wish to change the enterprise to achieve strategy or implement the operating model, but if you don't really plan that, is there still a need for the EA?

Indeed, there is: to enhance understanding of the enterprise operation, to provide a common vocabulary for stakeholders, to efficiently inventory the enterprise assets, to enable fixes to the current operation, to analyse resources allocation to processes...

"The term enterprise architecture is used in many complimentary ways. It is used to describe both a unique business practice and the aspects of a business that are being described.

Well this is a problem, isn't it? The definitions look different, even if complementary, each describing a different application or aspect of EA. Assuming we morph the definitions together do we still get the whole EA picture? I doubt it.

Author's note: the Wikipedia entry has been changed since then.

Enterprise Architecture entry in Wikipedia (ii)

Feb 10, 2012

http://www.ebizq.net/blogs/ea_matters/2012/02/enterprise-architecture-entry-in-wikipedia-part-2.php

Cont'd.

Wikipedia: "the United States Government describes enterprise architecture as an Information Technology function. Instead of describing enterprise architecture in relation to the practice of examining an enterprise, the U.S. Government defines the term to refer to the documented results of that examination."

EA is defined here as "documented results" and again as an IT function. May I conclude that the results document the government IT? I guess, I may.

So far, so good. EA has been defined as an IT or business function, a transformation process, but also as the documentation of the enterprise IT.

Wikipedia: "Practitioners of EA call themselves enterprise architects."

Kind of obvious. Worth noting though, that taking into account the continuous growth of EA architect population, the many interpretations and the lack of proper and agreed definitions and methods becomes worrisome to say the least, for the profession as whole.

Also, "An enterprise architect is a person responsible for performing this complex analysis of business structure and processes and is often called upon to draw conclusions from the information collected".

Well, perhaps not. EAs, as I know them, have not much remit to do analysis of the business structure and processes. Most, simply live in IT, as stated. They may hack a business capability map though, for their own work, a map that business seldom or never uses.

I've seen recently advertised positions of business architects that report to IT EA architects. This anomaly comes from the continuous confusion between the desired top business status of EA and its current incarnation in IT.

Next, according to the UK National Computing Centre EA best practice guidance[7]:

"EA takes the form of a comprehensive set of cohesive models that describe the structure and functions of an enterprise... arranged in a logical manner that provides an ever-increasing level of detail about the enterprise: its objectives and goals; its processes and organization; its systems and data; the technology used and any other..."

This comes closer to what I believe a technical bare bones EA is, or at least near to what the EA name promises.

But has EA been defined as the structure of the enterprise so far? Not that I could see.

Have a look at your house architecture or town plan or any architecture for that matter. Do they look like a process to you? The architecture of your house is a set of schematics and descriptions. It does look like a blueprint to me.

EA, as any architecture, is the structure of a system and its description. It is neither about what you plan to do with it or what that process of transformation should be (even though it could be extended to cover that). It simply describes the parts and interconnections (IEEE1471, ISO/IEC 42010) as seen through various stakeholders viewpoints.

As a pleasant surprise, (see this discussion) finally the realisation has come into being that the enterprise transformation does not equal EA; it is just one of the potential use cases of EA.

Still, this revelation has to be analysed in all its consequences for the current EA approaches. What does it mean for the current frameworks like TOGAF, which is nothing else but an enterprise transformation process after all, or the widely held views (see Wikipedia entry) that EA is about strategy translation into change or even that EA is about transforming the enterprise to achieve an operating model?

I won't hold my breath though. It takes time to turn around their own cart.

Had this EA entry compilation helped the emergence of a single view, the achievement would have been remarkable but perhaps debatable yet again and, I am afraid, unadopted. As it is though, it reflects the state of the art of the EA field. Puzzling for sure and not helpful, since not even the "greats" agree.

Another observation: Zachman does not appear at all. It is worth the mention though, at least because Zachman explains best for the executive audience, in a brief table, how a system (if not an enterprise) can and should be described in a systematic way by asking the cognitive "w" questions from all development chain perspectives.

Cont'd next time... but rather than further debating the current entry I'll come with my own.

Preview:

Had I been invited to produce an Wikipedia EA entry after the desire of my heart, I would start with tabula rasa and come up with views for which I would take responsibility.

The Enterprise Architecture definition in Wikipedia (iii)

February 15, 2012

http://www.ebizq.net/blogs/ea_matters/2012/02/the-ea-definition-in-wikipedia.php

After a decade (or even two) of banging around the EA concept, there are too many egos and vested interests at play that render the process of objectively defining EA harder than it should be.

Well, reputed fora, studiously ignoring each other, came out with different definitions sometimes complementary, at other times not. The EA Wikipedia entry proves that. None of the definitions in there acknowledges the others. Most are incomplete as well.

A proper definition should reflect as close as possible the meaning of the terms it consists of, in order to avoid misleading interpretations. Currently, too many EA definitions have nothing or little to do with the terms in the name.

As long as there is no consensus, no single meaning can be attached to the EA term. Practitioners are challenging then each other, each pretending to know better. There is nothing there to help arbitrate the debate. New entrants, employers, customers and recruiters are befuddled. Not knowing what to expect they too come with their unexpected expectations. The modus operandi for an EA architect is "Trust me, I know what I am doing". The one with more commercial clout, reputation or self confidence wins. In practice, the definition can be and is hijacked by the strongest players.

Let's go back to the beginnings to come with a definition and avoid the politics of EA. Let's assume we do not know what EA is and just look again at the words in the definition.

Rephrasing it, the EA is the Architecture of the Enterprise, I said it long ago and others have said it since.

While the expression is somewhat tautological, the definition suggests the decoupling of the concept of Enterprise from that of Architecture, against the tendency to morph them together and attach new unrelated meanings.

Then the logical way to define EA is to join the definitions of its two terms. This should be the reverse process of the initial naming of EA.

Simplifying a bit, if we equate architecture with the structure of a system and its blueprint, our commonly accepted view outside EA (the architecture of our house, the map of the town...), then

the EA is the structure and the blueprint of the enterprise.

Currently, many EA definitions often emphasise only one of the many purposes of this EA rather than describing what EA itself is. Not that that is wrong but it's narrowing the field leaving space for many other definitions. As such you may define a car by saying that you use it for driving to the office or to transport your farm product.

Similarly, you can use EA to implement strategy, business models, operating models... but these are just EA use cases.

We may aggregate all these purpose definition viewpoints together as long as the definition is logical and proper as above.

Say that EA is a reflection of the Business Model (BM) for instance. We could qualify this as an Enterprise BM Architecture viewpoint describing the business model alone. After all we have many other EA viewpoints such as operating model, ITIL, reporting, infrastructure architectures...

The critique of illuminated opinions on EA and frameworks (Deloitte)

Oct 1, 2010

http://www.ebizq.net/blogs/ea_matters/2010/10/the-critique-of-illuminated-opinions-on-enterprise-architecture-and-frameworks.php

Deloitte initiated, some time ago, a debate on "Does Cloud Computing Make Enterprise Architecture Irrelevant?" asserting that "*The world of business technology is shifting to "almost enterprise" applications - a network of smaller, more agile applications that are often hosted remotely, as in cloud computing. With less reliance on massive, monolithic enterprise solutions, it's tempting to think that the hard work of creating a sustainable enterprise architecture (EA) is also behind us. So, as many companies make the move to cloud computing, they anticipate leaving behind a lot of the headaches of EA.*"

It looks like Deloitte has its own definitions on the Cloud and EA. Unfortunately, not only professionals but reputed consultancies diverge in their opinions on EA a lot. Take for instance Gartner with their EA hypecycle where they crammed more "technologies" that we ever cared about, announcing the dawn of a new EA era only they know about. Gartner also seems to associate EA to strategic planning alone; but EA is much more. Or SOA guru David Linthicum saying that SOA equals   EA.

For Deloitte the cloud means the move "to smaller or more agile applications as opposed to massive, monolithic enterprise solutions". Deloitte also states that "we're outsourcing our EA headaches. No more having to manage the underlying IT infrastructure, operating systems and software patches".

For them EA appears to mean the management of IT systems. Coming from a reputed company like Deloitte, this adds to the profusion of confusion in the EA field. Most professionals would be surprised at that, since there were many definitions for EA but none like this, to my knowledge.

The truth is that the Cloud means outsourcing IT resources while the EA describes them to a relevant degree, no matter how large they are or who owns them. So we do not get rid or outsource EA with the Cloud. But IT and its management does part with the Enterprise, when in the Cloud.

The Cloud is about outsourcing your IT while EA is about discovering, documenting, and roadmapping your Enterprise to achieve its goals. EA is much more than IT management, outsourcing or architecture. You need EA even more when you don't have the outsourced systems expertise in house. You need the EA schema to make them work over the Cloud.

Now, moving on at ZapThink considerations on The beginning of the end for enterprise architecture frameworks. I haven' realised that ZapThink professes in the EA arena unless you consider SOA to be EA.

Again, EA is the discipline to describe your Enterprise so that you can control and plan it to achieve objectives. Enterprise wide SOA is about services, that is structuring your Enterprise on services. In short, SOA is mainly about services while EA is about the Enterprise blueprint. SOA, for most, is still an IT integration technology. It has no method attached and it does not aim to describe the Enterprise. SOA fails without the envelope of a proper EA framework and without business support and knowledge to organize the business as services.

That being said, I believe like ZapThink that the current EA frameworks are obsolete. I sadly learn how many people think they do EA using Zachman or TOGAF. But these frameworks leaves us short when it comes to describing the current and future states of the Enterprise.

DODAF though, incomplete and too specialised as it is, maybe a different matter.

Zachman is not a method or a framework. It's not even an ontology because it does not describe the elements of an Enterprise in their relationship. In fact, it refers little or at all to an Enterprise. It applies to any system. It has appeal to management because management often asks Zachman's questions to appraise an effort but do they ever apply the framework?

The lawsuit between Zachman and its former partner is of consequence in the sense that the "framework" is in the public domain, at least I thought so. That may raise questions about other public domain work. But, perhaps, too many borrow too liberally copyrighted information.

TOGAF is mostly a long story of classical proportions that few read given the propensity for reading these days. It makes an engineer or any structured mind for that matter, cringe. It pays to be certified, at least because you avoid reading the stuff and you enter the realm of EA architects, on paper. TOGAF mentions the known EA layers inside the process (?), and then ploughs on with random and unrelated detail. It is mostly IT despite other claims and as such of little relevance at the Enterprise level.

TOGAF does not even try to describe the components (or capabilities) of an Enterprise. It leaves that to us. How about having to describe, change and improve a system (like a bike) being given solely a process (TOGAF) or a way of thinking (Zachman) but no information about its component parts (no. of wheels, chain, speeds frame...)? Do we come to same or similar results?

After all, despite variations, most Enterprises are similar. There should be a root Enterprise schema that should be the core of the Framework.

Nevertheless, to conclude from here, as ZapThink does, that the EA frameworks are "at the beginning of the end" is hazardous, in particular when this is followed by a proposal to train and certify you the reader in their "down to earth", architect course.

But it is true that many EA architects work for too long to define own frameworks or limit themselves to listing, describing, reviewing and roadmapping the IT technology and solutions, all business as usual IT work.

In the end, yes, there is a veiled EA framework crisis because there already are so many EA architects that have no body of knowledge to do proper EA work. How can we classify them collectively as EA architects? Well, TOGAF, Zachman and variations play that role for now, with known results . We have to change that even though this is not an academic matter any longer since large vested commercial interests are already in play.

The question is for us if we do need an EA framework. Yes, we do because the framework embodies, in a structured manner, the long experience of the many of us and our companies. For those having worked in a consultancy, you know how many EA case studies piled up in the library and how little pattern discovery work has been done on them to uncover a framework.

The framework saves a lot of effort and costs since it leaves the architect focus on own Enterprise issues. It makes the EA development predictable and repeatable. And ensures that professionals are certified against a single standard.

"Enterprise Architecture as Strategy" book, is it about EA?

Dec 14, 2011

http://it.toolbox.com/blogs/ea-matters/enterprise-architecture-as-strategy-book-is-it-about-ea-49744

I browsed the book "Enterprise Architecture as Strategy" by Jeanne W. Ross, Peter Weill and David C. Robertson quite a few times, never quite making my mind about it. It is widely recommended though. But since it landed on the next desk, I decided to take the bull by the horns.

The book has an attractive title consisting of catchy buzz words like Enterprise Architecture and Strategy. The name conveys to me the idea that developing EA should be an enterprise strategy in itself. Which I agree with since the EA is the only way an Enterprise can consistently execute the strategy.

Quoting from the book, "EA is the organizing logic for core business processes and IT infrastructure reflecting the standardisation and integration of a company's operating model. ...EA boils down to these two concepts: business process integration and business process standardisation", page VIII.

So far, so good. Really?

The book appears to assume that the purpose of EA is the development of a company's Operating Model (OM). Well, this is a rather narrow view, in my opinion, since the Operating Model is just one aim of many of the EA transformation. The purpose of EA is much greater than the achievement of an Enterprise Operating Model. EA makes possible the implementation of new Products and Markets and in general of the Business Strategy as, in fact, stated in the title. EA is about providing a framework for strategy execution, decision making and investment...

EA is also a method of systematic description of the Enterprise and its organization logic. But there is little mention of that in the book. Without the Enterprise description, one can hardly think about standardisation and integration through which the desired Operating Model is realised.

Also architecture alone, as an organization logic, is not only reflecting integration and standardisation, but also grouping, encapsulation, service orientation,... aspects not really mentioned in the book. Besides, Standardisation and Integration alone barely render the EA business case positive.

In the Quadrant, the Operating Model is expressed, in terms of Business Process Integration and Business Process Standardisation but not in terms of technology and data, even though technology and data Integration and Standardisation are discussed later on - as they should be. EA though is not only about the organizing logic of Business Processes and IT (the book does not seem to refer to any other technology except IT) but also about people organization and its alignment, at least in my view. This is little mentioned.

The book abounds in examples of business transformations that realise various Operating Models. That is good. But have these transformations been executed by EA efforts?

EA should support all enterprise transformations, not only OM, and also the goals of every stakeholder in the enterprise. For instance, the Operations to fix defects, the

Development team to create new products, the Programmes to manage consistently projects in a portfolio, the business teams to improve processes... Well, the book does not cover these EA aspects.

There is not much advice on how to achieve the target Operating Model except the process band in the Operating Model core diagrams, that is sketchy. Ultimately, various (EA) methods could be employed to achieve the result. There is not much mention though of any other EA framework; how can one use Zachman for instance, TOGAF or any others, to implement the Operating Model of choice?

The book does not talk about Value Streams or Enterprise Capabilities either, both quite common in process improvement and EA developments today.

Moreover, it does not relate much or at all to Porter's Value Chain, a well known business analysis concept. As for example, would an enterprise Value Chain look different for various Operating Models?

Equally critical for the company, if not more so, are the current and target business models since they show how the enterprise delivers value to customers and returns profit to stakeholders. Well, business models are not discussed. But Business Models are very different in nature from Operating Models.

"Enterprise Architecture as Strategy" book, is it about EA?

Dec 28, 2011

http://it.toolbox.com/blogs/ea-matters/enterprise-architecture-as-strategy-book-is-it-about-ea-cntd-49796

The Operating Model (OM) strategy does not really apply to each and every company but to those which are geographically distributed and consist of a few similar business units. For most companies though Integration and Standardisation are architectural dictates, no matter the Operating Model.

The Unification OM may not be the ideal target state for many enterprises; it depends on the type of business the enterprise is in. For McDonalds, for instance, where the same/similar products are delivered in many outlets around the world, the ideal OM state could be Replication. The truth is that for many other companies a mixture of these Operating Models would apply. If the company is thought to be only temporarily part of the portfolio of the mother company there will be no integration with the rest of the family of companies.

Anyway, currently, the enterprise support services are typically shared these days by the divisions of an enterprise often called as such Shared Services. In effect, Unification already applies to most enterprise support services. But even in this case - take for instance for IT - services (or part of them) may still be replicated for each business unit for greater response and accountability.

Most companies achieve the Operating Model that is natural to their type of operation early in their lifecycle, without engaging in an EA effort.

It is also rather hard to believe that an EA architect, working in IT, would impose or even propose an operating model since this is essentially a business issue and decision.

The Operating Models core diagrams in the book are not really intuitive for an architect, at least because an architect would expect very different notations from an EA blueprint.

About the EA maturity model phases.

1. "Business Silos architecture" is the typical, current and initial state of an Enterprise transformation.

2. "Standardised Technology architecture" is not mentioned in the Operating Model quadrant. But should technology standardisation be happening before process standardisation? One first needs to discover and standardise the current processes then design and standardise the technology. Also, many processes can be standardised or executed by people, independent of technology. In the book it is stated that "EA is not an IT issue- it's a business issue" (page VIII). Still technology is the first transformation stage.

3. "Optimized Core architecture"; it looks to me though that "optimization" means more than process "standardisation".

4. "Business Modularity architecture"; modularity is not mentioned in the Operating Model at all; in fact, it may add another dimension to the OM quadrant - which may become a cube. Does this final state guarantees that the target Operating Model has been achieved? In fact, is there a connection between the Operating Model and the EA maturity stages model?

To summarise:

The book conveys little information on EA. It is limited to a discussion on the Operating Model which may be implemented by an EA or otherwise. The book should have been more properly called "The Operating Model as Strategy".

It is not a book for IT or EA for that matter. It is describing the Operating Model but as we are already used to, in isolation from all the other business concepts such as Value Chains, Value Streams, Business Models... The book rides on the popularity of the EA concept to introduce the Operating Model concept and the EA maturity cycle that are little related. The simplicity of its view greatly appeals to business readers though.

Were I to express the book in one picture I would choose the Operating Model Quadrant as I would chose the Matrix for Zachman and the ADM circle for TOGAF.

To paraphrase:

"EA is the organizing logic for core business processes and IT infrastructure reflecting" a lot more than "the standardisation and integration of a company's operating model..." "EA boils down to" much more than "two concepts: business process integration and business process standardisation". EA also "boils down to" managing complexity (simplification, reduction in duplication, streamlining processes...), alignment of technology to business operation and service orientation that enables agility and as such rapid business change.

In the end, like most other readers, I would recommend the book for the Operating Model concept but not for Enterprise Architecture.

IAF, Integrated Architecture Framework, analysis

May 22, 2009

http://it.toolbox.com/blogs/ea-matters/iaf-integrated-architecture-framework-analysis-31784

"Capgemini has been developing its own architecture approach that covers business, information and technology since 1993". Quote from Cap's web site. Here it is, IAF. As I studied the IAF I discovered that the E2AF framework looks similar.

While I won't copy the IAF picture in here, for copyright reasons, I will refer to it. You might open the URL above in another window.

What I want to understand is how it works and how it compares to other frameworks.

IAF reminds me of Zachman's because of a sub-set of its questions. They are shown as two dimensional thin bands crossing the rest of the framework's tri-dimensional elements, horizontally. The picture also shows us the four standard layers, found in any EA, in Spewak's work and later in TOGAF. The layers are not positioned top down, but from left to right and crossed by Zachman's questions, as thin bands.

Hence, the "What", "How", "With What" question bands cross

Business, Information, Information Systems and Technology Infrastructure layers forming a Matrix framework.

The "What" question is subtitled "Conceptual". I can see little association though. In Zachman's the two are different dimensions.

Zachman's "What" means, debatably, Information, for most practitioners. But Information is already another layer in IAF. So "What" does not mean Information in IAF.

As the question is applied to all layers it appears that a conceptual architecture is required for each layer.

The next question, "How" is associated with "Logical". Not that it matters a lot but it may confuse you since Logical and How, in Zachman's, are on different axes.

The "How" is again applied to all layers meaning probably four Logical architectures.

Does it make sense? At least, they would have to be aligned. I would have thought that a single logical architecture for the Enterprise suffices.

"With what" or "Physical", the 3rd question is a new dimension for Zachman. But "With what", to my mind, looks like pointing to the technology resources implementing the Business layer. That creates a problem: we already have the Technology Infrastructure and Information Systems layers. So, what is the meaning then?

I believe that the aim was to describe each EA layer in terms of concept, logic and physical, but layers don't exist as independent systems. They exist only in the context of one system, the Enterprise. Hence, I would say that a single conceptual and logical architecture would do for the Enterprise. The questions dimension then is unnecessary.

The "Information Systems" layer probably denotes mostly "Applications layer" because of the potential overlap with the "Technology Infrastructure" layer.

Security and Governance architectures have a three-dimensional body, unlike the question bands, but like them they extend the length of the layers.

But, if we have Security, we might like to have other views like Finance, Real Estate etc. Later.

The "Why" band is floating on top of the framework, touching nothing. In its isolation, it looks like it's posing the question "Why are we doing this?" at all levels.

All in all, I think IAF looks good for customers. It attempts to combine the goods of a few approaches. By using Zachman terms with different meanings it confused me though. I can see duplication between the "With what" and the IT (Information System and Technology) layers.

The question bands suggest Conceptual, Logical and Physical views at each layer which looks good but unnecessary as we have one single system, the Enterprise. If you remove the question bands, what is left is the four layers architecture we all know, which is still good.

All is well when it ends well!

THE STATE OF ENTERPRISE ARCHITECTURE AND ITS FUTURE

The state of Enterprise Architecture

Mar 5, 2007

http://it.toolbox.com/blogs/ea-matters/the-state-of-enterprise-architecture-14863

"Enterprise Architecture (EA) has promised a thorough transformation of the business world by aligning IT to business, improving investment and Enterprise planning, streamlining enterprise operations and documenting the company blueprint to enhance understanding, measurement and management of its operation. Although EA has been around for some time now, it's take off has been rather modest or inconsequential. But what are the factors hindering the EA adoption or its success?" Moreover, how can we overcome them?

I began this series of posts some time ago with the intent of analysing the EA key challenges. But the more I looked into it, the more I discovered that the roadblocks to EA success were more serious than I thought. So serious that they do explain why the EA has not taken off as forecasted. Nevertheless, we can do something about it both at a theoretical and at a program specific level. The future is not so gloomy after all that effort we all put in!

One of the first discoveries, not surprising though, was that the problem starts with the confusion in the EA definition, scope and frameworks. It is not clear or agreed what EA is, what it covers or what a framework should look like.

Furthermore, EA is surrounded by excessive hype and information overload from companies and individuals quickly jumping the hype bandwagon. This has created an equal strong rejection from the part of business for lack of comprehension of what it is, how it delivers and lack of trust in results.

IT is one of the significant business innovation factors but the practice of IT department of initiating and leading the EA developments, has done little to help, and even worse, has little chance to achieve the stated EA benefits since, simply put, the business workings or the organization charts cannot be readily changed by IT.

The reality is that in many cases the EA ends up with a few large IT applications diagrams, an infrastructure inventory and a few data definitions. Looking even from the IT stakeholders' perspectives, there is either too much or too little information for many of them: where are the firewall, email, IP telephony, call centre, DW/BI, B2B, BC, content management etc architectures needed by stakeholders?

After all, most Enterprises were created without a blueprint, have grown organically and have been working better or worse, ever since. With the advent of EA, too often the IT has the task of specifying the EA, part of which is the business architecture, the determining part of an EA, which has never been specified or documented. In fact, is this an IT task?

In the end, it is ultimately upon the business people to finish the business architecture task, that is, to document processes, business data, strategy and risks, because this is their core competency. This is not happening because business has few stakes in the EA process. More, people, part of and the weak link of most processes should be represented and organization should be re-aligned to the core business activities to provide ownership and responsibility.

Unless the EA is initiated by management and bought-in by business, there is little chance of IT succeeding, in isolation. The Enterprise architecture should be driven top down, cascaded to IT layers and not the other way around.

The roadblocks take place at every phase of the EA lifecycle, from inception to the Enterprise transformation execution, EA usage and maintenance. In the next few posts, I will blog a while about

- Defining and scoping the EA (is it a blueprint, program, plan, strategic planning...?)
- The relationship to other Enterprise programs (we are already doing SOA...)
- Definition and utilization of frameworks (how to choose one!)
- Stakeholders' participation (how to give them what they need!)
- Proper Enterprise transformation planning and execution (Best Practices)
- EA maintenance mechanisms (compliance team...) to make the EA last.

Enterprise Architecture - what's in store for it?

Jan 4, 2008

http://it.toolbox.com/blogs/ea-matters/enterprise-architecture-whats-in-store-for-it-21532

This looks like a legitimate question at the beginning of the renewal cycle of the new year, 2008. Is Enterprise Architecture going anywhere? It is, albeit slowly in the absence of an agreed practical framework and clear proof of its business case. The reason is straightforward: EA is a necessary "evil". Any system needs a blueprint enabling proper operation, maintenance, planning... To fulfil the expectations, EA needs to satisfy its many stakeholders in top management, business, technology/IT and organization. Here are a few trends, I can see, Enterprise Architecture progressing, in no particular order:

The EA evolves to increasingly cover business architecture rather than IT alone; the Enterprise Architecture will be the result of the fusion of IT, Business and Organization/People architectures; what is the value of an applications architecture, without the process it implements or the people operating it? EA will finally be recognized as a business discipline as well, having incorporated Value Chains, Business Models, Strategic Planning...

The governance for EA will be more & more business and top management heavy; this is because it would be used in mapping the strategy to components, to derive the enterprise transformation portfolio, make investments and take strategic and tactical decisions.

The EA development will be increasingly triggered by Mergers & Acquisitions and outsourcing activities; IT BPO, SaaS(ASP) outsourcing is riding a strong current right now.

The Enterprise Architect would be more and more called in the business decision making process; that is because the EA architect deals with the business logic, technology operation and strategy, is able to understand both worlds and use both business and IT vocabularies.

A combined EA framework emerges to take advantage of the strengths of various frameworks, such as Zachman, TOGAF, FEA and others.

SOA is recognized as part of the EA program as the target EA style of architecture and technology, rather than executed in isolation as it often happens

EA would be increasingly required by

shareholders/owners/investors to provide the blueprint of the business operation to describe assets, provide proof of regulatory compliance, map costs and profits on various operations and align strategy. Exactly like the US government demands it for the public sector. Would EA become a regulatory feature for public listed companies?

Well, there is another possibility that springs to mind, after all: the EA team, having failed to satisfy it stakeholders is gradually disbanded to man more tactical efforts. Would this happen?

The state of EA 2009

Jan 8, 2009

http://it.toolbox.com/blogs/ea-matters/the-state-of-ea-2009-29155

At the beginning of the new year, let me recap the situation of EA or SOA for that matter. Anything to be merry about?

Here is a point of view, in brief:

Overall, EA looks like business as usual. In fact, little really happened in the field for years now. Nothing of true value was added since Zachman's table and TOGAF. No substance was added.

Except that, in this void, certifications offerings are getting a foothold.

An external observer would say that people are satisfied with the state of the art, the methods, the frameworks, the results. I cannot speak for others; speaking for myself I would say "no way".

Since there is no academic or an agreed definition for an EA framework, many fora and companies have come with their own views that cover just aspects of the Enterprise, in various depths. For instance, some cover the development process; others, the business process map; some add stakeholders' views.

We often have to ask questions like: how do we map business strategy? Why is the human component "people" left out? How do we align organization, process and technology? What are the key artefacts?

Even though it is clear for everybody now that EA should cover business architecture, there is no agreement on what that is in the first place. Secondly the business side, pushed by IT, seldom buys into the concept of business architecture. They deal with Value Chains.

Since no major contribution has advanced the cause, most people wait and see, hoping for a miracle breakthrough.

People technically still use the four layers paradigm: business, information, applications and technology in various combinations sometimes adding the strategy view. Even so, each layer is described differently by different people.

The layers are poorly interconnected since there is no navigation between them. Sometimes, to compensate, architects add matrices of application interconnections, mappings of applications to technology systems, processes to applications etc. The mappings matrices are not intuitive and become out of synch rather easy.

I believe that a "standard" metamodel would be a cure; it would help jump start the EA framework evolution again. A metamodel would describe key artefacts in layers, their entities and dependencies. In other words, it would describe an EA framework in practical terms, would provide the EA vocabulary and clearly scope the basic EA. The metamodel will be the key structure for EA development, additions and tool.

EA remains confined in the space of IT where it is slowly depreciating since the business people have no incentive to use it. In fact they would prefer to outsource IT altogether as a too costly and troublesome distraction. They would like a clean contractual relationship to a rather chaotic cross boundary continuous debate with IT.

Business expects the EA to describe the Enterprise operation, which is not the case and as such ceases to employ the EA. The Enterprise operation is partly described sometimes by process maps and improved by frameworks as Six/Lean Sigma, but they still seem to remain independent approaches.

Yet, everybody agrees that EA is necessary despite its performance in terms of results and usage.

Enterprise Architecture and its state

Jul 5, 2009

http://it.toolbox.com/blogs/ea-matters/enterprise-architecture-and-its-state-31979

From time to time it is worth assessing the progress of Enterprise Architecture body of knowledge. Not much has happened in the past few years.

It was said SOA is dead or at least the hype. With the EA the problem is no better. It is barely moving. No remarkable results have been published. Most use own frameworks because the EA frameworks are what they are. But EA has yet a lot to deliver since the concept is very promising.

Zachman covers a high level philosophy, Socratic in that it asks various questions to define an entity. It is called sometimes an ontology or taxonomy. It is not practical, it does not take us too far. After asking the first few questions, the road ahead is too open to interpretation. There is no more guidance. It is appealing in its simplicity to top management as it enables an executive's analytical approach. But, at the next level of depth, another framework is required.

TOGAF covers extensively the process and its deliveries, ADM. Its technology standards chapter is said to be obsolete. TOGAF 9 adds a few hundred pages, some structure and Archimate, an architecture language which looks more like a metamodel. People are looking hard for examples because it is not clear how to use it. It introduces services and interfaces although most Enterprises, having evolved organically, cannot be described using the service concept. And that does not help TOGAF.

Neither of these frameworks is specific to the Enterprise, i.e. they can be applied to most technical systems. As such they can be called Architecture rather than EA frameworks.

Zachman covers a high level taxonomy while TOGAF a process. In a sense they are complementary. None of them provides guidance for the structure of an Enterprise which is essential for an EA framework.

As a result no two EAs outcomes are similar. Everybody pretends to know Zachman and TOGAF. It's easy to pretend to be an EA architect as Zachman's matrix is a straightforward one pager while few can verify that an answer is compliant or not with 800 pages of TOGAF.

FEA and DODAF are more prescriptive but specific. And even so no two departments EA look or feel quite the same.

EA frameworks should enforce repeatable or predictable results so that even if you build your EA in two different Enterprises in the same industry, they should still have the same fundamental structure and components. So you can compare apples with apples.

Some have delivery checklists but architecture is about diagrams not lists.

No framework offers reference designs (templates), not even for IT, except, maybe, for the old model-view-controller paradigm for software.

As with SOA, the first step is to design the EA Business Architecture. It is not the business of IT, in the first place, but IT understands "architecture".

The business schools, academia, management consultancies have not quite put together a business reference map to guide the architecture. What are the typical parts of an Enterprise? You would wonder why they don't need an EA in their work.

There are a few tries though at process architectures. (APQC, VCG, SCOR, eTOM...). They do not help too much though. They are virtually unknown in the IT domain. They are used by business people for benchmarking and quality improvement. The Value Chain concept, the closest attempt to an architecture in the business world, looks foreign to the IT world.

How can you build an Enterprise Architecture (essentially the Enterprise structure, operation and strategic planning) starting from technology, IT for that matter?

Imagine an electricity utility company that has other technologies. How can the EA IT architecture describe what the Enterprise does? It can catalogue the IT landscape and document front-ends, back-ends etc. But there are networks of transformers, transmission lines, couplers, switches, meters, SCADA systems not part of IT. Not to mention the people operations.

The natural expectations of business and management from the current EA i.e. to deliver the Enterprise blueprint, roadmap, transformation are far from being fulfilled then. The solution would be to limit the expectations to technology standardisation, reduced platform duplication and complexity and integration of the islands of IT.

To succeed, in its full meaning of structure and operation of the Enterprise, the EA has to be started top down from the business architecture in scope (for instance for the Operation or Shared Services) and then the supporting technology architecture. But the division between business and IT does not help.

The state of EA at the debut of 2011

Jan , 2011

http://www.ebizq.net/blogs/ea_matters/2011/01/the-state-of-enterprise-architecture-at-tge-debut-of-2011.php

At the beginning of the new year, let me recap again the situation of EA. Anything to be merry about?

Overall, EA looks like it always did. Little really happened in the field. No substance was added since Zachman and TOGAF. Except that, in this void, various trainings and certifications offerings are getting a foothold.

Since there is no academic or agreed definition for EA or its framework, many fora, individuals and companies have come with their own views that usually cover aspects of rather than the whole of Enterprise Architecture.

We still have to ask basic questions like: what is the purpose of EA, is it about strategy and change or about complexity management or...? How does EA achieve business alignment or support strategy? How does EA enable decisions and investment making activities? What are the key EA artefacts?

Since no major contribution has advanced the cause, most people wait and see, hoping for a miracle breakthrough.

An external observer would say that people are satisfied with the state of the art, methods, frameworks and especially with the results. That may be true only because expectations have been adjusted low.

EA is mostly seen as an IT discipline having more to do with IT strategy and target state rather than anything else. Typical work involves solution architecture reviews and IT roadmapping. The EA professional issues architecture principles, technology guidelines and creates applications, technology, connection inventories and eventually a business capability map. Architects are expected to know TOGAF, typical IT systems and quite often specific technologies.

People technically still use the good old four layers paradigm: business, information, applications and technology in various combinations. Even so, each layer is described differently by different people. Navigation between them is rather difficult since there is no overall framework to interconnect the layers. Good metamodels that help appeared though. Sometimes, to compensate for the lack of navigation, architects add matrices of application interconnections, tables of applications mapping to technology systems etc. The mappings matrices are not intuitive and become out of synch rather soon.

Even though it is clear for everybody now that EA should cover business architecture, there is no agreement on what that is in the first place. Business expects the EA to describe the Enterprise operation, which is not the case in today's EA that describes systems and technology alone. Business mostly deals with process maps, process improvement methods (BPM, xSigma...) and Value Chains analysis which are seldom part of EA. So why should anybody outside IT bother with EA?

It is also trendy to talk about business modelling but business models mean not business architecture.

Every EA development experience looks different. Without reference, architects treasure their own findings as a competitive advantage and share little. Every EA outcome is different, hard to compare.

As such, without definition, reference and guidance, the architect job description and selection criteria vary widely; the field is gradually invaded by people who think that's the title sounds good, certainly pays well enough and requires nothing concrete. Paying lip service to TOGAF gets one there. Certifications surely help. Nevertheless, stakeholders don't get to see an EA but they don't expect it any longer. In the end, EA diminishes.

The good news is that everybody still agrees that EA, in concept, as the architecture of the Enterprise, is still necessary despite its performance in terms of results and usage.

EA goes through the trough of disillusionment

May 2, 2011

http://www.ebizq.net/blogs/ea_matters/2011/05/enterprise-architecture-1.php

Enterprise Architecture goes through the trough of disillusionment.

There is confusion about its definition, scope, frameworks and deliverables.

In the main, EA is an IT discipline aiming to document the Enterprise, reduce duplication in process and platforms, integrate, standardise and roadmap them.

Still we talk about different things when we refer to EA because we have different definitions; thus we have endless debates, misunderstandings and we deliver different artefacts.

Recruitment goes wrong: how can one recruit an EA if there is no consensus on what an architect does or needs to deliver?

Business Architects are often recruited to do the job of a business analyst but there is still no agreed definition for business architecture.

The EA architect has to have structured mind willing and capable to analyse systems and discover patterns. And wide expertise in business and IT. But existing web 2.0 social media lowers the barriers of entry for many who speak business and IT platitudes in order to enter the EA world. As such, there are many EA architects and few Enterprise Architectures.

But EA, in time, becomes increasingly a must. Enterprises acquire companies; many are organised as functional silos. There is often duplication in products, processes and people. Projects duplicate platforms. We buy new applications that often duplicates existing functionality and offer standard processes rather than what the business really wants. A car or a system without a schematics and fiddled with would becomes progressively unknown and unstable as our enterprises do. The knowledge is in people's minds. EA does provide this needed documentation of

Enterprise knowledge.

To move on the Gartner hype cycle the EA needs:

- Single definition and scope

- An agreed framework

- Templates/reference models for business and technology

architectures

*A trusted organization that provides impartiality and leadership in defining these by analysing and selecting from existing frameworks

Critique of the Enterprise Architecture state

Jun 13, 2012

http://www.ebizq.net/blogs/ea_matters/2012/06/currently-there-are-too-many.php

Currently, there are too many EA frameworks that crowd the EA field, too many development approaches, too many insufficient metamodels... and too many parties that claim to hold the truth.

Since the approaches or parties have little in common they bewilder the practitioners. You will find that anybody can challenge everybody on what they do and how they do EA. And no judge of that. There is little consensus as a result of that. But nobody has taken a systematic approach to sift through the many approaches. There is no credible body for that. Well, there should be, so that we don't end up with many species of EA especially those that challenge each other.

The few leading contenders in the field seldom acknowledge each other if at all. And the existing frameworks do not deliver, at least not to common expectations.

Even when a body claims success the results are not available for confidentiality reasons they say. How can one judge then the validity of the claim?

The EA terminology (EA, framework, method, process, practice, ontology, taxonomy, function...), which has never been established in the first place, is still stirring sterile debates.

I finished a TOGAF course without being given the definition of EA. It was like I was taught TOGAF rather than EA. Many cadres have no EA practical experience but were chosen for their ability to teach in related fields alone which is good enough up to a point.

So many are expertly preaching EA now. The heavy use of the social media clouds the atmosphere. Obviously, these are not professional discussion fora. Debates have little purpose or scope.

Discourses take easy advantage of fora's lack of etiquette or regulation. Rules of engagement hardly exist. Statements cannot be verified. The "trust me" attitude prevails. The louder is the most convincing and successful at that. Nobody is hold responsible for a statement. As such, why not be controversial? Lack of accountability is the heart of the evil.

Since more often than not, an audience is not able to make an own judgment, it relies on the reputation of a participant or of the institution it represents. However many of these institutions had no contributions to the field and individual standing is based more on who has given them credit.

Overt self-marketing is well and alive. Those who can are supporting own frameworks.

There are practitioners that will tell you that that there is no best framework- the message for you is that only their own experience makes the EA work.

That EA is about strategy. EA enable it but it is much more than strategy.

That you have to collect requirements. You don't really. EA would synchronize the many enterprise projects which in turn would have to collect requirements. But the EA itself has to correlate and help implement the architecture principles, vision and strategy rather than collect requirements.

That the EA, method or framework depends from case to case. But there can be only one enterprise architecture no matter how you represent it and many ways to employ it to better the enterprise.

The Enterprise Architecture black hole

Apr 6, 2009

http://it.toolbox.com/blogs/ea-matters/the-enterprise-architecture-black-hole-30936

I would look now at the dark side of EA to regal that hidden audience just lurking under the surface, keen to express their distress with the EA state of art.

"Enterprise Architecture as a Black Hole" (to paraphrase a known title of an EA book) seems to be a proper name for many EA contemporary developments. To business, EA certainly looks like that. It sucks resources and energy and returns naught.

To IT, the EA often means an IT applications and technology architecture discovery and design exercise. No more than that. But, since long, IT appended to its technology the "Enterprise" denomination to demonstrate it can be used anywhere inside. But that created false expectations for business and other stakeholders.

Zachman, while developing the framework, initially for IT systems, extended it to the Enterprise. So people expect all the benefits of an Enterprise level architecture as opposed to those of an Enterprise level technology like JAVA, EAI, ESB... This mismatch between expectations and deliveries may ruin the EA prospects, in time.

I have surveyed the EA field for years now and I have to say that the state of affairs is bleak. We have pretty much the same few frameworks we had years ago, with a few twists. The EA scope can be anything you like.

The trouble is we have more EA architects and developments than ever. Are the EA developments fruitful? What do they deliver in fact? What keeps the architects busy? Do they feel secure?

What does an EA architect use for a framework?

Essentially, there are two schools of thought.

One, indeed, appears philosophical, looking into the approach to the discovery and design of a system. The EA architects like true Socrates' disciples, start asking questions like Why, What, How, Who, Where and combinations like Where is Who? Where is What? Who makes what? or who knows what or maybe who's who. The answers though, constituting the basis for the Enterprise artefacts, may have such a variability that is hard to forecast what you get. You are left on your own, with little guidance, soon after asking the questions. No two answers look similar.

Nevertheless, the management likes the questions as they convey the right scope avoiding the focus on IT only.

But, as with philosophy, those questions beget other questions rather than answers.

An EA framework should enforce similar predictable and repeatable outcomes, otherwise it fails to be a framework.

The Enterprise Architecture black hole (ii)

Apr 18, 2009

http://it.toolbox.com/blogs/ea-matters/the-enterprise-architecture-black-hole-ii-30951

On the other hand we have the "method" cult. This, in a "deus ex machina" manner, promises results if you follow the process provided.

In my experience, in a known company, the architecture development exercise was restarted three times, with different deliveries and management teams. While the results were different for each iteration they were similar nevertheless in their uselessness and quantity of tree paper. They did not address any stakeholder specifically.

The process alone did not help without a framework defining the artefacts, the relationships, the expected outcomes and their form.

The cult members have to be expensively certified to be accepted. They have a bible of many pages, describing in indiscriminate detail the workings of the EA architect's. How do you use it? You open it at a certain chapter and read the verse. "You have to do this and that!" There is no holy picture to show you the inner soul or structure of the Enterprise. The method is general enough to help you build anything and everything. Down the line, you start offering a stack of unrelated, uncorrelated artefacts, with lots of explanations. The customers of that, if any, are not clear. As a result, nobody feels served. The results, one might say, are not quite fit for purpose.

"Enterprise Architecture is about diagrams, not stories"; I would like to suggest it as a key design principle.

Our customers need interconnected diagrams to analyse interaction, costs and impacts, rather than heavy tomes describing whatever. And they are not interested in the methods we use, whichever.

That typically stirs negative reactions and bad press that render the EA process ineffective.

An Enterprise Architecture wish list

Mar 12, 2009

http://it.toolbox.com/blogs/ea-matters/an-enterprise-architecture-wish-list-28048

What would you like to have when delivering an Enterprise Architecture (EA)? Surely, we'd like to know what that is. To avoid this perennial discussion here, I would suggest the definition implied in the name, that is "the structure and the blueprint of an Enterprise".

We would also like to list the key artefacts a basic EA needs to provide and how would they be documented and navigated. The four EA layers do help classify artefacts on a conceptual level. But, in practice, we need more clarity.

A look at the existing frameworks reveals:

TOGAF serves at the EA development process and four layer architecture level. It also suggests the use of architectural views. Recently, in TOGAF 9, a content metamodel was introduced that adds concepts such as service and contract which link EA to SOA. This is of little help when documenting the current architecture where no or few contracts or services exist. Also, TOGAF does not really propose specific artefacts and relationships as DODAF does, for instance.

DODAF is one of the most endowed frameworks in terms of artefacts definition. Their type and diagrams are judiciously specified and interrelated. A metamodel shows the relationships between the components of the artefacts. But DODAF does not really attempt to serve the business community.

Zachman expresses the essence of an architecture design asking a few rather philosophical questions such as why, what, how, who, where... It does not go much further than that, even though the cells in the matrix are often lightly assimilated with EA artefacts.

I'll put now together my wish list for the EA key artefacts and deliveries:

For Business Architecture:

- Context/Stakeholders' view

- Business Reference Map with key Business Functions

- Key Business Process Diagrams with Information exchange

- The Value Chains, Business and Operating models of the Enterprise, customizing the configuration of the Business Functions according to model

- Information Map

- Business strategy

- ...

Applications Architecture artefacts

- Applications diagrams with key interconnections

- Interconnections matrix

- Data architecture

- Data items mapping to the Business Information map

Various Applications EA views for:

- Portal Architecture

- Content Management

- Access (Authentication and Authorization)

- Reporting, BI and Data warehouse

- ERP and CRM architecture views

- ...

IT Infrastructure artefacts

- Servers and Storage technology diagrams

- Office Architecture views(file, printing DB servers...)

- LAN/WAN/Voice Network architecture

- Applications and interconnections mapping to technology servers and networks

- Infrastructure Security architecture

Organization Architecture artefacts

- organization chart

- organization mapping to business functions

- organization roles in organization units and job descriptions

- ...

An Enterprise Architecture wish list (ii)

Mar 21, 2009

http://it.toolbox.com/blogs/ea-matters/an-enterprise-architecture-wish-list-ii-30501

I would like to restate that this is just a basic wish list to which many architectural views can be added.

The EA wish list continues here:

- A basic EA metamodel diagram to clarify the mapping and

 relationships between the elements in artefacts.

The diagram types used to illustrate the artefacts are on the wish list because they establish, once for all, the elements of the artefacts, i.e. the EA objects. As you add views, the metamodel should be enriched with the new objects and their links.

- Templates or Reference Maps and patterns to help the design of the

Business, Application, Infrastructure, and Organization architecture layers. The maps supply the typical "design" structure of the layer, the components and patterns. For instance, the Business Architecture discovery or design would start from the Value Chains of an industry and specific enterprise and the particular Business and Operating models and Strategy.

 - a Single Page Enterprise Architecture is key; it describes in one page a synoptic view of the Enterprise structure and operation showing a single EA picture to all stakeholders and developments

 - an EA framework showing all its key layers and views (artefacts in this list).

The EA entry GUI, enables access to and navigation between all artefacts and elements so that a stakeholder can rapidly select the information needed and navigate to technology and people.

 - the alignment framework between the EA and the on-going solutions architecture projects, i.e. how would the project artefacts have to be represented to be included in the EA and how is the EA guiding the solution architecture projects.

 - The EA program plan with EA deliveries part of the Enterprise Project Portfolio

 - The Enterprise Project Portfolio consisting of all Enterprise projects and the impacts to EA elements thus reducing project, resources, process and function duplications.

 - the documented EA building process to manage EA delivery

 - the EA governance

 - SOA design best practices, EA architectural principles to guide architects

 - maturity models for measuring the state of EA development

 - the Strategy mapping to business, organization and technology EA objects

 - the Business Case for the EA evaluating financial Payback and NPV and the Return on your Enterprise Architecture (RoEA) to enable financial support for the EA development

All the above you may find in the just published 3rd edition of the book "An Enterprise Architecture Development Framework" out now from Amazon, Trafford and other. Other topics:

- a common view of the EA, SOA, BPM, ERP, Lean/Six Sigma developments... This will help integration of all these developments in one to eliminate Enterprise wide duplication in efforts

- the definitions and scope of EA

- a classification and brief discussion of current EA frameworks

- an EA development exercise

- how to use the proposed EA framework in practice for ITIL, Merger and Acquisitions, Outsourcing, business Start-ups...

- organization design models

- current drivers for business and IT in Commercial and Government sectors

- typical IT developments of this decade: MDM, single customer view, reporting consolidation

- EA inhibitors and triggers

- EA politics and sell, culture and EArchitect's leadership

- The Cloud Enterprise of the future, the Virtual Enterprise based on

SOA and Cloud Computing

The state of EA, revisited

Jan 22, 2011

http://it.toolbox.com/blogs/ea-matters/the-state-of-ea-revisited-43842

At the beginning of the new year, let me recap again the situation of EA. Anything to be merry about? Overall, EA looks like it always did. Little really happened in the field. No real substance was added since Zachman and TOGAF. Except that, in this void, various trainings and certifications offerings are getting a foothold.

Since there is no academic or agreed definition for EA or its framework, many fora, individuals and companies have come with their own views that usually cover aspects of rather than the whole of Enterprise Architecture. We still have to ask basic questions like: what is the purpose of EA, is it about strategy and change or about complexity management or...? How does EA achieve business alignment or support strategy? How does EA enable decisions and investment making activities? What are the key EA artefacts?

Since no major contribution has advanced the cause, most people wait and see, hoping for a miracle breakthrough. An external observer would say that people are satisfied with the state of the art, methods, frameworks and especially with the results. That may be true only because expectations have been adjusted low. EA is mostly seen as an IT discipline having more to do with IT strategy and target state rather than anything else. Typical work involves solution architecture reviews and IT roadmapping. The EA professional issues architecture principles, technology guidelines and creates applications, technology, connection inventories and eventually a business capability map. Architects are expected to know TOGAF, typical IT systems and quite often specific technologies.

People technically still use the good old four layers paradigm: business, information, applications and technology in various combinations. Even so, each layer is described differently by different people. Navigation between them is rather difficult since there is no overall framework to interconnect the layers. Good metamodels that help appeared though. Sometimes, to compensate for the lack of navigation, architects add matrices of application interconnections, tables of applications mapping to technology systems etc. The mappings matrices are not intuitive and become out of synch rather soon.

Even though it is clear for everybody now that EA should cover business architecture, there is no agreement on what that is in the first place.

Business expects the EA to describe the Enterprise operation, which is not the case in today's EA that describes systems and technology alone. Business mostly deals with process maps, process improvement methods (BPM, xSigma...) and Value Chains analysis which are seldom part of EA. So why should anybody outside IT bother with EA? It is also trendy to talk about business modelling but business models mean not business architecture.

Every EA development experience looks different. Without reference, architects treasure their own findings as a competitive advantage and share little. Every EA outcome is different, hard to compare. Without definition, reference and guidance, the architect job description and selection criteria vary widely; the field is gradually invaded by people who think that's the title sounds good, certainly pays well enough and requires nothing concrete. Paying lip service to TOGAF gets one there. Certifications surely help. Nevertheless, stakeholders don't get to see an EA but they don't expect it any longer. In the end, EA diminishes.

The good news is that everybody still agrees that EA, in concept, as the architecture of the Enterprise, is still necessary despite its performance in terms of results and usage.

By the way my EA book latest edition "An Enterprise Architecture Development Framework" here and in UK has just been published in Kindle e-book format on Amazon.

"The book attempts to answer a few of the most asked Enterprise Architecture (EA) questions. What is the problem? Why EA is the solution? What is EA and what is an

EA framework? What is Business Architecture, what is SOA and how do they relate? What are the existing EA frameworks and related business developments such as BPM, Lean and Six Sigma, ERPs and what is their relationship to EA?

A proven EA Framework, the associated metamodel, a novel single page generic Business Architecture and enterprise reference architecture templates for business, people organization, IT applications and infrastructure layers are then provided. The framework looks like a content page showing the components of an EA as placeholders, without actually describing them, but illustrating how they fit into the whole. It enables navigation between business and the technology layers implementing the business processes. Navigation makes possible technology alignment to business operation, business change impact analysis and new business models implementation. The templates enable the professional to jump straight into own Enterprise description phase with no waste of time on EA framework specification.

The book then shows how to document and build an Enterprise Architecture, the development process, architecture principles and design method, best practices in EA and SOA development, delivery checklists, EA patterns, tooling and repository, integration to the mundane solution architectures design and implementation, typical EA use cases, a simple EA development example, how to measure the EA maturity and value delivered, what are the typical triggers and roadblocks and how to build an EA practice, its governance, organization, funding and site.

A unified strategy specification and mapping and roadmapping process is illustrated in order to identify the future states and the target architecture of the Enterprise.

The Enterprise Architect job description, selection criteria, leadership skills, politics of the job. cultural issues and how to effectively sell EA are then discussed.

In essence, the book describes all aspects of why and how to build an Enterprise Architecture with emphasis on the fact that EA is more than IT: EA is about documenting and alignment of the Enterprise business processes, organization and technology to deliver the strategic intent."

The Enterprise Architecture state and root causes (i)

Aug 25, 2012

http://it.toolbox.com/blogs/ea-matters/the-enterprise-architecture-state-and-root-causes-i-52799

There's been no news in the EA space apart from the continuous growth of the body of professionals.

Demand for practitioners though comes in all sort of forms and shapes such as EA SAP architects, EA software development, finance, enterprise solution, Java architects and so on.

Nevertheless, few are EA roles, in reality. That is an architect that has to organise and deliver EA and support the stakeholders in employing it.

It's like the EA prefix is added to any other IT profession we know. In reality, the demand is for a multitude of roles housed selfishly under the EA banner.

Ads demand business architect roles that report to the EA IT manager which role is in IT!!!

Understandably though, since the senior business analyst role seems to be increasingly called the enterprise business architect.

Increasingly, people who had and have nothing to do with EA pretend to be EAs only because they are somewhat experienced in IT or in a few business administration methods. That is indeed true if one defines EA to suit own views. But who can stop them if it's your opinion against theirs?

And what happened to the architecture part in the EA title? It looks like EA today does everything but architecture. The term architecture is interpreted as strategy, alignment, operating model...

Yet, what are the present outcomes of the EA profession? Hard to say. In any case, I have not seen an EA sample yet or even a framework that may lead to an EA.

Yet, many keep dispensing advice on the process, strategies, the soft skills... or how to convince the CEO of the EA worth, citing references that have little to do with EA but sound professionally erudite.

What do EA architects do? Police the work of the solution architects, typically, and talk about IT strategy.

Also, If you watch to the EA discussions, it looks like the EA has an increasingly indiscriminate, octopus like reach that covers more and more the territory of other established enterprise disciplines such as strategy, planning, governance, business models, business organization, BPM, xSigma, UX design, culture, social architecture, change management, decision making, leadership...

And that does not do any good to the EA since it ultimately means the EA works at times against the rest of the enterprise in attempting to do anyone else's job.

Enterprise Architecture state and causes, (ii)

Oct 6, 2012

http://it.toolbox.com/blogs/ea-matters/enterprise-architecture-state-and-causes-ii-52946

There is much hype, few visible results and a great number of professionals who still ask what EA is and what is it for, even if they already "practice" it.

The state of frameworks is dire. Too many that do too little.

Frameworks like TOGAF explain ad nauseam concepts that have to do with IT project management but less to do with EA and, in particular, with the business EA.

Zachman's is just a table reminding us that we have to ask the W questions from the perspectives of all participants in the delivery chain, before embarking in a design effort. And it leaves us there.

FEA is for government use, DODAF for defence and so on.

Others talk about EA either as an operating model or a business model. Both are true but cover little of what EA is and does, that is the architecture of the enterprise.

Some are listing a number of objects, whatever they are (models, efforts, to do items...), present them as an EA recipe and eventually call them grandly with an acronym made of its first letters.

Many hear the buzz words such as strategy or strategic advantage and jump the wagon. They contend they know better even if they never worked in EA and never will. We all recognize them but given etiquette and the "democracy" of the Internet, what can one do to deal with such cases?

Experienced IT practitioners just proceed to call themselves EA architects even if they do not deliver EA architecture.

Who's or what's stopping them to become EA architects?

Social media makes things worse, even as it means to democratise the issue. Perhaps democracy does not produce results when people are expressing views in domains they are not qualified to speak about.

Hundreds of different answers are the norm for a simple question about EA. Nobody has a qualm in expressing a superficial view or a new definition.

It's like we are just creating the EA now. Perhaps this is what we do.

But these kind of open discussions lead nowhere, time and again, since there is no leadership to direct the course of the debate and separate the wheat from the chaff. Yet, they demean EA in front of our customers and the other business or IT disciplines.

Still, we all agree that the EA concept has value.

That we cannot even agree on what EA is, is a key issue.

That few EA approaches return results according to expectations, the expectations we created, is another issue.

To me, a core problem remains though the collective contentment with the EA state of art. It looks like we prefer the status quo to rocking the boat. Why so though?

Enterprise Architecture state and causes (iii)

Oct 12, 2012

http://it.toolbox.com/blogs/ea-matters/enterprise-architecture-state-and-causes-iii-

To me, a core problem remains though the apparent contentment with the state of art of EA. It looks like we prefer the status quo to rocking the boat.

 Why so though?

A. In the first place, many practitioners seem not to care about the status quo, not as long as they can still call themselves EAs. The EA body of knowledge does not serve them well, obviously. But most practitioners are not going to invent new EA frameworks since that is not part of their role.

True, professionals are still debating what framework to employ. The end result seems to always favour a minimal approach made up of various and different bits and pieces, used according to skills experience. But there is no new method here.

Yet, if everybody comes up with own "bits and pieces", perhaps we are not talking about the same EA. What is clear though, is that existing methods are shunned.

If you ask a few teams to come with the EA for the same enterprise you would most likely end up with many different outcomes.

B. Known players seldom acknowledge each other, if at all, and bother little to evaluate other EA approaches or to align or merge their definitions not to mention their methods in a common outcome. They have an interest in the status quo.

Practitioners though struggle to understand how frameworks compare, overlap or complement each other or what are their strong points and when to use one or another.

But what practitioners discover is that in practice, after the magic and steep costs of the training and certification, most frameworks are of little use.

C. The famous parties monopolise the attention. As such, there are also lots of practitioners that pay lip service to them, serving themselves in the process, as well.

Many take advantage of the situation for own commercial benefit. They continue to milk their own success to the bone, ignoring all others or belittling them.

This looks like fierce competition between frameworks without a shred of collaboration. But this is the system, right? A few win, the rest loses. The enterprise though is the biggest loser.

D. Few, if anybody, share EA results.

Confidentiality? Perhaps.

Intellectual property? Few would want to disclose the way they did it because too many fish around for that, while pretending to preach EA to you.

Anyway, you'll soon see your ideas, either explained by someone else, as I've seen mine at times, or used without credit. Or both.

And, and I believe that this is the most frequent case, the outcomes are too unstructured to be of any use to anybody else, if of any use at all.

In some cases no EA is delivered at all, even if the EA team continues to painfully exist.

E. There probably are a few good EA approaches (I maintain that mine covers and returns results) but there is too much opportunistic literature (books...) available today to confuse one for a century. Besides, in this brave world we live in, without references, solid advertising or belonging to a strong party, the chances of an anonymous to succeed are minimal. Nobody would readily recognise value as many avoid the stand alone critical thinking and instruction necessary to do that.

F. All in all though, while customers are not complaining, nothing can be done. This is the main reason for lethargy. Why are customers not complaining though?

Because, the visibility of the EA function is low since for one, EA happens in IT for IT. And even in IT, it has a scarce audience. Not many customers to cry as such.

Because the expectations from an architect are low, since surely, everybody knows by now the dire state of the EA art. The architects are not even hired nowadays with the expectation that they deliver EA. EA architects do not deliver EA these days.

Because EA still fulfils a useful IT governance and design function, which is to establish standards and principles, regulate the solution design and technology utilisation, do roadmapping, IT strategy and too often though do solution architectures, while not doing EA.

EA architects are professionals for sure but they lack the tools to do the job.

Mind you, the EA function can be quite expensive when not delivering. Only the EA tools can cost a fortune, on an ongoing basis, and even if they are little used.

Then there is the amount of attention (and time) the EAs demand only to justify themselves again and again.

Beware also of the EAs policing aggressively the IT development. That typically stirs negative reactions and bad press.

Enterprise Architecture state and causes (iv)

Oct 27, 2012

http://it.toolbox.com/blogs/ea-matters/enterprise-architecture-state-and-causes-iv-52895

And what does EA deliver during this status quo to manage to survive though?

EA stays alive in IT, as always, by delivering architecture reviews, IT roadmaps and perhaps strategy. Still, the EA function does not deliver the EA, that is, the architecture of the enterprise that should stand reference for every other EA activity.

To make the EA profession succeed to expectations, that is to truly deliver the blueprint of the enterprise, we have to think critically and constructively, as opposed to paying lip service to the established. We need to

a) find out what that target EA method we'd like to achieve would look like because we have to know what we want first. This is the most important step since currently most proponents define methods or frameworks differently and rather incompletely

b) then analyse the EA frameworks landscape to find out what methods are out there that may map out onto our target EA method.

c) and then propose the target EA method made of from the chosen bits and where missing, fill the gaps in with proposed creative pieces.

Overall, we have to consider that an architecture has to raise above IT where it is currently taking place.

It also has to come down from the big picture rather than come upwards from various bits designed in isolation than would not fit the whole. Politically, we must be able to recognise the value that exists in other methods and promote it meritocratically. We have to honestly listen and collaborate rather than keep bragging.

Then we would be armed to do EA. Questions remain though.

Who can and is willing to do that? Since few would be able and fewer would be willing to do so for various reasons explained in previous posts.

Perhaps a group of us who are able to be impartial to a degree, enough independently minded and can see the win-win in doing that rather than continuing to feed the status quo.

Well, I might not be the best example, since I believe that I already have the answer consisting in the FFLV-GODS method that returns the expected results, since it provides

- the EA development process

- the EA governance (principles, organization, control...),

- the EA framework (in which the EA parts fit in to give the whole)

- the EA metamodel,

- the EA generic models to get you instantly started

- the design method (diagrams, language/UML..., sequence).

It covers business architecture (GODS), people (organization)

alignment and technology blueprints. A kindle book, a web site and a training course would help you go through the process.

The design starts from the big picture, the one page architecture, from which all parts cascade, building the whole to the last detail.

It is not simple though to embark on this road alone. There are few fundamental issues for most frameworks, that can stop you along the way.

For instance the difference between functions, capabilities, processes, value streams, value chains... should be sufficiently clarified before even attempting to integrate them in the EA framework and whole.

Or how to integrate the information architecture? How SOA and security architecture fit in? What is the EA business case? How to measure the EA value and progress?

Enterprise Architecture state and causes in ten points

Nov 30, 2012

http://it.toolbox.com/blogs/ea-matters/enterprise-architecture-state-and-causes-in-ten-points-52765

The causes for the current Enterprise Architecture dire state of art:

1. The enterprise is indeed complex and in need of a systematic description approach because human processes are intricate and hardest to formally describe.

Moreover, enterprises have never before been formally and consistently described.

A jumble of methods from IT and business such as UML, value chains, process models, business models, organization charts... have been/are employed to model aspects of the enterprise in separation.

Still, EA should provide the consistent and integrated description of the enterprise.

2. There is no agreement of what EA is and, for that matter of what its parts, scope and deliverables are.

We need a proper definition for the enterprise (and for the architecture term indeed), even before we start.

EA scope is too variable. It typically begins with the IT architecture but it often ends with strategy, culture...

Since each and every EA architect uses own definition and scope, the outcomes may vary wildly. This situation also derails most EA debates on unproductive paths.

The answer is simple though:

The enterprise is a group of people organized to make and deliver the products, using various technologies.

EA is the overall enterprise blueprint.

EA covers the whole enterprise.

3. The EA's lack of mandate to cover the whole Enterprise

Therefore, the ever promised EA benefits at the enterprise level are never realised and the EA reputation declines.

And there is no mandate because EA does not deliver to business expectations.

4. There is no complete method (even if there are some out there) that enables the systematic description of a complex system, never mind the enterprise.

Most EA architects struggle with the method, that is with the how to describe the enterprise rather than with the depiction itself.

As such the EA looks like a disjoint set of representations.

5. The multiplication of the existing orthogonal EA "frameworks" produced by organizations and individuals that ignore all other approaches.

There are too many self centred EA practitioners, gurus, organizations, consultancies and tool providers who push their own agendas ignoring all others, creating hype and chaos as such.

Yet, most frameworks describe EA development processes or cognitive approaches that ask the "W" questions but stop short of proving useful in practice.

Architects create as such their own blended approaches.

In the end, two or more EA architects or teams would most probably come with different approaches and outcomes for the same enterprise, outcomes that one cannot even compare.

People don't even know how an Enterprise Architecture looks like. How can one be able to compare EA results and frameworks?

There is a plethora of pseudo Enterprise Architectures that provide disjoint artefacts that fail to offer the synoptic view of the enterprise, which is what EA is all about.

We already have many isolated artefacts in an enterprise today, unfortunately all designed independently, disconnected and hence failing to enable the end to end analytics and development of the enterprise. Thus what we call EA, a disjoint set of representations, had existed for a long time in the enterprise.

6. The proliferation of EA architects that having had plenty of experience in IT and strategy and having eventually been certified in TOGAF, suddenly pretend to be Enterprise Architects. One can easily discover the pretenders by watching any EA discussion forum.

A result is that it is hard to distinguish the architects from the pretenders in particular because the customers do not know what to expect. The pretenders take the jobs. And they muddy the waters even worse.

7. There is no able regulatory forum but too many training and certification bodies with have very different EA curriculums.

Some organizations, such as Open Group end up certifying EAs through two different and unrelated programs such as Open CA and/or TOGAF.

8. The lack of business confidence in EA since the EA does not deliver to expectations comes back to haunt the EA. As such EA cannot surpass its condition.

9. And a root cause is the lack of critical thinking from the masses of practitioners, client organizations, professional services firms, and recruiters that accept unblinkingly, without questioning what the guru organizations say, without bothering to form an own opinion, encouraging as such the perpetuation of this dire state of EA.

If G... said that it must be okay.

10. Lack of customers pull. If EA does not deliver why don't they react?

Because EA is hosted in IT. And the IT management is satisfied with the results. The lack of the big picture of the enterprise or the business or people architectures does not bother them. It's not their concern.

For instance, while I design the big picture of the enterprise including the business, technology and people views, many EAs produce solution architectures, organise review boards and sketch IT roadmaps, work that may satisfy the IT management but it represents just a small part of the EA whole. It cannot even be properly done without the EA blueprint.

Many points above are a consequence of or dependant on other points. To break the vicious cycle, practitioners have to think critically and act meritocratically in promoting an EA framework.

A proper framework would set EA on its right path.

The architects would adopt it, adapt it and deliver EA. Results would be finally observable at the enterprise level.

Business would sponsor the effort.

New practitioners would get the proper training and proceed to work at effectively describing their enterprises rather than spending time debating again and again the same elementary issues.

Certification bodies would align to the method and between each other to promote the true EA architects. Recruiters would know what they are after rather than continue to demand TOGAF.

EA becomes as such a competitive advantage for the enterprise because it enables fixing its operation in no time, process improvement, alignment of technology to business needs to respond fast to market demands and management of complexity, roadmapping and strategic transformation to implement vision. The better the EA the easier the transformation.

Enterprise Architecture status quo

Oct 13, 2012

http://www.ebizq.net/blogs/ea_matters/2012/10/enterprise-architecture-status-quo.php

To me, a core EA problem is the apparent contentment with the state of EA art. It looks like we prefer the status quo to rocking the boat.

Why so though?

Since the EA body of knowledge is not mature, many practitioners are not armed to produce the EA. They are still long debating what framework to employ. They struggle to understand how frameworks compare, overlap or complement each other or what are their strong points and when to use one or another. But what practitioners discover is that, in practice, after the magic and steep costs of the training and certification, most frameworks are of little use.

But few are going to invent an EA framework since that is not part of run of the mill work. Most use a mixed EA approach made up of different bits and pieces from various methods, chosen according to skills and experience.

Hence, as long as they can still call themselves EAs, practitioners' attitude is of wait and see.

Yet, as critical commentary, if everybody ends up with own "bits and pieces" method, perhaps we are not getting the same EA. If you ask a few teams to come with the EA of the same enterprise, the outcomes would be vastly different.

Known players seldom acknowledge each other, if at all, and bother little to evaluate each other's approaches or to align or merge their definitions or methods in a common outcome. Apparently, they have an interest in the status quo. No progress, means they can still sell their own frameworks.

As famous parties monopolise the attention, there are lots of practitioners that pay lip service to them, serving themselves in the process, as well. Many take advantage of the situation for own commercial benefit. They continue to milk their own success to the bone, ignoring all others or belittling them.

This looks more like fierce competition between frameworks and practitioners without a shred of collaboration. But this is the system, right? A few win, the rest lose. The enterprise though is the biggest loser.

Few, if anybody, share EA results. Confidentiality? Perhaps.

Intellectual property? Few would want to disclose the way they did it because too many fish around for that, while pretending to preach EA to you.

In any case, you'll soon see your ideas published without credit by someone else, as I've seen mine at times.

And, and I believe that this is the most frequent case, the EA outcomes would be too unstructured to be of any use to anybody else, if of any use at all.

In some cases no EA is delivered at all, even if the EA team continues to painfully exist.

There probably are a few good EA approaches (I maintain that mine covers all aspects and returns results) but there is too much opportunistic literature (books...) available today to confuse one for a century.

Besides, in this brave world we live in, without references, costly advertising or belonging to a strong party, the chances of an anonymous to succeed are minimal.

Few would readily recognise value as most do not exercise the necessary stand alone critical thinking. As such "smaller" but progressive approaches may not be adopted.

All in all though, while customers are not complaining, nothing can be done. This is the main reason for lethargy. Why are the customers not loudly shouting though?

Because, the visibility of the EA function is low since, for one, EA happens in IT for IT. And even in IT, it has a scarce audience. Not many customers to complain as such.

Because the expectations from an architect are low, since everybody knows by now the dire state of the EA art. The architects are not even hired nowadays with the expectation that they deliver EA. How does an EA look, in fact? Most EA architects do not deliver EA these days.

Because the EA still fulfils a useful IT governance and design function, which is to establish standards and principles, regulate the solution design and technology utilisation, do roadmapping, IT strategy and way too often though, do solution architectures, while not doing EA.

EA architects are professionals for sure but they lack the tools to do the job

Mind you, the EA function can be quite expensive when not delivering. Only the EA tools can cost a fortune on an ongoing basis, even if they are little used as it is usually the case. The EAs are expensive choices too for solution architecture.

Then, there is the large amount of attention and costly time the EAs demand only to justify themselves and the EA, again and again.

The Enterprise Architecture 10++ commands

Sep 16, 2009

http://it.toolbox.com/blogs/ea-matters/the-enterprise-architecture-10-commands-34156

Gartner has recently defined 10 EA pitfalls. I take this opportunity to post here my own 10++ EA commands, best practices and key success factors.

1. Define clearly EA and its scope

2. Build the EA business case, communicate specific stakeholder's benefits and sell EA

3. Using the business case, ensure business and management support and top sponsorship from the beginning

4. Adopt a combined EA framework covering approach, structure, behaviour, process, method...

5. Define the EA metamodel, vocabulary, principles and standards and Solution Architecture guidelines

6. Specify business architecture so that the technology architecture is linked to business operations

7. Integrate in the EA effort other Enterprise level activities (Six Sigma, Organization improvement, Business Strategy...)

8. Delegate work to the domain experts once the framework is in place

9. In roadmapping and planning, prioritise business operational, tactical and strategic objectives; deal with the EA trigger cause first and deliver what was requested, listen to your stakeholders

10. Observe potential EA roadblocks from the very start; bottlenecks have to be quickly discovered and eliminated

11. Create an EA site, provide FAQ to avoid confusion, training and display the EA progress dashboard on the Web for transparency

12. Select a quality EA team since it is the major risk; the EA team must have a vast knowledge spanning business, IT and people issues and be socially and politically astute

13. Employ agile processes with frequent iterations and deliveries in consultation and agreement with stakeholders

14. Make the EA process transparent with neat accountabilities, i.e. governance

15. Police development work, solutions architecture, install EA compliance controls (checkpoints) in all relevant development and change processes, confer with stakeholders for feedback and requirements

16. Measure the Value of EA as seen by stakeholders and track progress

17. Empower the EA Architect role

18. As the EA gets documented and implemented create an EA task force to deal with EA on a permanent basis.

SOA AND ENTERPRISE ARCHITECTURE

SOA, Architecture Style or Technology?

Jul 5, 2007

http://it.toolbox.com/blogs/ea-matters/soa-architecture-style-or-technology-17440

A definition of architecture states that it is the structure of a system and the description of its components and interconnections. As a structure, the architecture exists in any system, no matter how convoluted; and it can be described by an architecture diagram. For the target state of a system, a blueprint is drawn to describe the desired logical architecture of the system, that is its components and interconnections.

This architecture blueprint enters then a design phase where technologies and products are selected for each component and interconnection. The end result, the Design blueprint consists of detailed drawings of the interconnected applications components. The design is ready now for implementation and as such, at last, the architecture is implemented in a physical system out of interconnected applications.

SOA, a style of architecture, consists of recognisable and reproducible architecture patterns. The style is applied to a target architecture which, after the design phase, is implemented in a system. SOA is at the same time an integration technology for services rather than applications. This is what vendors try to sell you: ESB, registries... based on SOAP/XML, UDDI, WSDL etc. SOA technology integrates and interconnects rather than implements the services of a system. But vendors also offer, in addition, business process (and rules) engines, B2B systems, application servers, service management and other products in their SOA offer.

SOA, as a style or even technology, can be applied to a complex application design or to the target architecture of an Enterprise. The business component design of SOA is what people say you must do, not buy. You do have to specify your business services first and then interconnect them with a SOA technology. Can you say implement SOA services once you specified them? You probably can. And then integrate and orchestrate them with SOA and BPM technologies.

Now, you may find more answers in this book, the 2nd edition just published: "An Enterprise Architecture Development Framework" (subtitle "Business Case, Best Practices and Strategic Planning for the Enterprise"), available from Trafford at www.trafford.com/06-0421 and soon on Amazon.

Some of the content might be of interest to you although the book is not entirely aimed at IT people. The book describes an EA framework consisting of business, technology and people/organization architecture, EA frameworks classification and mapping, an EA development exercise to clarify the process and deliverables of the EA process at every step, the link between the Value Chain, business model, EA functional architecture and UML stakeholders' Use Cases, an EA maturity model, inhibitors and politics, relationship to SOA, BPM, ERP, Enterprise Architect role...

SOA versus BPM

Jul 30, 2007

http://it.toolbox.com/blogs/ea-matters/soa-versus-bpm-18008

The relationship between SOA and BPM has been the subject of some debate recently. No wonder since in an Enterprise, there are different professional groups, magazines or activities to address them.

I would place them both in the Enterprise context, since SOA, for instance, may be applied, as well, to an application architecture. Then I would look into the conceptual and the technology sides of BPM and SOA.

BPM was in vogue in the 90ies as BPR, Business Process Reengineering. As a concept it is about discovering your processes, improving and automating them to reduce human error, delays and reduce costs. There are notations and languages to describe business processes. There are models that help evaluating the maturity of processes in a domain and frameworks, such as Six Sigma, for process improvement to reduce the percentage of errors in a manufacturing environment.

Business processes are also a part of the Business layer of the Enterprise Architecture (EA). The Enterprise processes would be described by a current and target process architecture described respectively by an As-Is and To-Be EA. Processes are still abstract in that they still have to be performed by humans and/or machines.

From a technology viewpoint, BPM is offered at the EA business layer, as Business Process and rules design, execution and monitoring engines.

SOA, on the other hand, is a business architectural style which might originate in the Object Oriented (OO) distributed technology and Web Services. But, the concept of service is not new at all, you can find it in the Yellow Pages. SOA, like the OO, is about providing data and processing, encapsulated and accessed only through a published interface. But, as opposed to OO, which addresses the SW development community, SOA aims at services business can understand and eventually orchestrate to implement end to end Enterprise processes.

In a SOA architecture, the business workflows will consist of orchestrated SOA services that encapsulate both process and the technology implementing it.

SOA is supposed to be implemented in the target architecture of an Enterprise; it does not exist in the current architecture. SOA, as a technology, is typically offered as an ESB (Enterprise Service Bus) product for services integration and UDDI/WSDL discovery and interface description catalogue. Web Services may be thought as a SOA implementation over the internet.

In a few words, SOA is a target style of BPM where processes are designed and implemented as a sequence of loosely coupled SOA services. SOA is an evolution of BPM aiming to hide, encapsulate complexity in business services. Business process engines are now offered as part of an overall SOA proposition, since they become SOA services orchestration engines working over an ESB.

EA, ERP and SOA

Mar 19, 2007

http://it.toolbox.com/blogs/ea-matters/ea-erp-and-soa-14178

ERP application suites, covering many Enterprise functions (manufacturing, supply chain, payroll, procurement, accounting, finance, inventory, order fulfilment, task scheduling, resource management etc.) aim to provide the EA application layer and the Enterprise business processes, in a rather proprietary and monolithic approach. That may be changing with the advent of SOA.

Historically, ERP application suites were successful as they reduced the hassle of integration of many different Enterprise applications from various vendors. Today though, ERPs are too tightly integrated hampering as such the opening of the Enterprise to competitive, Best of Breed solutions. In simple words, Enterprise's agility is at stake from too tight integration which does not allow for best of breed 3rd party Enterprise applications integration.

I would argue that it's not in the ERP suppliers' interest to open up their products to SOA or advertise EA when they already claim to provide most of the applications an Enterprise needs to operate. But ERPs, having embedded processes, do not promote the same visualization or comprehension of the Enterprise operation potentially offered by an EA or the agility to change of SOA. SOA appears to threaten traditional ERP application suites which tend to provide the Enterprise services and integration as a very large package at the cost of reliance on one single supplier.

At this stage though, there are not enough off-the shelf SOA services to compete with ERPs. In some cases that means collaboration with your application vendors to package applications as services. Replacement of your ERP solution may prove prohibitively expensive from a cost and time perspective. An iterative development, starting small and adding services as you go may prove to be the best approach for SOA introduction. Integrating the existing ERP with your other applications would be a safe decision.

EA may re-use the ERP applications suites, provided ERP modelling is performed to document the business processes.

SOA, to do or to buy!

Feb 1, 2008

http://it.toolbox.com/blogs/ea-matters/soa-to-do-or-to-buy-21904

A definition of architecture states that it is the structure of a system and the description of its components and interconnections. As a structure, the architecture exists in any system, no matter how convoluted; and it can be described by an architecture diagram. For the target state of a system, a blueprint is drawn to describe the desired logical architecture of the system, that is its components and interconnections. This architecture blueprint enters then a design phase where technologies and products are selected for each component and interconnection. The end result, the design blueprint, consists of detailed drawings of the interconnected components of the systems.

The design is ready now for implementation and as such, at last, the architecture is implemented in a physical system out of the interconnected products. A style of architecture consists of recognisable and reproducible architecture patterns. SOA is a style of architecture applied to a target system. SOA, as a style, can be equally used in an application or in the target architecture of an Enterprise. SOA architecture, after the design phase, is implemented by the systems delivering the SOA business services.

SOA is at the same time an integration technology for services rather than applications. This is what vendors try to sell you: ESB, registries... based on SOAP/XML, UDDI, WSDL etc. SOA technology integrates and interconnects rather than implements the services of a system. Vendors also offer, in addition, business process (and rules) engines, B2B systems, application servers, service management and other products in their SOA offer.

The SOA business services design and orchestration is what people say you must do, not buy. You do have to specify your business services first and then interconnect them with a SOA technology. Can you say implement SOA services once you specified them? You can. But you can equally say that you buy SOA technology to integrate the systems delivering the business services.

SOA, business processes and shared services

Feb 16, 2008

http://it.toolbox.com/blogs/ea-matters/soa-business-processes-and-shared-services-22343

Business processes are linearly arranged in a sequence of cascaded activity steps. A business process is part of a single end to end (e2e) process or workflow. In contrast, an SOA service may be called by many e2e processes; it is designed and implemented once with reuse in mind. The SOA service:

- supports concurrent users calling from client processes

- provides the same access interface and messages (not necessarily the same version) to all users

- is designed for scalability to satisfy all potential customer demand

- delivers security and privacy of data and communication

- provides provision for enforcing QoS in SLA agreements & KPIs

for measuring the quality of delivery and usage

- supplies a management interface

- is managed on behalf of all users

- it often supports Web Services standards

- it is easily provided by an external supplier

What about Shared Services, are they a SOA type of development? They are and they aren't. They are because they are reused by many Lines of Businesses (LoBs) in an Enterprise. They are not since they are mainly used by people rather than applications. Often shared services are performed by a mixture of humans and systems. SOA is mostly talked about in the IT domain although, in principle, it applies to people or/and technology services. Since Shared Services are frequently about Enterprise support services, they are often implemented in ERP technology. SOA in comparison, often applies to the whole Enterprise.

Shared Services are an important step towards SOA since the practice of sharing is already agreed upon. Shared services are SOA candidates. Once a SOA service is implemented, outsourcing becomes an option too since interfaces and SLA are already in place.

SOA, the real benefits

Aug 30, 2007

http://it.toolbox.com/blogs/ea-matters/soa-the-real-benefits-18703

More often than not, agility and technology reuse are the major benefits associated to SOA. The reality is that SOA, frequently approached outside an Enterprise Architecture context, is developed incrementally, without the benefit of the big picture the Enterprise Architecture delivers. As a consequence, the promised agility is achieved late, towards the end of the SOAisation of your Enterprise when technology reuse may require costly redesign.

It is worth mentioning though that Business process reuse rather than IT is the advantage since SOA identifies similar business activities and groups them in a service. SOA reduces process replication followed eventually by the application de-duplication. Nonetheless, there are a few other major SOA benefits which should be more easily achieved, understood and accepted. Invoking these advantages would make SOA a joyous sell rather than the reported stressing experience.

1. Business service accountability, improving business and IT governance. Applications and suites, usually a bundle of many functions, provide many services; in practice, a large group of business and IT people will share the responsibilities for the data and behaviour of applications. But who can hold accountable such a group of individuals with many other responsibilities? Neither the stick nor the carrot would work in such an environment where neither accountability or authority can be assumed. On the other hand, for a SOA business service, there is a specific function or group assigned responsibility: it does not matter it is an IT or business issue, there is one single point of contact which will assume blame or the praise.

2. IT technology virtualisation behind SOA business services, reducing the Business and IT divide and enabling audit for a regulatory compliant architecture.

This a major achievement since your applications and technology are hidden behind IT services with contract interfaces supplied to the business. From a business perspective this is what really counts. IT becomes a service provider offering business services at a QoS secured by an SLA, well comprehended, quantified and eventually paid for by the business. No more blame culture. The separation of concerns pacifies the parties with no more business and IT divide as an additional advantage. The access is logged as well for various reasons such as regulatory.

3. Untangling the applications providing a clean architecture, reducing the side effects of change.

There is no more random access to parts of applications or databases which makes any change a burden and any modification of an application a major risk because of unforeseeable effects.

4. Extended lifetime for your legacy applications, reducing the immediate pressure to replace them.

Although there are other increasing costs related to legacy technology, there is no more pressure to replace it; you can do it at your own convenience when a viable alternative exists. This is an extension of the technology virtualisation.

SOA, dead or alive?

Jan 14, 2009

http://it.toolbox.com/blogs/ea-matters/soa-dead-or-alive-29187

The good questions about SOA such as the relation to Enterprise Architecture (EA), is it architecture or integration and its success rate have recently re-emerged in dramatic public discussions.

With poor results, SOA disappointed the business people. Very true. It was said that SOA has died - this rushed away justifications since SOA pundits felt the sting - while its offsprings such as mashups, BPM, SaaS, cloud computing are alive and kicking. I would like to remark though that BPM, SaaS as ASP, and cloud computing as IT data centre outsourcing, existed before SOA came to the fore. Mashups look more like "offsprings" but even they are an implementation of the existing Web Services technology. SOA had its contribution though in this spiral evolution.

Before making any judgment I would like to review what SOA is. It is a style of architecture based on services that can be flexibly orchestrated in end user processes. Integration is only implied here by orchestration. SOA can be applied to a software application or up to a full Enterprise as part of the target Enterprise Architecture. It depends on the scope of your endeavour.

The architecture side of Enterprise SOA, consisting of business services design and their orchestration in processes, would belong to the business people rather than IT. It is their job to "design" the business, if they need it. SOA is something that "you have to do" as pundits say. It is not really "you" in IT, but the business people.

SOA as architecture eases integration by providing modularization, encapsulation and "standard" interfaces for services. It does not specify the protocols or the technology choice though.

The integration implied in SOA belongs to the IT even though SOA is primarily about architecture. IT provides, in fact, all the technology - ESB, BPMS... - that facilitates services orchestration, integration, discovery, security, SLAs... This is the SOA you "buy".

SOA failed. The truth is that Enterprise wide SOA projects failed. The reason is simple: it was promoted, manned and driven by IT, solely. Business did not ask for it. It is the result of IT hype and push. It is not the job of IT to design the business.

The EA wide attempts at SOA fail for lack of support from Enterprise Architecture, business people and management.

In practice, had business been aware that SOA is about re-engineering the Enterprise operation, their reaction towards IT would be swift and lethal. In fact that lead to the SOA obituary.

From an IT viewpoint, SOA technology is an evolution of distributed components concepts and technology that continues to evolve, and as such, it does not really die. Being not necessarily SOA specific, the technology would survive the premature SOA fate.

The application (suite) SOA should be also well and alive. IT and software houses can engineer applications as software services e.g. SOA at IT applications or suite level, and integrate them with web services and ESB technologies. That is what happens in WOA, the side of SOA that IT can do. This is where SOA was successful, even driven solely by IT. SOA at application level is not dead and will not die soon. For instance, many ERPs are re-engineered now on SOA principles.

What would revive SOA at Enterprise level? Business people look more and more at the Virtual Enterprise, VE,(in business tongue also networked Enterprise, boundaryless company) even if they do not call it as such. The VE is made of partner companies cooperating to implement the processes in the value chain to deliver the products. Parts of a business, links in the value chain, are, in reality, outsourced to partners. This is where SOA needs to be incorporated into the bigger business context to provide the architectural framework for the VE. Cloud computing, SaaS, i.e. outsourcing IT to 3rd parties, become part of the Virtual Enterprise.

Enterprise SOA failed for lack of business support, drivers and proper preparation, given the project size and implications. The technology usually associated with SOA (ESB, BPMS, WS) for orchestration, discovery, integration is alive and well. Idem, SOA at the application and suite levels. Take for instance the trend to design applications suites observing SOA.

The Virtual Enterprise of the future, composed of orchestrated business services provided by partner companies will drive SOA along B2B to provide the agility and technology for interconnecting the networked Enterprise. IT needs to take a lead.

SOA or SOEA, Service Oriented Enterprise Architecture

Jan 31, 2007

http://it.toolbox.com/blogs/ea-matters/soa-or-soea-service-oriented-enterprise-architecture-14157

Service Oriented Architecture (SOA) appears to be at the top of its hype curve. Definitely it gets a lot of attention. It is promoted as a cure to the evils of Today's Enterprise. It reduces costs through service re-use and by promoting modularity at service level, it enables the flexibility and agility required to respond to the greater than ever pace of change.

But what is SOA? Is it a technology, an architecture, a program or a product? Is it a business or an IT development? And what is the relationship to Enterprise Architecture (EA)? After all, the EA is supposed to remedy similar malfunctions of the Enterprise and both SOA and EA are about the Enterprise and its architecture. It's just that SOA appears to attract an even more IT oriented audience than EA. The question is: should we implement SOA and EA or SOA or EA, if any?

To begin with, SOA is a style of architecture design which may be applied to Enterprise Architecture, to the target EA to be explicit. It enables a Business Oriented Architecture (BOA - sorry, my new acronym) by allowing the business to define Enterprise workflows around re-usable business services. The granularity of the service is targeted at the business cognisant rather than at the software application developer. As a matter of fact, SOA is more than IT although it looks like its origins are in IT, more precisely, in the evolution of the distributed component architecture towards best of breed, technology and vendor agnostic high granularity business service components.

SOA in a W3C definition is "a set of components which can be invoked and whose interface definitions can be published and discovered". From an IT point of view, a SOA service is a component providing a business service which exposes an interface hiding the internal implementation technology, published in a registry and dynamically discovered. Web Services have been implementing for a while now, the SOA paradigm over Web protocols. As a result SOA is often associated to Web Services and its technologies (SOAP, XML, UDDI, WSDL...).

A SOA service would require definition and enforcement of SLAs to control the service consumption within defined usage limits and the quality of the service delivered. Security is another important aspect of SOA as it regulates access and enforces privacy and integrity of the information exchange in a distributed environment.

Nevertheless a SOA service may not necessarily be implemented by software or provided by IT technology. From a business point of view, one may think of a SOA service as an internal postal service with a pigeon hole interface provided by a team of people, no matter what technology.

SOA harbours under its umbrella developments which are in the scope of EA. SOA does cover architecture but it does not specifically cover business process automation or IT alignment to strategy, even if it helps, and it does not aim to document the As-Is state as EA does.

SOA requires a large Enterprise processes re-engineering and re-design effort, with significant consequences, at EA process, applications, infrastructure and people layers. Services will be re-used, access will be enforced by SLA contracts, and a new SOA governance will be in use affecting the existing organization and applications suites which might be replaced by best of breed services from various vendors.

Ultimately, SOA is an architectural style which may be implemented by a technology as Web Services, there are products as Enterprise Service Buses (ESB), Business Processes Orchestration and Rules engines, Service Registries and management tools supporting SOA and there are many SOA development programs. But SOA services definition is in the realm of business; services should be specified by business people since they are not an IT concern or in the IT domain of expertise.

As SOA is usually initiated by IT, it may have a careful adoption rate, similar to EA, because of the lack of business stakeholders' engagement and firm's management support and funding which may foil its success.

SOA, a partial EA development in disguise, may hide the recognition and complexity of an EA program (even though it is not an EA "inhibitor" per se - see previous posts). SOA, given its scope and ambition, should be a joint business and IT effort, a key part of a full EA development and not considered in isolation as a light IT Enterprise Integration effort.

Service Oriented Enterprise Architecture, SOEA would better describe the positioning of SOA with regard to EA. EA may be implemented without SOA, although not advisable, while a standalone SOA development, mainly driven by a service orientation architectural requirement will tend to ignore business requirements.

SOA, Enterprise Architecture and a word of caution

Mar 26, 2010

http://www.ebizq.net/blogs/ea_matters/2010/03/soa-enterprise-architecture-and-a-word-of-caution.php

This is to draw caution. Service Orientation and Enterprise Architecture are without a doubt, the way. But a careless execution could spell failure for both.

SOA, in a W3C definition, means "a set of components which can be invoked and whose interface definitions can be published and discovered." A dram too simple to my liking.

From an IT point of view, SOA is an integration technology for application services. A service is an application component which exposes an interface (hiding the internal implementation technology), published in a registry and eventually, dynamically discovered.

Web Services have been implementing the SOA paradigm over Web protocols. As a result, SOA is often associated to Web Services and its technologies (SOAP, XML, UDDI, WSDL...).

From a business angle, SOA is a style of business architecture design and, ultimately, a way of structuring your business. It enables a Business Oriented Architecture by allowing the business to define Enterprise workflows around reusable business services. The services and their interfaces have to be designed by the business cognizant, rather than the application developer.

SOA imposes a new business process design, implemented as an orchestration of loosely coupled SOA services. It is an evolution of BPM aiming to encapsulate and hide complexity in business services. In SOA, the business workflows will consist of orchestrated SOA services that encapsulate process, information and the technology implementing it.

What is the relationship between SOA and Enterprise Architecture (EA)?

A "Service Oriented Enterprise Architecture," SOEA, defined as an EA with an SO style of target architecture, would better describe the positioning of SOA with regard to EA.

The EA sets in place a method to achieve technology and organization alignment to business processes, strategy, and objectives.

SOA does cover architecture, but it does not specifically address business process automation, IT alignment to strategy..., even if it helps; it does not document the As-Is state like EA does; and it does not provide guidance for the development program as EA frameworks do.

SOA, as a style of business architecture, is adding value to the EA by enabling modularity at the business service level, and, as such, agility, reuse, Quality of Service, facilitating payback mechanisms and service contracts.

EA may be implemented without SOA at the cost of flexibility and agility. A stand-alone SOA development, solely driven by a service orientation architectural requirement, would fail to achieve the business needs and goals and would lack method.

SOA requires a large Enterprise process re-engineering and re-design effort, with significant consequences, at process, applications, infrastructure, and people Enterprise Architecture layers. Services will be reused, access will be enforced through SLA contracts, and a new SOA services governance will be in play, affecting the existing organization. SOA, given its scope and ambition, should be a joint business and IT effort, a key part of a full EA development, and not considered in isolation as a light IT Enterprise Integration effort.

Enterprise SOA, Success Factors

Jan 15, 2010

http://www.tmforum.org/community/groups/frameworx/blog/archive/2010/01/15/enterprise-soa-success-factors.aspx

SOA, from an IT perspective, is an Enterprise Integration technology consisting of service definition, orchestration (BPMS/BPEL), description (WSDL), registration, discovery (UDDI) and distribution (ESB) technologies. Nevertheless, SOA is more than IT although its origins are in IT.

From a business viewpoint, it is a way of structuring a business as

clusters of loosely coupled services.

SOA, apart from agility and reusability, enables:

- The Business to specify processes as orchestrations of reusable services
- Technology agnostic business design, with technology hidden behind service interfaces

- A contractual-like interaction between business and IT, based on service SLAs
- Accountability and governance, better aligned to business services

- Applications interconnections untangling by allowing access only through service interfaces, reducing the daunting side effects of change

- Reduced pressure to replace legacy and extended lifetime for legacy applications, through encapsulation in services

- A Cloud Computing paradigm, using Web Services technologies that makes possible service outsourcing on an on demand, utility like, pay-per-usage basis.

Nonetheless, SOA harbours developments that are in the scope of EA. It does not specifically address IT alignment to business and strategy, documentation of the As-Is Enterprise state or guidance for the development program as EA frameworks do.

As both SOA and EA are usually initiated by IT, the lack of business stakeholders' engagement and top management support may foil the success of SOA.

SOA does require a large Enterprise re-engineering effort, with consequences at all EA layers: business, applications, infrastructure and organization.

The Enterprise SOA Critical Success Factors (CSF):

- Should be primarily approached as a business development, a Business Architecture, a way to structure the Enterprise, a style of target Enterprise Architecture and only then as an IT integration technology

- May only succeed if developed inside an EA effort since SOA does not cover the Enterprise transformation process

- Driven only by IT, both SOA and EA are prone to fail; the business stakeholders' engagement and firm's top management support are key to success

- Business process re-engineering, a new governance around services and ultimately re-organization.

Enterprise SOA was pronounced dead because these CSFs were not really met. Application level or Web domain SOA are alive and well though.

Once implemented, an Enterprise wide SOA becomes a competitive asset based on business services accessed independently of technology and geography, agilely orchestrated for change and ready for outsourcing in the cloud."

This post was published September '09 in the 21st edition of the Microsoft Architecture Journal, as a column, downloadable here .

The virtualisation of the Enterprise and SOA

Jun 16, 2007

"*In business, a Virtual Organization is a firm that outsources the majority of its functions*", a Wikipedia definition. The concept is similar to the virtualisation described in the previous post: an Enterprise, consisting of outsourced business functions and a governance function that coordinates and identifies the company, becomes "virtual".

The Virtual Enterprise (VE) is composed of business functions belonging to different outsourcing parties participating in the VE Value Chain. A business function is described by a few typical Enterprise Architecture layers: business, applications, information and infrastructure. To these, one might add people/organization and non-IT technology which are often neglected. Effectively, all processes, data, technology and people belonging to a business function are outsourced together. Take for instance a SaaS outsourced application. This layered view conveys a first dimension to the Enterprise virtualisation.

All the same, each and every layer (process, information, applications, infrastructure) of an Enterprise Architecture can be virtualised, that is, an abstraction layer can be introduced to standardise communication to its functionality and hide the complexity and implementation. This is the way to handle the ever increasing complexity. This is the way it was done in the networks OSI (Open Standard Interconnect) standards where each layer provides a number of functions and an interface to the layer above to hide its implementation. The encapsulation of business functions and applications follows a similar paradigm to the HW industry where microprocessor chips encapsulate so much functionality.

The virtualisation of the IT infrastructure, a hot topic now, in the Enterprise, is , in essence, about providing an abstraction of the IT technology: servers, storage and networks. It is about providing an interface hiding the infrastructure implementation and its platform types. The benefits appear to be compelling: server utilization grows significantly and inverse proportionally to the number of servers and the cost of the occupied real estate and cooling. Virtualisation provides light and less costly business continuity and easier management. Ultimately the infrastructure can be outsourced to a 3rd party and paid per usage. There is no more need for getting skilled people, training employees, buying hardware, upgrading HW/SW every so often, depreciating or disposing the hardware. No more headaches.

What virtualisation promises? Independence from the HW infrastructure. Multiple applications and OSs run on one physical or multiple servers. Virtualisation is supported by blade systems where processing power is modularly scaled on demand.

Processing power can be consumed "on demand" (IBM parlance); MIPS can be purchased in an "utility" like model (HP talk). Storage will be retailed as a commodity from a pool and I/O is ultimately virtualised. An analogy can be made to the networks world where the leased lines evolved into virtual circuits, VPNs etc. where, newly, QoS and SLAs matter. Same for virtualised infrastructure. Same for services, provided by an outsourcing company that have to be delivered, according to SLAs at a particular QoS, for every customer eventually, over a shared, virtualised infrastructure.

Rapidly, the virtualisation seeps upwards, from HW to OS, to applications and business processes. In fact, since long Java had introduced a virtual machine abstraction layer between the applications and OS. Application servers are providing even more abstracted functionality today.

At the application layer, virtualisation is provided by SOA through standard interfaces and encapsulation, hiding the implementation technology. More, SOA provides the standard integration technology. As such communications are implemented over standard protocols and interaction is described by interfaces accessed in a standard manner. SOA provides an abstraction layer above applications hiding the communications and applications implementation technology. It should not matter any longer how the applications and network are realised or what are the platforms. Applications are in effect virtualised as services.

There is still the issue of standardising business services and their operations; this may fall into the remit of the application suite vendors, industry standardisation bodies or your own business people having a good knowledge of the specific processes and services.

THE CLOUD AND THE ENTERPRISE

Transition to the Cloud

Apr 15, 2010

http://www.ebizq.net/blogs/ea_matters/2010/04/transition-to-the-cloud.php

I have recently seen a request for information on the process of transition to the Cloud Computing business model. Is there such a process? You tell me. But I guess you have your experiences you may want to share. Here is my best try at good practices.

My view is that one needs to start small, to test the waters, to understand the issues; the Cloud makes that easy. And the Cloud is a real alternative for your IT because, even before, companies have entirely outsourced their data centres, applications management, networks, helpdesk... in a much more unstructured manner.

Ultimately most IT can be outsourced to the cloud. But it's not only IT, business functions can be entirely outsourced as well, that is with all IT and expertise. So

Create a working team for Cloud evaluation.

Consult stakeholders to decide what to outsource and priorities. Research market, potential suppliers, assess them.

Calculate benefits. List and compare alternatives.

Evaluate security and data privacy issues and check suppliers solutions. Consider a Virtual Cloud architecture where a combination of in-house and in-cloud solutions would be the norm.

Select a relevant service in the Cloud (SaaS, PaaS, IaaS) and test before buy. The Cloud Computing business model is "lease" rather than buy or build and Opex rather than Capex spending, that is, pay as you go, pay for what you use, no big commitment upfront.

You need to understand upfront the outsourcing big picture because mixing too many suppliers and different models of SaaS, PaaS, IaaS would create unnecessary integration problems.

I would start with SaaS for complex applications that demand costly maintenance, licensing, upgrades, in-house expertise...; IaaS may be suitable to host for most applications you still own but you or someone else manages them for you.

Then design an Information architecture prior to moving your applications in the Cloud so applications use compatible information in exchanges. I believe that during the process an MDM implementation would significantly help harmonize the integration information exchange.

Also design the Integration Architecture based roughly on services. Evaluate integrator companies and Cloud brokers.

Specify the Business processes that have to be checked end to end, orchestrating the services and model them over prospective Cloud services.

Essentially if you document a high level Enterprise Architecture from the As-Is to To-Be states you would be better off because you discover your current capabilities, your IT landscape and you can sketch you options on the plan.

The experience is essentially that of plain outsourcing; the cloud comes though with less published, tested, on-line interfaces, faster to deploy and probe, easier to revert from.

The Cloud will offer increasingly more choices and portability to other suppliers. So it's less risky and less difficult, i.e. doable.

The good news is that we would manage for the first time the divide between business and IT through formal contracts. And we can really control and plan IT spending. We have some choice too. What do you want more?

The Cloud and the Enterprise IT Value Chain

Jun 5, 2010

http://www.ebizq.net/blogs/ea_matters/2010/06/the-cloud-and-the-enterprise-it-value-chain.php

What will be the impact of the Cloud on the Enterprise IT and the IT Enterprises (i.e. supplying IT)? Let me post a few thoughts in answer to that. The Cloud represents an enhanced business model of supplying the IT resources supporting your Enterprise operation through outsourcing. It is enabled by today's virtualisation, infrastructure scalability, SOA, Web, and increasingly capable network technologies. The Cloud offers independence with regard to the outsourcing location and implementation technology. It is easy to take up, configure or renounce since there is no more ownership of IT resources. It presents an IT "lease" business model with pay as you use charging.

IT would become separated from the Enterprise and IT concerns would be separated from business ones. New Cloud supply firms would appear. Business people would control the IT capabilities through self service under contract with these firms. The outcome would be evident: no large IT departments in an Enterprise, no own data centres, cooling and energy bills, no more IT skills, licenses, training, etc. The Enterprise would be truly nimble and agile. The Cloud would facilitate easy ramp up and upgrades through self service. B2B at its best.

Enterprise Architecture becomes essential now to describe the business functions and the distributed outsourced supporting systems and their interconnections since a problem may lay in any of a few systems distributed in various Clouds. There must be a blueprint for analysis, defect fixing and evolution. The Cloud would signal nonetheless the end of the old division between business and IT.

Nowadays, the IT Enterprises, supplying equipment and applications, and outsourcing suppliers are both serving the customer Enterprises. With the Cloud, the IT supplier would mainly supply the Cloud provider even though the IT Enterprise might also choose to become a Cloud supplier. In time, the IT infrastructure suppliers, would have to switch from their large customer base of many Enterprises to a few Cloud suppliers. Less customers but more gear though. The applications suppliers may choose to go SaaS themselves or provide their application as a service over a Cloud infrastructure supplier.

It looks like a win-win... situation for most parties. An impact would come though from the consolidation of outsourcing suppliers since few companies could provide the large scale and the necessary reliability of operation. Gigantic Cloud centres have to be build and managed.

Another rather expected consequence is that the IT people would have to migrate from the many Enterprises they work for today to a few Cloud providers. But that is already happening with legacy outsourcing.

The Cloud is still immature nevertheless and standards are not quite there yet to enable, for instance, portability between Clouds and with it the major growth.

Applications Suites or Best of Breed in the Cloud?

Jul 24, 2011

http://www.ebizq.net/blogs/ea_matters/2011/07/applications-suites-or-best-of-breed-in-the-cloud.php

Lauren Carlson asked a question in the Application Strategy 2.0 that most IT departments had to, are or will be confronted with. Do you chose an Integrated Suite or Best of Breed (BoB) solutions? The answer looks more complicated now by the growing Cloud adoption trend.

A Suite adoption decision, while apparently difficult, has been made more often than not. Difficult because one has to adopt all functions in a suite at the same time. Because the transformation is not really a transition but more of a cutover. Typically, ERP like enterprise functions would be implemented as a Suite. Suites often mean though dependency (costly to migrate from) on one provider.

The Best of Breed solutions will allow you to pace the transformation. Usually this is the case for core applications.

Integration is critical though. But integration was always a problem in the enterprise, mostly implemented as an afterthought.

The Enterprise Application Integration (EAI) technology was introduced to alleviate the issue. Then SOA. But SOA was buried alive. And dead it is, because few SOA endeavours succeeded to deliver. The service oriented principles are alive though. The problem was that SOA was treated as a technology alone rather than a business design paradigm based on Enterprise services. And business was not enticed to support the efforts. It didn't help that services had to be re-invented in various forms and shapes in each and every enterprise even though they are pretty similar in nature, at least for an industry. Also, services are part of end to end processes, which were and are still not standardised either. Have these problems been solved? Not really.

Suites often won because they delivered both functionality and integration. Does the case change with the Cloud though? The Cloud provides an on-demand, pay as you go business model for both Suites and BoBs. Quick adoption, provisioning, scaling and no upfront CAPEX. And SaaS services are effectively SOA services in the Cloud. Moreover, today, business would often bypass IT to procure these outsourced services. This is because the Silo culture is still alive and well and well, IT is not really necessary in the process.

How does one integrate these services though? You will see probably IT system integrators waving their flags to design it for you. And service aggregation brokers that do the integration in their own cloud.

We need though a hybrid cloud that is, a mixture between on-premise and on-cloud. How do we integrate the two worlds from a functional, security and management viewpoint?

Is there a Cloud Integration Middleware, a Cloud Service Bus (CSB) or a Cloud Integration Service? There are.

Boomi provides a Cloud integration platform Atom Sphere integrating "on-premise and cloud computing environments in a seamless and fully self-service model... users could build and deploy integration processes visually using a design "canvas" with familiar point and click, drag and drop techniques". Or CastIron, an IBM company now.

But does the Cloud integration make BoB solutions more attractive to adopt? Yes, when end to end processes will be extended over many SaaS clouds, that is integration is applied not only at the application but at the process and rules level.

i.e. process Orchestration in the Cloud. See Loraine Lawson's interview on Hubspan.

How does one choose between a Suite and BoB? Suites are also been moved to the cloud. Suites for ERP like functionality maybe still the choice. Because they offer integration at data and process level as well. For core business applications, BoBs maybe the choice though with Cloud integration platforms.

But where does all this slowly lead us to, i.e. BoBs or Suites in the cloud? To the Cloud Enterprise I dare say.

Systems integration in the Cloud, SOA and best practices

Jun 4, 2010

http://it.toolbox.com/blogs/ea-matters/systems-integration-in-the-cloud-soa-and-best-practices-37979

With the advent of the cloud, systems can be placed on premise, outsourced to an off-site cloud or to a number of them. For instance, two or more SaaS systems that connect back to the on-premise applications and infrastructure. Integration of these systems works in various ways.

Between the private (own systems) and a public Cloud there may be a Virtual Cloud approach deployment that makes integration almost transparent through a secure VPN.

Inside a Cloud, the supplier should provide connectors between applications and other services like storage and communications.

Between Clouds there can be a number of solutions because Clouds are not quite standard yet. But there are a few Cloud integrators that link selected SaaS applications: CastIron, Beowulf, Boomi, Pervasive, Informatica...

One also has the traditional System Integrators.

Of course, it helps if your applications are SOA and Web Services based since integration becomes almost transparent. A SOA service should hide both the technology and the location of the service and offers access to functionality solely through an interface reducing as such the integration crisscross. That is why a SOA implementation becomes best practice before Cloud adoption.

Another best practice is to harmonize the Information architecture of the SaaS and on-premise applications and make sure the data formats are aligned or translated properly. One might have to deploy an MDM hub.

Not least, one should verify that key processes and transactions still work, end to end, over the distributed Cloud applications.

Aggregation Cloud brokers may be used to combine multiple existing services into one, taking the burden of data and process integration from the client. A broker means both a provider and a distribution technology.

The broker would also take care of revenue sharing between Cloud Providers.

Is SOA needed?

For integration between multiple Clouds and on-premise applications, a clean SOA architecture simply eliminates the internal integration fur-ball spreading in the Clouds. For a single application in the Cloud, outsourcing to SaaS without SOA may be still all right.

An Enterprise Business Architecture is the 3rd best practice recommended since it supplies the big picture of the Enterprise, its functions, the systems executing them and the internal organizational units and Cloud providers supplying the services.

The Cloud impact on Enterprise IT

Jun 11, 2010

http://it.toolbox.com/blogs/ea-matters/the-cloud-impact-on-enterprise-it-39291

What will be the impact of the Cloud on the Enterprise IT and the IT Enterprises (i.e. supplying IT)? Let me post a few thoughts in answer to that.

The Cloud represents an enhanced business model of supplying the IT resources supporting your Enterprise operation through outsourcing. It is enabled by today's virtualisation, infrastructure scalability, SOA, Web, and increasingly capable network technologies. The Cloud offers independence with regard to the outsourcing location and implementation technology. It is easy to take up, configure or renounce since there is no more ownership of IT resources. It presents an IT "lease" business model with pay as you use charging.

IT would become separated from the Enterprise and IT concerns would be separated from business ones. New Cloud supply firms would appear. Business people would control the IT capabilities through self service under contract with these firms. The outcome would be evident: no large IT departments in an Enterprise, no own data centres, cooling and energy bills, no more IT skills, licenses, training, etc.

The Enterprise would be truly nimble and agile. The Cloud would facilitate easy ramp up and upgrades through self service. B2B at its best.

Enterprise Architecture becomes essential now to describe the business functions and the distributed outsourced supporting systems and their interconnections since a problem may lay in any of a few systems distributed in various Clouds. There must be a blueprint for analysis, defect fixing and evolution. The Cloud would signal nonetheless the end of the old division between business and IT.

Nowadays, the IT Enterprises, supplying equipment and applications, and outsourcing suppliers are both serving the customer Enterprises. With the Cloud, the IT supplier would mainly supply the Cloud provider even though the IT Enterprise might also choose to become a Cloud supplier. In time, the IT infrastructure suppliers, would have to switch from their large customer base of many Enterprises to a few Cloud suppliers. Less customers but more gear though.

The applications suppliers may choose to go SaaS themselves or provide their application as a service over a Cloud infrastructure supplier.

It looks like a win-win... situation for most parties. An impact would come though from the consolidation of outsourcing suppliers since few companies could provide the large scale and the necessary reliability of operation. Gigantic Cloud centres have to be build and managed.

Another rather expected consequence is that the IT people would have to migrate from the many Enterprises they work for today to a few Cloud providers. But that is already happening with legacy outsourcing.

The Cloud is still immature nevertheless and standards are not quite there yet to enable, for instance, portability between Clouds and with it the major growth.

Enterprise Architecture and Cloud Silos

Aug 24, 2010

http://it.toolbox.com/blogs/ea-matters/enterprise-architecture-and-cloud-silos-40796

In "The danger of cloud silos" David Linthicum writes that we create silos while moving to the brave new world of the Cloud. True.

To avoid silos, you should consider integration from start. That may come with a simple Enterprise Architecture picture showing all key business functions, applications and infrastructure on premise and in the clouds.

A simple EA picture would illustrate the whole issue. You can easily judge what stays, what goes and what are the interconnections that traverse security zones between on premise and the clouds systems themselves. EA would provide the connectivity information that you need to link your applications and infrastructure in the clouds. You should be easily permitted to add new connections.

Indeed SOA would be highly desirable before you move to the cloud since then the interactions would be simple to add and rather standard.

But what good is the integration if the transmitted information is not understood by all systems in the cloud? It's time to discover, design and implement your EA information architecture as you move into the clouds. This ensures that an order has the same structure and content across the Enterprise.

Cloud Computing and Enterprise Architecture

Dec 24, 2009

I cannot resist the temptation to blog about Cloud Computing. Everyone does. I'll do that in the context of Enterprise Architecture (EA) though.

Cloud computing is an overloaded term and vague at that. Nonetheless, I would define it in brief as the outsourcing of your IT services - applications and technology - over the Web. What is new? Nothing much, except, I think, the combination of powerful technologies such as SOA, Web Services, the Internet, Virtualization, Blades, VPNs... The utility like, on demand service consumption and charging is still the novel element of the Cloud.

The Cloud is, in fact, a business concept, even though created by the IT world, because it is about the business outsourcing IT functions. But so are SOA and Enterprise Architecture.

The Cloud should include only the services provided to your Enterprise. Each and every firm may have its own Cloud, that may be supplied by the same multi-tenant service providers. The Cloud symbol, coming from the networking world, signifies Internet distribution.

Any Enterprise Architecture consists of a few basic layers: Business, Information, Applications and Technology. An I would add the People layer. The Cloud covers both the IT application and technology layers of an Enterprise Architecture. Imagine the EA Business Architecture layer resting on top of a fluffy Cloud of outsourced IT Application and Technology layers. How would this map to our TM F Frameworks? In the next posts. Mind you, you still need to do the overall Enterprise Architecture, but you need not bother with technology detail any longer.

Is the Cloud a technology? To start with, it is the business concept of outsourcing IT services, really. But it is constructed on Virtualized infrastructure, Web Services...

To recap, the term Cloud Computing, from an EA perspective, means the outsourcing of Enterprise Architecture IT applications and technology layers over the Web.

For those worried about Security here is some good news:

"*San Francisco, CA, Dec 17, 2009 – The Cloud Security Alliance (CSA) today issued here the second version of its "Guidance for Critical Areas of Focus in Cloud Computing".*"

The Cloud Security Alliance is a not-for-profit organization with a mission to promote the use of best practices for providing security assurance within Cloud Computing, and to provide education on the uses of Cloud Computing to help secure all other forms of computing. The whitepaper, "Guidance for Critical Areas of Focus in Cloud Computing – Version 2.1", outlines key issues and provides advice for both Cloud Computing customers and providers within 13 strategic domains. Version 2.1 provides more concise and actionable guidance across all domains, and encompasses knowledge gained from real world deployments over the past six months in this fast moving area."

Cloud computing, SOA and Enterprise Architecture

Jan 27, 2009

http://it.toolbox.com/blogs/ea-matters/cloud-computing-soa-and-enterprise-architecture-29406

Cloud computing is an overloaded term and vague at that. In short, I would define it as the outsourcing of your IT services - applications and technology - to 3rd parties over the Web.

Remote access only to these services may sound incomplete since it suggests interaction with people rather than applications integration, and leaving aside the outsourcing and subsequently the utility like service consumption that are the novel elements of the Cloud.

The Cloud is, in fact, a business concept even though created by the IT world. But so are SOA and Enterprise Architecture. And it should refer only to the services cloud of your Enterprise. Each and every firm may have its own cloud, that would overlap sometimes at multi tenant service providers. As a simple picture, it looks like an Enterprise Cloud of Services surrounding and serving your core company.

It consists of a few component service concepts (types of outsourcing services): SaaS, PaaS (XaaS)... (Application, Platform, Infrastructure, Security... as a Service).

PaaS (platform) and all its variants, part of the computing cloud, offer the opportunity to outsource not only your data centre but platforms for your Web presence, content management...

Integration as a Service is an emerging service providing the orchestration and integration of the XaaS services.

The cloud covers both the IT application and technology layers of an Enterprise Architecture. Imagine, the EA Business Architecture layer resting on top of a fluffy Cloud of distributed, outsourced IT Application and Technology layers. The cloud symbol, coming from the networking world, signifies Internet distribution. Mind you, you still need to understand the overall Enterprise Architecture, but you need not bother with technology detail any longer.

Because of the mapping between various XaaS. a few business models are possible. At one end, your applications would be outsourced to different SaaS providers in the Cloud providing their own technology layer. At the other end, applications from various providers are housed e or more Infrastructure/Data Centres providers, managed by 3rd parties.

Is the Cloud a technology? To start with, it is the business concept of outsourcing IT services, really.

As with SOA, companies such as Amazon, Google, Salesforce.com, Microsoft... provide various technological platforms/centres for you to use. If not relying on the Internet, I found them called private clouds. A number of these platforms may become part of your Enterprise cloud.

THE GODS BUSINESS ARCHITECTURE AND ONE PAGE EA

A Single Page Enterprise Architecture

Apr 1, 2009

http://it.toolbox.com/blogs/ea-matters/a-single-page-enterprise-architecture-30755

One of the most useful reviews of my early EA book was Paul Harmon's of BPTrends. He suggested, among others that, while I mentioned that an EA picture is worth a thousand words, I haven't really supplied it. Instead, I provided only a general framework. True, stakeholders show little interest in the complexity and subtleties of an EA framework. The framework is for the EA architects to construct and use. (The critique was taken in consideration: blueprint design and samples provided in the 3rd edition, now available).

Most stakeholders are in fact after a single picture showing only their own concerns mapped over a single page Enterprise blueprint that describes the basic structure of the Enterprise. The picture provides a common set of objects for all designs, the common EA vocabulary.

How would this EA blueprint look like though?

Let me begin by saying that an EA not only should look like but should represent the map of an Enterprise: "A map is a visual representation of an area, a symbolic depiction highlighting relationships between elements of that pace such as objects, regions..." (Wikipedia).

Simplifying even further, which map do we typically use to represent an area? given the fact that there are so many types of maps. Wikipedia saves us again: "road maps are perhaps the most widely used maps today, and form a subset of navigational maps...".

From an Enterprise Architecture perspective, how would this road map look like?

A Single Page EA blueprint would like a road map depicting the key connections and objects of the EA. Ideally, we should be able to zoom and navigate electronically with a tool.

The single page EA blueprint is one of the most important deliveries of an EA effort since it will be used by all stakeholders alike. An EA picture is not going to replace the EA though but should evolve and synch with all other EA views. The key stakeholders can map and add their information to create a view which should be added to the EA set.

The single page EA blueprint should be aligned with the business architecture based on the Value Chains of the Enterprise.

The Essential Business Architecture

October 25, 2010

http://www.ebizq.net/blogs/ea_matters/2010/10/essential-business-architecture.php

Business Architecture (BA) is the most important layer or component of an Enterprise Architecture (EA). This is because it shapes all other layers. For instance, Business functions and processes described in the BA dictate the type of technology and organization architecture that implement them. It is true though, that the availability of people and technology resources constrain business operation as well.

But what are the essential parts of an Enterprise? At the beginning of the '80es, Michael Porter suggested that any Enterprise consists of two categories of activities:

Michael's Porter Value Chain

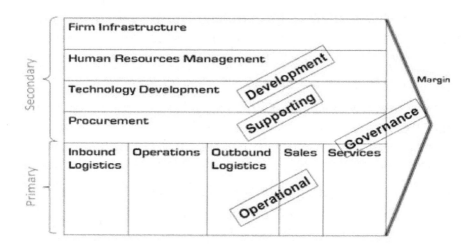

Primary activities, which are the operational processes that deliver the product such

as inbound logistics, Operations. Outbound logistics, sales and services

And Secondary activities that are all other supporting activities , as for example human resources, technology development, procurement etc.

Taking into account the dynamics of today's economy, I concluded though that Development activities are worth a category in themselves since a great chunk of them, such as strategy and business

development, new products and capabilities development or R&D ensure the competitive edge of the Enterprise and its continuity.

In a world that spins faster and faster, more and more activities are outsourceable and outsourced, even Operations, once a core activity. This is why, the only part that stays put in the today Enterprise is the newly added Governance function, since it coordinates all activities, outsourced or not, and ultimately identifies the company.

This is how the GODS Enterprise structure came into being. GODS stands for: Governance, Operations, Development and Support. Since primary activities are often outsourced to specialized firms, they become autonomous chain links in what Porter called Value Systems or Networks.

I found that the Operations function can be further subdivided in three large Flows or Chains in the Operations Value System.:

1. Marketing & Planning

2. Production & Delivery

3. Selling & Servicing

GODS Enterprise Structure and Porter's Value System

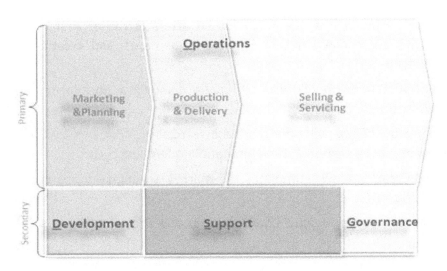

Adrian Grigoriu

A generic One Page Business Architecture, cnt'd

October 27, 2010

http://www.ebizq.net/blogs/ea_matters/2010/10/a-generic-one-page-business-architecture-cntd.php

The essential generic business architecture (gBA) shows the main Enterprise Functions and Processes that describe, in one page, both the Enterprise structure and behaviour.

gBA illustrates a full product cycle from forecasting and planning, to demand creation, product delivery, sales and orders, revenue accrual and customer services for both production and services types of industries. It also depicts the Governance, Development and Support functions. It builds on the concept of Value Chains.

As such, besides operations/production, support or IT, gBA addresses all Enterprise activities and thus stakeholders from marketing and planning, sales, customer services, finance, etc.

It is a reference Business Architecture in the sense that it describes generic business elements in interconnection - rather than a disjoint list of capabilities disconnected from the Enterprise value flows -, that can be used to describe any/your Enterprise.

It is also a business architecture because it does not describe technology alone as so many other frameworks do. Still the EA IT architecture of today can be easily aligned.

gBA is part of the EA though. Business and other EA Views can be linked to gBA to show further process detail and the systems implementing the business functionality. FFLV, the related method described on this site, can be further used to build the whole EA.

By comparison, Zachman is a taxonomy for EA artefacts rather than a BA or an ontology of the Enterprise (that is Enterprise elements and relationships) as sometimes claimed.

Here is a description of the key Enterprise Functions and Flows that form the generic Business Architecture:

- The Planning Flow begins with the market investigation, followed by forecasting; this Flow prepares all Operational, Development and Support cycles.

- The Demand Creation Flow stimulates the market, through various channels, to acquire the products

- The Production Flow or Supply Chain delivers the Products, from sourcing to distribution

- The Demand Flow or Sales & Ordering is the process through which the customers obtain the products

- The Revenue Flow or Money Flow charges the customers at sales and ordering,

306

bills and invoices them and accrues the revenue attained for the firm

- The After-Sales Flow or Customer Services depicts the customers' feedback/complaints, product returns and repairs Flows

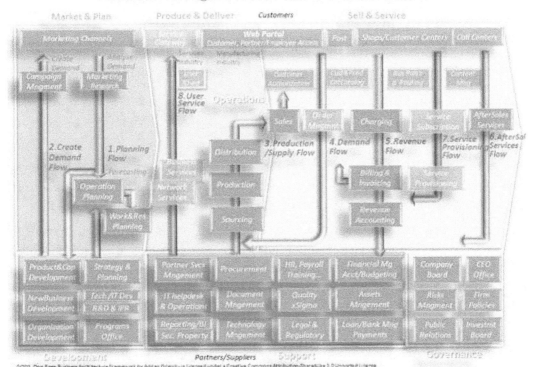

The Services Industry Flows looking slightly different

- The Service Provisioning Flow describes how the customer acquires membership to a scheme, or subscribes to a service

- The Service Delivery Flow depicts how the customer, once identified , claims and uses the service, often provided by a business partner; analogue to the Production Flow

There are also shown a few typical business functions that are supporting the interaction with customers, such as: Customer and User Authorization, Products Catalogue, Business Rules and Request Routing and so on.

In principle, the Customers channels and interaction are represented at the top of the diagram.

The Development, Support and Governance Flows, even though important, are not shown here; the corresponding Functions are illustrated in the picture.

A note: I might have called the Flows, Value Chains, Streams or Processes but each terminology comes from a different domain, with baggage and meanings I wanted to avoid. Also, Functions are part of Capabilities which capabilities include physical resources as well.

On a practical plane, you will have to

Customise this business architecture to illustrate your own Business Operation.

Align the Technology and Organization Architectures to the Business Architecture.

Map the Strategy objectives to the overall Architecture to enable strategy execution and transformation of the Enterprise.

Value Chains, streams, capabilities & one page architecture

Mar 15, 2012

http://it.toolbox.com/blogs/ea-matters/value-chains-streams-and-capabilities-in-an-one-page-architecture-and-the-integrating-ea-framework-50789

An enterprise typically needs four types of functions to operate: **G**overnance, **O**perations, **D**evelopment and **S**upport. This is the GODS taxonomy, produced having in mind Porter's Value Chains concept.

The Governance (Management if you like) function is introduced because it becomes more and more visible today with the increasing trend of outsourcing all the other Support, Development and Operational functions.

Ultimately Governance maybe the only function that remains to define the company.

Think of companies that outsource all manufacturing, product design, strategy specification, the IT -to the Cloud -, HR and Payroll, Fleet... They just do, as such, the coordination and management of the links in the value chain. They effectively consist of the Governance function alone.

In Operations (similar to Primary activities in Porter), Create Product is not included, because it is not part of a normal production cycle.

You develop a new product once in a while but you make and deliver the product many times afterwards. They are part of different enterprise cycles.

Operations do include planning, source, make, deliver, sales and service activities. Market research and, in particular, subsequent planning become part of the chain since they support the sizing of the offer, and the necessary resources for the specific demand.

While Development activities include R&D, new product, capability or business development, organization improvement, strategy...

Overlaid on the GODS taxonomy are the key flows (a.k.a. value streams) of an enterprise, the customer interaction and the business functions (a.k.a. capabilities).

Here is the representation of this generic business architecture.

The work aims to describe in a single page, a generic enterprise, as much as possible, in terms of structure, behaviour and interfaces to customers.

All three concepts of Value Chains (from business academia), Value Streams (Flows) (from Quality improvement methods) and Functions (Capabilities in Enterprise Architecture) are mapped in this approach unifying in fact, rather independent approaches from different domains of activity.

You can use this model by starting to customise it to your enterprise: that is adapt the value chains, business functions (capabilities) and flows (value streams) to your own enterprise. From then on, just add and link the next architecture levels 2, 3...

The model offers you more insight than all approaches - value chains, capability and process maps - taken together or in isolation. It is an integrated and complete model of all these views.

The architecture is technology independent; it is in fact a business architecture. But you can add the IT/Technology and organization layers at later times.

To integrate these layers together you may use the FFLV (Function-Flow-Layer-View) EA framework (and navigation , definitions and integration) described elsewhere in my blogs and site.

As such GODS would describe your basic business structure and operation while FFLV would add the technology and people resources tiers in and link all components and artefacts together, to give you the whole picture of the enterprise.

Depending on enterprise, there may be more (GODS like) business units which can be organised in various ways (as for instance all Support activities as Shared Services.

Also the various business units (represented as GODS models) in your enterprise can be standardised and integrated according to an Operating Model, in the case of geographical distribution of the enterprise operation. As for instance standardise and integrate the Development functions, or standardise the "make and deliver" Operations processes.

The enterprise Business Models can be described now over GODS-FFLV in terms of

 - the associated functions and processes in the business architecture (GODS flows),

 - interfaces to customers (channels),

 - the resources implementing them (the technology and people layers) added with FFLV

 - and indeed by the value proposition taking into account the costs associated with each business function resources versus the overall profit.

Give it a try for your EA. Start with GODS and add technology and people with FFLV. In the book and on site there is a basic metamodel, supporting the EA framework. You can use TOGAF ADM as a process (because it is too stuffy, you may use a development process described succinctly in bullet points in the book) and Zachman, if you think you need it, for scoping and EA justification.

What architects can do with a single page Business Architecture

November 15, 2010

http://www.ebizq.net/blogs/ea_matters/2010/11/most-enterprise-architects-are-not.php

The question was raised in a LinkedIn discussion. Do Enterprise stakeholders need a simple business architecture like the one proposed in previous posts?

True, most Enterprise Architects are not asked to do Business Architecture. A reason is that, it is not the business of IT to describe how the enterprise operates or to describe the business flows. Most of us are called Enterprise Architects without ever producing in fact a BA or an EA for that matter. As Forrester found in a 2009 survey, EA architects do mostly IT solution architecture, reviews and strategy. Some do loose capability maps that prove sufficient for the limited purpose of IT.

For the new emerging breed of business architects this is a different matter though since they are tasked to produce the overall picture of the Enterprise and its operation in terms of flows and functions.

We already have many views of an Enterprise. Every team has a diagram in a drawer showing how the Enterprise part of concern operates. The Views do not re-use though components and interconnections though, they overlap... have various naming conventions, diagramming types, are produced with different tools and stored all over the place.

The problem a proposed single page generic business architecture is trying to solve is the fusing of these Views into a single consistent integrated Enterprise architecture by linking and building the Views from the same the top level business architecture picture. Without a simple BA showing the key Enterprise reference functions and flows, stakeholders and architects would keep reinventing them only to add to a disjoint stack of views.

What is the single page GODS generic business architecture good for? Your practical business architecture would be a customisation of it, representing your own Enterprise. Any Enterprise stakeholder needs a picture to understand how the Enterprise operates. As such, business people and IT would talk on and build from the this same single page BA picture. It would relieve the tension between the business and IT, having now same terms of reference.

Various segments in business and IT can link their Views to this top architecture: BPM and xSigma people would expand business Flows to work on improvement and automation, organization improvement groups to align organization, business development people to configure new business models, executive management to pinpoint issues...IT to discover, map, document and roadmap every IT system in the Enterprise now, by looking at parts of the Enterprise they never considered before, for instance the system used for campaign management.

IT systems and technology can be mapped to the business flows they execute and as such their performance evaluated by business. Systems serving Service Provisioning,

Content Management, User Identification... could be linked and aligned to the corresponding business functions needs, goals and strategy. A system can be analysed now in the context of the business functions and flows it serves.

A solution architecture project to replace or add a system would benefit from the BA description of functions and flows it has to implement.

Many see EA/BA in terms of strategy, future states and change. But how can one do roadmapping without knowing the systems described by a current architecture? That aside, strategy is one of the many other use cases. EA/BA can be used for comprehension, simplification, agility enhancement, technology alignment...

Ultimately, companies like IBM (Component Business Model) and Microsoft (Motion) have their own business frameworks (for consultancy assignments or to help sell their own systems) which are similar in nature and purpose to this. This generic business architecture expands these frameworks by adding to business capabilities, end to end business flows that complete the Enterprise picture and engage in the EA effort all Enterprise stakeholders form the business side.

Benefits of the GODS generic business architecture model

Nov 30, 2010

http://it.toolbox.com/blogs/ea-matters/benefits-of-the-gods-generic-business-architecture-model-42814

Here are a few benefits of the generic business modelling, presented in the previous post (http://it.toolbox.com/blogs/ea-matters/a-generic-business-architecture-42616):

• It is complying to IEEE/ANSI 1471 since it consists of both business functions and flows, that is components in relationships, rather than either capability maps or business flows in separation.

• It makes distinction between business capabilities, processes and flows that are not clearly distinguishable today in other business modelling approaches.

• It aims to be complete at the top in that it describes all categories of functions of a typical enterprise Value Chain (as GODS), and all flows of a typical business cycle.

• It represents customer's interaction and channels consistently - at the top of the diagram - for every flow of the Value System so that one can trace and improve the customer journey from prospect to after-sales.

• It represents the top tier of an EA framework, elucidating the first steps of an EA development

• It is technology and organization neutral in that it does not contain elements of them; nevertheless, the IT architecture can be readily aligned to the BA within the same EA. Architectural Views can be linked to BA to reveal necessary detail, systems and organization roles that execute the business architecture functionality.

• It supplies the functional vocabulary and business objects repository.

• It represents a reference architecture that can be tailored to industry and company to create a specific framework for own business operation discovery, documentation and roadmapping. Your practical business architecture would be a customization of it, representing your own Enterprise as a common model shared around the Enterprise. It would be the single most used artefact of an EA.

• Ultimately, it enables the fusing of the current business modelling methods in a single approach uniting the Business Capability Maps of EA with the Value Chains and Business Models...of Business Management and Value Streams of xSigma and Quality Management disciplines.

And benefits for enterprise stakeholders:

• It reaches a wide audience besides the typical operations/production, support and IT functions since it addresses most other Enterprise activities such as R&D, product development, marketing, sales, customer services, finance, etc.

• It relieves the tension between the business and IT that have now the same terms of reference. Any stakeholder needs a picture to understand how the Enterprise operates. As such, business people and IT would talk on and build from the this same single page BA picture.

Here are also a few practical Use Cases:

• Single page reference architecture for development of specific business architectures for industry and firm.

• Top tier of an Enterprise Architecture framework.

• Business Functions Map design for technology resources and

organization alignment.

• Key business flows (Value Streams) discovery for process analysis and improvement for BPM and Quality Management efforts such as xSigma.

• Business and Operating Models mapping, analysis and

implementation.

The generic business architecture integration to EA (IT)

Dec 21, 2010

http://it.toolbox.com/blogs/ea-matters/the-generic-business-architecture-integration-to-ea-it-43265

Since EA is primarily IT these days, how do we add and integrate business architecture late in the process? How do we integrate other Enterprise efforts?

The generic business architecture (see this) is just a part of an overall EA framework which would allow navigation from business entities in the business architecture to the IT implementing it. Thus we can inspect assets, resources and evaluate actual performance.

We also need to integrate the EA work and collaborate with existing BPM, Sigma efforts in the Enterprise, rather than working in isolation.

Here is an oversimplified scenario of using GODS for integration of business modelling efforts to EA

1. tailor the GODS Value Chain for your business

2. customise and develop the next hierarchical level of value streams for BPM/xSigma effort from GODS business flows

3. customise GODS business functions to create your EA functions map

4. Align your technical architecture to the business function map

The truth is that you need a proper EA framework to render the EA big picture components. Most existing EA frameworks practically ignore business modelling. TOGAF and Zachman, FEAF... only tell you that BA exists not how it looks like or how to integrate or navigate between business and technology architectures.

FFLV is such an EA framework that can help you in this endeavour, as noted earlier. It integrates the one page generic GODS business architecture (that is the Functions and Flows, the FF part of FFLV).

FFLV stands for Functions-Flows-Layers-View and is described here and in the book. Layers are essentially the Enterprise tiers of People and Technology that implement the Business operation.

The Views concept of FFLV (and 1471) are filters through layers that enable a stakeholder to see solely the part of interest of the Enterprise (be it business process, technology or/and people resources), but conserving the overall integrity and consistency of the Enterprise model.

THE GODS-FFLV FRAMEWORK

A Practical Enterprise Architecture Framework

Oct 17, 2007

http://it.toolbox.com/blogs/ea-matters/a-practical-enterprise-architecture-framework-19687

Any Enterprise consists, at its basics, of business processes delivering the products and the Technology and People resource layers implementing the business processes. As such Business, Technology and People become the key layers of an Enterprise Architecture (EA).

For practical reasons, each layer is further described by Views, filters showing only the aspects of interest to a stakeholder: for instance, the business layer consists of process, information, strategy, value chains, business models...

The people layer is more often than not, left out since, frequently, the EA framework covers solely IT. The Technology layer consists of IT Applications and Infrastructure architectures and other non-IT technology. Information is spread across layers: conceptually it exists in the business layer but in physical form, in all layers.

Any Enterprise structure is shaped by its Value Chain. Fundamental Enterprise Functions, such as Operations (delivering the product), Development (developing the product & capability, R&D...) and Support (HR, technology management) are consistent with the Value Chain representation. Each of these functions consists of lower level business functions. The Operations function, for example, can be further described by Porter's Value Chain (sourcing, inbound logistics...), the Supply Chain framework SCOR, eTOM or other frameworks. A Governance function is specifically defined here, since it is the centre of a Virtual Enterprise concept; it is managing the Enterprise, coordinating all other Functions and it, ultimately, identifies the Enterprise.

Here is now an EA framework built on these components: business Functions, Flows (Processes), Layers and Views (FFLV) and the GODS (Governance, Operations,

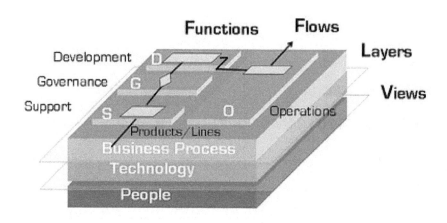

The FFLV Enterprise Architecture Framework

Development, Support) structure.

Each business function consists, vertically, of at least a process and the technology and organizational role executing the process.

In a Flow (process) diagram, any line between Functions or between Functions and stakeholders can be described in terms of an output of a process which can be a Product (part) or Information (bill, order, message) and a connection which is the transport for the product/info implemented by a network, a mechanical transport band, a courier etc.

The framework could initially be implemented with a minimum of Functions and Flows describing the primary products delivery and a minimum number of Views. As the framework is open, Flows, Functions and Views can be added at later times.

For federated architectures, with a few Lines of Business (LoBs), the same framework applies: each LoB has its As-Is architecture, ultimately merged in a single To-Be architecture with a few LoB Operations and shared support and development functions, in fact reusable services in a SOA design.

Layers, Views and the FFLV Framework Metamodel

Nov 16, 2007

In fact any FFLV framework (see previous post) object - Function, Flow, Line - is described by three Layers - Business, Technology and People - and ultimately the Views describing them. Business consists of process, strategy and other Views at various degree of detail. Same, Technology consists of IT applications, infrastructure and non-IT technology...

An FFLV workflow (flow) will look like a sequence of business Functions, consisting of Business processes, Technology and People.

A View, is the graphical representation of all objects in a repository and their interconnections which have been selected because they reflect a specific aspect of concern as for instance the Content Management View. The selection of the attribute can be done from the EA cube GUI or menus. Attribute combinations can be selected by an SQL like statement, automatically generated at the menu selection or mouse click on the graphical EA framework representation.

Largely, a metamodel, from an EA tool point of view, describes the object metadata, i.e. the structure of the Enterprise objects. The metamodel is a reflection of the EA framework at the EA object level. An EA architecture framework is incorporated in the EA object metadata: the attributes of EA objects describe the layers and the structure of the framework the EA object is part of.

Starting from the attributes of an object, the diagrams of interconnections and relationships between objects could be drawn. This is also the way some EA tools generate dependencies diagrams on the selection of specific Enterprise objects attributes from the repository.

For the proposed FFLV EA framework, a Function, as the basic unit of the Enterprise, may be represented by a single object in the metamodel. The Function object may be decomposed in lower level sub-Functions but ultimately, all Functions consist of the three Layers - Business, Technology and People - which are described by an unlimited number of Views . As a result, an object in the metamodel, is described by many attributes representing the Views the object belongs to.

An EA Development Framework GODS-FFLV

Jun 25, 2010

Any Enterprise consists, at its basics, of business processes delivering the products and the Technology and People resource layers implementing the business processes. As such Business, Technology and People become the key layers of an

Enterprise Architecture (EA).

Each layer is further described by Views, filters showing only the aspects of interest to a stakeholder: for instance, the business layer consists of process, information, strategy, value chains, business models...

The EA framework is built on business Functions, Flows (Processes), Layers and Views components (FFLV) and the GODS (Governance, Operations, Development, Support) structure.

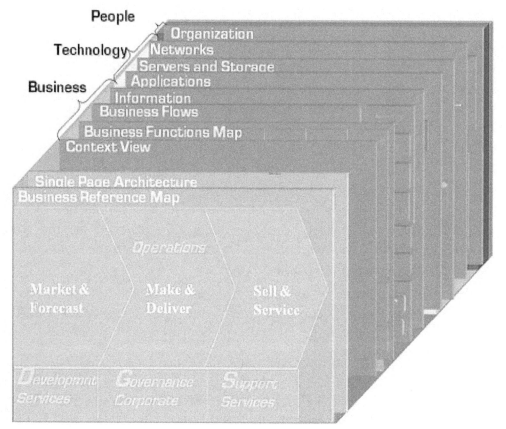

Any Enterprise business structure is shaped by GODS and Value Chains.

GODS describes the top business structure of an Enterprise, the key parts. (G-Governance - coordinates all other, O-Operations - deliver the products, D-Development - develops the products and the organization, S-Support - provides the other functions with technology, people, finance).

GODS structure supplies the Enterprise Architect with a standard capability map.

In the GODS framework this is the horizontal dimension.

Vertically, each GODS function is further described in this proposed EA framework by the People and Technology layers executing the functions.

Any function is fully described by its Business processes, information, rules, strategies... but also by its IT Technology and People implementing them.

Flows describe the processes delivering the products. Here is a graphical representation that can be used as a navigation GUI.

A View, is the graphical representation of all objects in a repository which have been selected for a specific purpose - as for instance the recruitment View.

Each business function consists of at least a process and the technology and organizational roles/units executing the processes.

The Business Reference Map is a standard template used to ease the development for all and everybody. It consists o GODS and a Value Chain such as Planning, Operations (Product delivery), Sales and Service.

A Single Page Architecture is the reference business blueprint for all stakeholders since it describes the basic structure and operation of the Enterprise in one page. It is a key EA delivery.

The extended EA framework also covers metamodel, references maps for business and templates for technology, best practices, development process, EA value assessment, business and operating models, organizational design and alignment, EA design method, security, information and SOA architectures, maturity evaluation, culture, EA architect role and leadership... are all described in my EA book, 3rd edition (Trafford, Amazon...).

The EA framework and a novel EA development method

Oct 18, 2010

http://it.toolbox.com/blogs/ea-matters/the-ea-framework-and-a-novel-ea-development-method-41951

A framework helps you build and decompose a system; it represents the meta architecture, that is the architecture of the architecture of a system.

What does a framework consists of? As a (meta-)architecture, a framework should consist, according to the ISO42010, of the elements of the system (that is the common elements of any architecture) in interconnection.

I found these elements to be the Functions, Flows, Layers & Views. Any system could and should be described by these elements.

The Functions describe the structure, the Flows the behaviour of the system, the Layers, the physical resources (implementing Functions and Flows) and the views, the many angles the stakeholders see the Enterprise which, put together and properly aligned, form the EA.

My initial "views" concept was called "planes" since I represented the framework as a cube (three dimensions: Functions, Flows and Layers+Views) where planes looked like CT scan cross-sections in the body of the Enterprise. If you need to see the BI architecture, just select a cross-section in the technology layer.

A system, in my view, should be described by both a logical and an implementation (the physical realization) architecture.

The FFLV framework consists of three layers: logical, i.e. Business, and implementation that is, Technology and People.

An EA development process is part of an extended framework.

Spewak's, TOGAF... mainly describe the EA development process. Because of that most professionals would expect such a development process to be The framework. And the process is useful indeed.

I felt the need to develop an overall EA method, rather than a framework alone, that contains:

- an EA framework (FFLV) and the necessary definitions, vocabulary

- EA reference models to ease up the modelling of the Enterprise (not everyone affords the time to uncover the Enterprise patterns)

- an EA Design that shows the key design artefacts that map on the framework and use the metamodel elements

- an EA development process

You'll find this "EA approach" on my website illustrated in four A3 posters (The Framework, The Process, The Models, The Design) each containing lots of diagrams. This work is meant to be public under a Creative Commons license: essentially, you can use it for any purpose and add to it, if you mention the author.

This EA approach, compressed in posters, is meant to contain everything an EA architect needs to do its work with, from business case modelling to the strategic transformation process, the EA organization, site, governance, maturity assessment, reference maps and models, framework, metamodel, reference business architecture...

The FFLV-GODS Enterprise Architecture framework

Mar 27, 2012

http://it.toolbox.com/blogs/ea-matters/the-fflvgods-enterprise-architecture-framework-50886

Its name is FFLV+GODS EA framework standing for Functions-Flows-Layers-Views + Governance-Operations-Development-Support.

Its purpose is to represent the EA structure on which individual EA elements and artefacts should be plugged-in to form the EA.

The scope: Business, Technology and People/Organisation Architecture. Technology covers more than IT.

FFLV is a meta EA (the architecture of EA) consisting of the interconnected elements that describe an EA:

- the business Functions (capabilities),

- the business Flows (value streams),

- the Layers: Business, Technology and People and

- the Views, the architectures representing aspects of interest to specific stakeholders.

In clear text, any Enterprise can be described by its Functions (structure) and Flows (behaviour) in the business layer, by its Technology and People resource layers, executing the business Functions and Flows, and by any number of Views of the above need by stakeholders.

Information is part of the business Functions and Flows and is represented as data in the Technology Layer.

The FFLV is based on a metamodel that shows the links between Functions, Flows and entities in Layers and Views.

FFLV was built by comparison with the human body anatomy and physiology descriptions you can see in any book. You are already used to it. Body parts are Functions, body flows (end to end vital processes) are business Flows and the nervous or blood system... look like EA Views.

GODS is the functional structure of a generic business consisting of

- Governance: the business Functions coordinating of all activities

- Operations: the business Functions making and delivering the products/services

- Development Functions developing the products and the enterprise itself

- Support Functions providing technology, financial,

HR, transportation, procurement ... support to all other Functions.

GODS aligns to Porter's Value Chain model. Functions are also known as Capabilities and Flows as Value Streams.

Any Business Architecture (the EA business layer), can be built on the GODS template. In addition to Functions GODS describes the key business Flows and the interaction with the customer at all times in the customer experience lifecycle.

The FFLV-GODS framework can be represented tri-dimensionally, as a cube and can be navigated across business flows and functions to analyse performance, executing systems and human resources, the impact of change or for roadmapping and strategy design and implementation purposes.

An extended FFLV-GODS framework is covered in the book "An Enterprise Architecture Development Framework" available on Kindle and elsewhere. It describes an EA development process (many times shorter than TOGAF), best practices, principles, the information architecture built, business and IT architecture templates, EA maturity, value delivery, EA evaluation method, business case, strategic planning with EA, SOA design. It also looks at the EA practice construction, governance, architects skills and selection, the role of culture and even a virtual case study.

The book also describes how to formulate and map strategy and how to do roadmapping.

It is not a stuffy process as TOGAF ADM is. It is much more than a system design taxonomy like Zachman. The framework itself is an ontology. It exhibits an extendable metamodel.

The framework (and metamodel) interconnects all your EA artefacts and offers generic template for business and IT architectures to start with.

FFLV+GODS unifies the EA (and IT) with the Business Process world and business theory.

It is the result of a long effort to understand what frameworks like TOGAF, Zachman, eTOM (Frameworx), DoDAF, FEAF, TEAF... do. From that experience a new framework was built that does all the above and much more.

Enterprise culture, EA governance, roadblocks, architects skills are also discuss in the book and on the web site.

MISCELLANEOUS

The EA Development Framework, book contents

May 13, 2009

http://it.toolbox.com/blogs/ea-matters/the-enterprise-architecture-development-framework-book-contents-31619

I interrupt the current series to list the contents of my EA book. I realised after reading and browsing a few EA books that, in many ways, each and every one is different. Like the EA frameworks. This book, the 3rd edition (see footer for URL) is intended to go past the existing taxonomy and development process frameworks to help you justify the EA, build it, based on best practices, reference maps and patterns and sell it. The book introduces new ways and information not yet available in the EA field. It shows how to avoid EA roadblocks, how to select an Enterprise Architect and what are his tasks. What is the governance of the EA practice. How to design and map strategy to IT. What are the Business and IT Architecture templates like. It tells you that ITIL is the business process architecture EA of the IT department. And more like the Virtual Enterprise, Cloud Computing, EA and SOA.

Here is a list of topics discussed in the book.

- the Enterprise, Architecture and EA definitions and scope; styles of architecture

- a classification and discussion of current EA frameworks

- current drivers and trends in business and IT for the commercial and government sectors

- the EA drivers, benefits and value proposition

- the Business Case for the EA, evaluating financial Payback and NPV;

the Return on your Enterprise Architecture (RoEA)enabling management support and business participation in your EA development

- an EA framework, integrating Business, Technology and People/Organization views; the extended framework includes the EA metamodel, development process, governance, standards...

- A basic EA metamodel diagram to clarify the mapping and relationships between the components of the key artefacts. As you add EA views, the metamodel should be enriched with new objects and links

- the EA navigation GUI for moving between layers and views, so that stakeholders can select the information they need and analyse supporting technologies, people and impacts

- the Business Architecture discovery starting from Value Chain and in particular the Business and Operating models

- Business modelling showing how products/services, and in general value, is delivered to stakeholders by business flows over functions

- the Business Reference Map

- a Business Process framework

- EA templates/reference maps and patterns to help the design of the Business, Application, Infrastructure, and Organization architecture layers. The maps supply the typical "design" structure of the layer, the components and patterns.

- the EA basic deliveries checklist

- the essential technology architecture reference map

- the Single Page Enterprise Architecture with examples, the key EA delivery; it describes a synoptic view of the Enterprise structure and operation in a single picture serving as a common vocabulary and architecture for all stakeholders

- the Information/Data architecture design

- the alignment of the EA and solutions architectures and projects, (how would the project artefacts be represented in the EA and how is the EA guiding the solutions).

- organization design models to help alignment of the business and technology architecture to people organization

- the Enterprise strategic planning starting from business vision, goals and business strategy

- EA architectural principles to guide architects

- SOA as part of EA (SOEA)

- SOA design

- EA standards references

- Technologies supporting the EA: BPM/R, Lean/6 Sigma, ERP, WS...

- typical IT developments for now: MDM, single customer view,

- an EA development exercise, abstract case study

- the EA building process

- the EA governance

- a Strategy specification process

- the business strategy mapping to business, organization and technology EA objects; IT strategy

- The EA planning and the Enterprise Project Portfolio consisting of all Enterprise projects in alignment to EA

- maturity models for measuring the state of EA development

- about EA tools

- the EA team and the Enterprise Architect's role and leadership

- how to use the proposed EA framework in practice for ITIL, Merger and Acquisitions, Outsourcing, business Start-ups...

- a common view of the EA, SOA, BPM, ERP, Lean/Six Sigma... helping the integration of all these developments to reduce duplication in efforts

- EA inhibitors and triggers

- EA politics and sell, culture and the EArchitect's leadership

- The Cloud Enterprise of the future, the Virtual Enterprise based on SOA and Cloud Computing and the role of EA and SOA

The Enterprise Architecture training course content

May 17, 2009

http://it.toolbox.com/blogs/ea-matters/the-enterprise-architecture-training-course-content-31697

I have finalized a training course in Enterprise Architecture and SOA. It cover issues from business case, framework, to single page EA and examples, business architecture, IT applications and technology templates, to soft issues like culture and leadership, EA inhibitors, maturity etc. The course is based on my EA book (textbook with student questions...). Here it is, the training course, available on demand:

Day 1

Enterprise state, problem and drivers for change

Enterprise Architecture (EA), the solution

Enterprise Architecture Benefits

- The EA Key Benefits Indicators table

- The Enterprise Architecture Business Case (NPV, Payback...)

EA frameworks overview and critique

- History and overview

- Zachman framework

- FEA, TOGAF, DoDAF

- Other EA frameworks

- EA framework types

- The EA frameworks classification

Enterprise Architecture related technologies and issues

- WS, SOA, ERPs...

- Business Process Management, BPEL, BPMN, B2B

- 6 Sigma, Capability Maturity Model (CMM)

- ITIL, COBIT, Val IT

- Compliance issues

- Balanced Scorecard

Day 2

Specification of the EA development framework

- The Enterprise Architecture anatomy and components

- The Enterprise context, stakeholders and Use Cases

- Enterprise Business Functions

- Enterprise Business Flows

- The Enterprise layers

- The logic/functional architecture

- The EA GODS: Governance, Operations, Development, Support

- The Technology Architecture (IT Applications + Infrastructure)

- The People and organization architecture

- Stakeholders' Views (Location, Planning, Finance, Performance...)

- The Information Architecture View

- Architecture principles and technology platforms guidelines

Enterprise Reference Maps

- Enterprise Value Chains

- Business and Operating models

- EA Business Reference Map/Template

- EA Applications Reference Map/Template

- EA Infrastructure Reference Map/Template

- EA node and line patterns

The Single Page Enterprise Architecture

The FFLV EA framework

- The FFLV framework three dimensions

- The EA decomposition tree

- The EA navigation cube

- The EA key views of the basic EA framework

- The basic EA navigation

The EA framework metamodel

Day 3

FFLV framework mapping to Zachman, TOGAF and DODAF

Enterprise IT architecture

- The Role of IT

- IT obsolescence

- Business drivers and requirements from IT

- Typical IT developments

- Applications and Infrastructure inventories

- Applications Interconnections table

SOA - Service Oriented Architecture

- SOA, what is it? WOA.

- SOA design best practices

- EA versus SOA and WS

- SOA versus ERP, SaaS

- SOA benefits

- SOA, lessons learnt

Strategic Planning and EA alignment to Business Strategy

- Environment Analysis: Porter's Five Forces, PESTEL

- Company analysis

- Stakeholders' needs, Financial analysis, Process improvements

- Strategies specification

- Strategy balancing against stakeholders

- Assess strategies for suitability, acceptability criteria

Strategy mapping to the EA tree and execution

Best Practices of the EA implementation process

- Discover As-IS at all layers

- Map strategy and specify To-Be Enterprise State

- Assess gaps and roadmap the Enterprise Transformation

- Execute transformation and re-iterate

Day 4

An EA development exercise(practical exercise): your EA

- Capture Enterprise Mission, Business Strategy and Objectives

- Outline Enterprise Products, Stakeholders and Use Cases

How to use the EA framework for outsourcing, M&A ...

EA program and architects

- EA governance, program and site taxonomy

- EA triggers and roadblocks

- EA maturity and sell

- EA compliance

- EA tools

- EA politics and the Enterprise culture

Day 5

The Role of the Enterprise Architect

- Current kinds of EAs

- EA Architect selection

- EA architect leadership

- EA architect tasks

The EA current state

The EA future outlook

The Virtual Enterprise

- EA layers virtualization

- Enterprise outsourcing

- The Cloud Enterprise

Recap: Enterprise Architecture and Strategic Planning

Why EA and why choose this FFLV framework

EA: To Be or Not To BE

Review of "An EA Development Framework" book

Oct 28, 2009

http://it.toolbox.com/blogs/ea-matters/review-of-the-latest-edition-of-an-enterprise-architecture-development-framework-book-34985

A review of the 3rd edition of the Enterprise Architecture book has been recently added at the Angry Architect. The previous edition was reviewed on the BPTrends.

Here it is, a copy of the review:

"I don't like buying the same thing twice. On first inspection one might think that was what one was doing. This new edition of a book we've already reviewed will look familiar to those who have the previous volume; even the number of pages in each section is similar.

I'm also suspicious of later releases that are substantially bigger than the original work; the previous edition weighs in at 220+ pages while this work has stacked on another 130 pages. Which you would think is a bit of a warning sign, but it wears it surprisingly well. I didn't feel like it was that much of an imposition. In fact, it's a feature of the book how already succinct sections have actually been trimmed even further allowing more room for the expansion of the important stuff.

While maintaining the orientation of the original work Grigoriu has addressed the short comings of the previous edition. His framework is now much more securely seated in the foundations of Zachman and Spewak without losing that business process and organizational focus that made the original work stand out. Something that's not easy to achieve.

While the book takes a cursory look at the usual framework suspects it does so mainly to establish its own credentials. The bulk of the new material is not surprisingly an elaboration of Function, Flow Layer and Views (FFLV) Framework and the result is coming of age, a framework that can punch it out with the best of them! The bar has been raised and if you're not one of the TOGAF mind slaves the FFLV has to be a serious contender. Accept its business process focus and use something else for the more abstract end of business strategy, but for the mechanics of execution this could be it.

I think it's fair to say that this is the book that Grigoriu always wanted to write and that its production has been a bit of a journey, but the best things always take time. I criticized the previous edition for not being as complete as it should have been, well that's been answered and while nothing is ever perfect I found myself thinking I've got to get a copy of this!

This is not a book for managers. This is a book for architects. It's a good set of alternative views in an alarmingly increasingly monoclonal world. This book will extend most architects' horizons, experienced or novice and is a worthy successor to the previous edition. It's time to upgrade your library. This could be the "little black book of EA".

The Mobile Broadband Growth Law

Dec 2, 2011

http://www.ebizq.net/blogs/ea_matters/2011/12/mobile-broadband-growth-law.php

Adrian's Mobile Broadband Law a factor in the Digital Transformation.

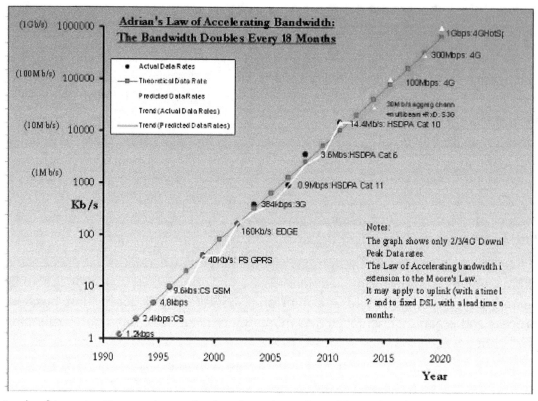

Lack of imagination perhaps. At the time, I produced it in the desire to forecast the rates to come in the mobile arena, so that I could understand what kind of mobile products, applications and terminals should be available to take advantage of it. It would be a good indication what your iPhone can do in the near future.

According to my calculations then (now lost in the vacuum of time), to be able to get this broadband on a similar scale with the fix broadband, an investment to quadruple the number of base stations in the network is necessary.

Also, the average mobile downlink speed would be around an order of magnitude lower compared to that of the co-existing fix broadband, if I remember well my own conclusions.

Essentially it is an extension of Moore's law. Adrian's Mobile Broadband Law says that downlink speed will double every year and a half. Simplistically put, my explanation is that every gain in this domain is achieved nowadays through digital signal processing. Therefore there is a direct dependency between the processing power (still obeying Moore's Law) and the transmission rate. The assessment was verified only to a certain degree though. So use it with care.

Who owns Intellectual Property?

May 3, 2008

http://it.toolbox.com/blogs/ea-matters/who-owns-intellectual-property-24117

Have you ever thought what are your rights on your own blog? I haven't, until now. Can anyone use it without accreditation? I suppose so.

In search of an answer, I found a debate on Intellectual Property, "Who owns Intellectual Property" initiated by Harvard's Business School professor Jim Heskett. I did not voice my view but seeing the profusion if not confusion of opinions, I realized too late that I feel strongly about it and I don't even know my IP rights. I specifically refer to the many comments on the site of this kind: " ... pirating intellectual property ... for the good of society", "stewardship ... a more realistic term today (with regard to IP) ... (in contrast to) Ownership ... a term from the days of the 'industrial revolution'", "ownership rights only limit the growth of innovation".

Judging by this, the answer seems to be obvious, anyone can use it, in the name of the greater good or at least this looks to be the public opinion. Why not, most people do not create IP, so why not freely use the others' IP. But, to start with, isn't IP about *property* that is the foundation of our economy and society since the very beginning? What if your own property is misappropriated?

IP is about recognition and eventually reward. The Open Source phenomenon appeared from an IP set free in the desire of peer recognition, not material reward. Nonetheless IP returns financial benefits which are your property. Isn't and wasn't IP a key differentiator in this increasingly competitive business world? Some companies live solely out of IP royalties, indeed. Is it not the American meritocracy about recognition? Everyone placed according to his merits. Happiness is about recognition. It was proved that it is worth to us more than money.

What happens in a company or even society where the IP ownership is not respected? I used to work for a company where it was said that everything of any value once revealed entered the public domain, appearing in other people presentations soon after, with no care for accreditation. In time, this "free to use IP" culture has been reflected in the company performance. This discovered, meetings became the place for platitudes where nothing ever happened and documents revealed little substance since people stopped communicating any worthy ideas.

Have you remarked how many articles published today - by reputed companies also - are so content poor? Well, this may be a defence mechanism against IP hijacking, but in the end it looks like it contributes to information pollution.

IP in our everyday job is another serious concern since it is about ownership of your own ideas, result sometimes of many years of intense study and hard work. At start, you are asked to sign that you surrender the IP created while at work. But your contract is about your regular work, you are not remunerated to innovate; it is not in your job description to invent. You do it because you are different. And companies cannot own what they have not contracted you to do! That is why I believe that the powers that be should take steps to clearly "regulate" the IP issue since otherwise innovation would slow down.

On the other hand, the royalties for music, films, sports, TV shows and personalities... in general in the entertainment industry, with the massive global market achieved nowadays, are disproportionate, fact that may create resentment against or these types of opinions about IP.

Beyerstein's pseudo-science criteria

Mar 19, 2010

http://www.tmforum.org/community/groups/frameworx/blog/archive/2010/03/19/beyerstein-s-pseudo-science-criteria.aspx

What are the characteristics of pseudo-science? Here is Beyerstein's list of characteristics of pseudoscience as exposed in Patrick's Lambe's post on "*Is KM a pseudoscience?*":

1. Isolation – failure to connect with prior and parallel disciplines
2. Non-falsifiability – no means to invalidate hypotheses
3. Misuse of data – leveraging data out of context or beyond validity
4. No self-correction, evolution of thought – often centred round a single 'thought-leader'
5. Special-pleading – the claim that this is a special-case that can't be measured in any other terms
6. Unfounded optimism – unrealistic expectations
7. Impenetrability – an over-dependence on complicated ideology and obfuscation, or bluster in place of debate
8. Magical-thinking – such as "the belief that good things will result from willpower alone"
9. Ulterior motives – particularly ulterior motives of a commercial kind
10.   Lack of formal training – including certification schemes that link back to #4
11. Bunker mentality – such as complaints about being 'misunderstood' by others, and often linked to #5 and #7

And perhaps Lack of replicability of results – especially replicability by others under controlled conditions.

It sounds familiar though. I would dare apply the criteria to technology not only scientific work. Does this apply to what we do, frameworks, standards, best practices?

Is this valid for what you do? I'll leave you think about it. The list is thought provoking and worth checking.

ABOUT THE AUTHOR

Adrian is an executive level consultant in enterprise architecture. He used to head the enterprise architecture at Ofcom, the spectrum and broadcasting U.K. regulatory agency. He is a former chief architect of the TM Forum, an organization providing a reference integrated business architecture framework, best practices and standards for the telecommunications and digital media industries.

Previously, he worked as a high technology, enterprise architecture and strategy senior manager at Accenture and Vodafone, and a principal consultant and lead architect at Qantas, Logica, Lucent Bell Labs and Nokia.

He is the author of a book on enterprise architecture development, speaks at industry conferences and has published presentations on line (just google with name + enterprise) articles with BPTrends, the Microsoft Architecture Journal and the EI magazine.

www.ingramcontent.com/pod-product-compliance
Lightning Source LLC
LaVergne TN
LVHW060039070326
832903LV00072B/1136